# PENGUIN BOOKS
## I was there!

Bob Brockie is a graphic artist and biologist. He has spent much of his life working for the DSIR where he researched hedgehogs, possums and forest ecology. Currently he is working as a research associate at the School of Biological Sciences at Victoria University. Until recently Bob was a consultant developing the Natural History gallery for the Museum of New Zealand Te Papa, Wellington.

In addition to his solid background in science Bob is a political cartoonist who creates the famous Brockie cartoons, reads history for entertainment and has worked and travelled extensively overseas.

### Also by Bob Brockie

*Inside Down Under* (with Ian Grant)

*Bones of Contention* (with Warren Mayne)

*A Living New Zealand Forest: A Community of Plants and Animals*

*Doctor Bob's Amazing Nature Facts*

*City Nature: A guide to the plants and animals of New Zealand cities and towns*

# I was there!

*dramatic first-hand accounts*
*from new zealand's history*

*Edited by*
**Bob Brockie**

**PENGUIN BOOKS**

PENGUIN BOOKS

Penguin Books (NZ) Ltd, cnr Airborne and Rosedale Roads, Albany,
Auckland 1310, New Zealand
Penguin Books Ltd, 27 Wrights Lane, London W8 5TZ, England
Penguin USA, 375 Hudson Street, New York, NY 10014, United States
Penguin Books Australia Ltd, 487 Maroondah Highway, Ringwood,
Australia 3134
Penguin Books Canada Ltd, 10 Alcorn Avenue, Toronto, Ontario,
Canada M4V 3B2

Penguin Books Ltd, Registered Offices: Harmondsworth, Middlesex, England

First published by Penguin Books (NZ) Ltd, 1998

1 3 5 7 9 10 8 6 4 2

Designed by Mary Egan
Typeset by Egan-Reid Ltd
Printed in Australia by Australian Print Group, Maryborough

Cover photograph: New Zealand troops embark for the Middle East on the
transport *Sobieski*, Lyttelton, 13 February, 1940. *War History Collection, Alexander
Turnbull Library, Wellington, New Zealand. F-7119-1/2-DA*

# CONTENTS

# Preface

A few years ago, I read John Carey's book *Reportage*, a catalogue of world events over the last 2000 years, as reported by participants or eye-witnesses. Some of Carey's stories were world-shaking—from Tacitus' account of Rome burning to Neil Armstrong's account of the moon landing. Other stories were intimate, such as those describing a priest ministering to a dying galley slave, Fanny Burney's mastectomy (without anaesthetic) in 1711, or an English boy shooting his first rabbit. *Reportage* is an engaging, often hair-raising and blood-curdling read.

Coincidentally, I came across several first-hand accounts of New Zealand events which were as engaging, hair-raising and blood-curdling as any in Carey's world anthology. More and more stories came to light— and so originated this collection of New Zealand eyewitness stories.

Some events reported here are on an epic scale, such as Rutherford's atomic discoveries, or the New Zealand forces' part in the World Wars. Other events, such as the settlers' wars, the local massacres, disasters and sporting triumphs, convulsed the nation but created few waves beyond our shores. It would be easy to produce a long catalogue of disastrous and triumphant New Zealand events, but to give a more balanced picture of our short history, I have tried to match the more spectacular stories with accounts of homely or intimate events, and comic with tragic events. I have also selected roughly the same number of stories from each decade since the 1840s, from all corners of the country, from different levels of society, and from a fair spread of young and old writers. Otherwise, the selection is quite idiosyncratic.

Most of the events related here happened in New Zealand but many of the country's defining moments happened overseas, so I include several accounts from other lands and dramas on the high seas.

Wherever possible I have chosen accounts from participants in these events rather than reports from professional journalists. However, newspaper journalists were sometimes the only people to leave coherent descriptions of events, so some of their writing is included here.

Apart from word of mouth, we get most of our news through intermediaries—journalists, writers, editors and TV directors who stand between us and the events they portray. Or we hear from historians who must reduce the kaleidoscopic detail of the past to manageable themes and generalities. These intermediaries are constrained by the limitations of their medium, the expectations of their audiences and the sensibilities of their day. So they edit, filter, reshape and pigeonhole stories, often dramatising or downplaying events, interpreting yesterday's events through today's eyes, sometimes romanticising or demonising the past or the future. With the passage of time, many significant events fade from public memory. In this way, our perception of the past drifts further and further off course and many of us carry a caricature of history in our heads.

Which is why eyewitness accounts so often take us by surprise. Here is fresh, clear-eyed, unvarnished experience, bringing us closer to events of the day and the flavour of the action. Among the slick radio and TV soundbites of the late twentieth century, these accounts provide us with correcting, calibrating ground-truth.

Perhaps the most striking thing about the early New Zealanders, as revealed in these accounts, was their physical energy, endurance and indifference to hardship. They took long treks on foot or horse, or uncomfortable and perilous boat trips, and many endured years of solitude, hunger and cold. Shelter, food, clothing and medicine were primitive, and pleasures simple. Newer and more comfortable means of transport and faster communication have reshaped our relationship with nature and with each other. Our pleasures have also multiplied.

Equally striking, is the devotion of early New Zealanders to the Crown and Empire. We thought of ourselves as part of Britain. In times of war, young men flocked unquestioningly to the British flag and royal visitors threw the country into fervid imperial convulsions. The visit of Queen Elizabeth and the Duke of Edinburgh in 1953–54 marked the last full flowering of royal hysteria. Subsequent visits have been greeted with polite but tepid enthusiasm. Today, those old colonial loyalties, standards and expectations are almost beyond our comprehension.

The utopianism of early New Zealanders is also impressive. Public utterance and private writings confirm that, until the 1970s, nearly every New Zealander believed the country was on an endless, upward road of social and economic progress. This untrammelled optimism began to wane when Britain cast us adrift in the late 1960s and we cut ourselves off from our military alliance with the United States soon after. Ever since, we have drifted on anxious, uncertain seas, bewildered by our new independence in a volatile, runaway world. It has become harder to recognise, let alone measure, progress of any kind.

Many of the issues and enthusiasms which we think are overwhelmingly important today were of little or no consequence to New Zealanders only 40 years ago. It is astonishing for us to look back at their social motives and landmarks. But, given another 40 years, our children and grandchildren will almost certainly look back on many of our frets, worries and passions with equal astonishment and incredulity.

In putting this collection together, another message has emerged. These days, fashionable shamans enjoin us to embrace mythology, religion, sacred books and texts, mysticism, art, antique protocols, rituals, obscurantism and ambiguity. Only thus, claim the postmodernist gurus, will we find our lost direction, soul, spiritual guidance and inspiration. These urgings and fictions leave me cold. Fiction we can take or leave, but we ignore real people and real events at our peril—Abel Tasman in trouble; Captain Cook, Joseph Banks and Peter Snell on a roll; Te Uatorikiriki and Hiropi in their despair; the anguish of Captain Jonas, James Cox, Arthur Allan Thomas and Zita Edmunds; the exhilaration of Ensign Best, Ernest Rutherford, Jean Batten, Sidney Holland and David Lange; Ruth Park and Jill King in the crowds at Auckland and Stratford; Charlotte Godley, Julius von Haast, Robert Muldoon and Tom Scott all having a good night out—all these accounts have a dimension, a bite, a message and a pathos which fiction lacks.

Our eyewitnesses, ancient and modern, have great charm and power. Sure, they entertain us, but collectively they can direct, guide and inspire us. They can 'extend and educate our sympathies', inform and shape our decisions and make us more human.

*Bob Brockie*
Wellington

## Author's Thanks

My warmest thanks go to Janet Braggins, Brian Easton, Ray Grover, Lloyd Jones, Margaret Orbell, Alison Parr, Chris Pugsley, Jim Traue, Anthony and Paul Treadwell for bringing stories to my attention and sorting some hassles. I am especially grateful to Colin Clark for recalling events of 1951, and Jill King for writing about her part in the Queen's 1954 visit. I want also to thank David Armstrong, Barry Ashwin, Max Avery, John Banks MP, Pat Booth, Raewyn Dalzeil, Sonja Davies, Robyn Du Chateau, Maryanne Gardiner, John Glennie, Charles Edmunds, Mary, John, Adam, and Anne Fyfe, Keith Holyoake, Rt Hon. David Lange, Sir Robert Jones, George Luoni, Pat Morrison, Alan Mummery, Ross Meurant, Olly Newland, Therese O'Connell, Ross O'Rourke, Alison Parr, Jane Phare, Te Ahukaramu Charles Royal, Kevin Ryan QC, Tom Scott, Peter Williams QC and John Watson for permission to reprint their, or their antecedents' stories. The book would be impossible without the obliging services of Alexander Turnbull Library (New Zealand National Library) Wellington, particularly archivist Margaretta Gee; the National Archives; the Kippenberger Military Archive and Research Library, Army Museum, Waiouru; the Canterbury Museum; Te Papa National Museum of New Zealand; the Home of Compassion, Wellington; The Peabody Museum, Salem, USA, and Radio New Zealand. Editors Geoff Walker and Nicola Strawbridge smoothed the path of the book as did Linda Sorensen in a thousand ways.

I have tried to find copyright holders of most excerpts in the book. Nearly all copyright holders were very generous in allowing their material to be reprinted here. However, I have quite a pile of enquiries returned 'Gone. No Address'. I apologise for any errors or omissions in the list of copyright holders and would be grateful to be notified of any corrections that should be incorporated into the next edition of this volume.

# I was there!

## New Zealand Espied *13 December 1642*

### Abel Tasman

Towards noon Saw a large high elevated land, had it South east from us by 15 miles, made our course to South east, direct for land; shot a shot and after noon had the white flag flown, whereupon the officers of the *Zeehaen* came to our ship, when we jointly resolved; to make said land, as soon as At all possible . . .

*18 December* . . . we have with the officers of the *Zeehaen* resolved that one should try to get into this land, and Try to find convenient harbour . . . after noon our skipper Ide Tiercxsz and pilot major ffrancoys Iacobsz, with the sloop together with the small boat of the *Zeehaen*, with the Merchant Gilsemans and one of the under-mates went ahead, to seek by the Land an anchor also water place, with the setting of the sun, we have since it became calm, dropped out anchor in 15 fathoms good firm bottom, in the evening about one hour after Sunset, Saw many lights on land and four vessels near the shore, 2 of which betook themselves towards us, when our two boats returned to the ships . . . after our people have been on board about one glass, those from the 2 canoes begin to call out to us; in a gruff hollow voice but we could not in the least understand any of it, however we called back to them in token of answer, when they began again several times, but did not come nearer than a stonepiece's shot, blew also many times on an Instrument which gave sound like the moor's Trumpets, we had one of our sailors (who could play somewhat on the trumpet) blow back to them in answer.

*Four months out from his home port of Batavia, Captain Tasman, aboard the* Heemskerk *and accompanied by the sister ship* Zeehaen, *came across a new land. Tasman named the new country 'Staeten Landt'—'States Land'—meaning the land of the States General of the Netherlands.*

## VIOLENCE AT MURDERERS BAY        *19 December 1642*

### Abel Tasman

. . . in the morning early a vessel of this people [the Maori] having in it 13 men approached our ships to about a cast away, they called out several times, which we could not understand . . . we waved to them many times that they Should come to the ships showed white cloth and some knives, from what Were given to us as Cargo, but however they did not come nearer but paddled finally back again meanwhile the officers of the *Zeehaen* appeared on our ship and this people (as it seems) is Seeking friendship, we Saw 7 more craft come from land, one of which (projecting in front high and sharp, manned by 17 men) paddled round behind the *Zeehaen* and a second (in it 13 sturdy men) came before the ship not half a cast from us, both of which occasionally called out to each other, we waved and showed them (as the previous) white cloth &c but they continued nevertheless to lie still, the Skipper of the *Zeehaen* Sent his quartermaster, with their small boat in it 6 rowers to the ship; to tell the under-mates if this people wanted to come to the ship they Should not let too many on board . . . when the small boat of the *Zeehaen* set out back to the ship They who lay before us, between the two ships began to Paddle So vigorously to it, that about a little more than half way to our ship, they struck the *Zeehan's* small boat with their stem on the Side, Dashed over the Same violently, whereupon the foremost in this canoe of rogues, pushed the quartermr Cornelius Ioppen in the neck several times with a long blunt pike so fiercely, that he had to fall overboard, whereupon the rest of them set to with short thick pieces of wood and their paddles, overpowering the small boat, in which violence 3 of the *Zeehaen's* people were killed, and the fourth through the heavy blows was mortally injured, the quartermr and 2 more sailors swam towards our ship and we Sent our sloop to them into which They got alive, after this monstrous deed and detestable Thing, the murderers let the small boat drift, have pulled one of the dead into their canoe and drowned another. We and those of the *Zeehaen* seeing this shot hard with muskets and canon, but although we did not indeed Hit them, they nevertheless hastened back, and paddled for land out of shooting range, we fired many shots with our forward upper and bow guns by and about their vessels, but struck none our Skipper Ide Terkxsen Holman rowed with

*Tasman's ships attacked in Murderers Bay*

our sloop well manned and armed, towards the small boat of the *Zeehaen* (which these accursed men, luckily for us still let drift) and returned with the Same quickly to the ship, finding one of the dead and the mortally wounded one therein, we raised our anchors and went under sail. we Saw 22 canoes by the Land, from which 11 (swarming with people) came off towards us, we kept quiet until we could shoot some of the foremost; when we made 1 to 2 shots with our pieces from the gunner's room but in vain; those from the *Zeehaen* shot also and Hit in the foremost canoe (who stood with a small white flag in the hand) So that he fell down; we heard the shot also strike in and Against the canoe, but what more effect it had remained unknown to us, as soon as They had received this shot, they turned with speed for land . . . since the detestable act of these inhabitants shown to four of the *Zeehaen's* people this morning is a teacher to us [we resolved] to hold this land's inhabitants as enemies; that one Shall therefore run east along the shore, following the stretch of the Land to see whether somewhere we may find convenient places, where there should be some supplies and water to obtain, as more fully by the resolution is mentioned, in the Murderers place (which we have also given the name of Murderers Bay).

*Tasman never set foot in New Zealand. On his return to Batavia, the East India Company demoted Tasman and docked his pay for failing to explore the country. Tasman later became a pirate, attacking Spanish treasure galleons off the Philippines, and was in trouble again later when, drunk, he tried to hang two sailors with his bare hands. Murderers Bay was later renamed Golden Bay.*

## FIRST EUROPEAN TO SET FOOT ON NEW ZEALAND

*7 October 1769*

### Captain James Cook

Gentle breezes and settled weather. At 2 PM saw land from the mast head bearing WBN, which we stood directly for, and could but just see it of the deck at sun set.

*8 October.* Gentle breezes between the ENE and north, clear weather. At 5 PM seeing the opening of a Bay that appear'd to run pretty far inland, hauled our wind and stood in for it, but as soon as night came on we kept plying on and off untill day light when we found our selves to Leeward of the Bay the wind being at the north. By noon we fetched in with the SW point, but not being able to weather it we tacked and stood off. We saw in the Bay several Canoes, People upon the shore and some houses in the Country. The land on the Sea-Coast is high with white steep cliffs and back inland are very high mountains, the face of the Country is of a hilly surface and appeares to be cloathed with wood and Verdure.

*9 October.* Gentle breezes and clear weather. PM stood into the Bay and anchored on the NE side before the entrance of a small river . . . After this I went ashore with a party of men in the Pinnace and yawl accompanied by Mr Banks and Dr Solander, we landed abreast of the Ship and on the east side of the river just mentioned, but seeing some of the natives on the other side of the river whome I was desirous of speaking with and finding that we could not ford the river, I order'd the yawl in to carry us and the Pinnace to lay at the entrance. In the meantime the Indians made off, however we went as far as their hutts which lay 2 or 3 hundred yards from the water side.

*Aboard the* Endeavour *and six weeks out from Plymouth, England, Cook landed beside the Turanganui Stream in Poverty Bay. He named the nearby headland Young Nick's Head after 12-year-old Nicolas Young, who first saw the land from the masthead.*

*Captain Cook's signature.*

## 'DR SOLANDER AND MYSELF . . . LANDED WITHOUT MUCH DIFFICULTY'  *21 October 1769*

## Joseph Banks

This Morn at Day break the waterers went ashore, & soon after Dr Solander and myself, there was a good deal of Surf upon the beach, but we landed without much difficulty; the natives sat by our People, but did not intermix with them; they traded however for Cloth cheifly, giving whatever they had, tho' they seemed pleased with observing our People, as well as with the gain they got by trading with them, yet they did not neglect their ordinary occupations; in the Morn several boats went out fishing; at Dinner time everyone went to their respective homes, and after a certain time returned; such fair appearances made Dr Solander & myself almost trust them; we ranged about the Bay, & were well repaid by finding many plants & shooting some beautifull Birds, in doing this we visited several houses, & saw a little of their customs, for they were not at all shy of shewing us any thing we desired to see, nor did they on our account interrupt their meals, the only employment we saw them engaged in.

In the proper Season they certainly have plenty of excellent vegetables; tho' we have seen no sign of tame animals among them except Dogs very small and ugly; their Plantations were now hardly finished, but so well was the Ground till'd, that I have seldom seen, even in the gardens of curious People, Land better broke down; in them were planted sweet Potatoes, Cocos, & some one of the cucumber kind as we judged from the Seed leaves which just appeared above the ground the first of these were planted in small hills, some ranged in rows other quincunx all laid out by line most regularly, the Cocos were planted on flat Land, & not yet appeared above ground the cucumbers were set in small hollows or dishes, mush as we do in England; these Plantations were from 1 or 2 to 8 to 10 acres each, in the Bay might be 150 to 200 acres in cultivation tho' we did not see 100 People in all; each distinct patch was fenc'd in, generally with reeds, placed close one by another, so that scarce a mouse could creep thro'.

When we went to their houses, Men, Women and Children received us, no one shew'd the least signs of fear; the Women were plain, & made themselves more so by painting their faces with red ocre and Oil, which generally was fresh & wet upon their cheeks and foreheads, easily transferable to the noses of any one who should attempt to kiss them, not as they seemed to have any objection to such familiarities, as the noses of several of our People evidently shew'd, but they were as great coquets as any Europeans could be, & the Young ones as skittish as unbroken fillies: one part of their dress I cannot omit to mention, besides their cloth which they decently rolled around them, each wore around the lower part of her waist a string made of the leaves of a highly perfumed grass, to this was fastened a small bunch of leaves of some fragrant plant which served as the innermost veil of their modesty tho' the Men did not so frequently use paint upon their faces yet they often did, one especially I observed whose whole Body and Garments were rubb'd over with Dry ocre, of this he constantly kept a piece in his hand, & generally rubb'd it on some part or other of him.

In the Evening all the Boats being employed in carrying on board Water, we were likely to be left ashore till after dark the loss of so much time in sorting & putting in order our specimens was what we did not like, so we applied to our friends the Indians for a Passage in one of their Canoes, they readily launch'd one for us but we in number 8 not being us'd to so ticklish a convenience, overset her in the surf & were very well sous'd, 4 then obliged to remain, and Dr Solander, Tupia, Tayeto, & myself embarked again, & come without accident to the Ship, well pleased with the behaviour of our Indian friends, who would the second time undertake to carry off such clumsy fellows.

*Joseph Banks, the English gentleman biologist, and Dr Solander, the Swedish botanist, came off Cook's Endeavour, and landed at Anaura Bay, Hawke's Bay.*

## FRENCHMEN FRATERNISING WITH THE SAVAGES IN THE BAY OF ISLANDS     *5 May 1772*

### Julien Crozet

Many canoes came along filled with savages, who brought us their children and their daughters, all coming unarmed and with the greatest confidence. On arriving at the vessel, they commenced singing out Taro, the name they give to ships' biscuit. We gave small pieces to everyone

*Maori road and pa.* [From Crozet's journal]

and that with the greatest economy, for they were such great eaters and so numerous that if we had given them according to their appetite, they would soon have consumed our provisions; they brought large quantities of fish, for which we gave them glass trinkets and pieces of iron in exchange. In these early days they were content with old nails two or three inches in length, but later on they became more particular and in exchange for their fish demanded nails four or five inches in length. Their object in asking for these nails were to make small wood chisels of them. As soon as they had obtained a piece of iron, they took it to one of the sailors and by signs engaged him to sharpen it at the millstone; they always took care to reserve some fish wherewith to pay the sailor for his trouble. The ship was full of these savages, who appeared very gentle and even affectionate. Little by little they came to know the officers and called them by their names. We only allowed the chiefs, the women and the girls to enter the chart room. The chiefs were distinguished by the feathers of egrets or of other aquatic birds stuck in the hair on the top of their head. The married women were distinguished by a sort of straw plait which confined the hair on the top of the head: the girls had no such distinctive mark, their hair hanging naturally over their neck without anything to bind it.

It was the savages themselves who pointed out these distinctions and who gave us to understand by signs that we must not touch the married women, but that we might with perfect freedom make advances to the girls. It was in fact not possible to find any more approachable.

As soon as we discovered these distinctions we passed the word round the two ships so that everyone might be circumspect with regard to the married women, and thereby preserve the good understanding with savages who appeared so amiable, and not to cause them to be ill-affected towards us. The facility with which the girls were approached was the cause that we never had the slightest trouble with the savages on account of their women during the whole time that we lived amongst these people.

*The French ship* Mascarin *was surrounded by more than a hundred Maori canoes. The amiable relations between the crew and Maori fell apart when some Frenchmen broke a tapu, and the Maori killed 24 crewmen and Captain Marion du Fresne. In revenge, the French shot about 250 Maori in a hectic battle. Crozet took over du Fresne's command.*

## MODERN MAN MEETS ANCIENT MAN AND HIS DAUGHTERS

*1773*

### Captain James Cook

The man could not help discovering great signs of fear when we approached the rock with our boat. He, however, stood firm; nor did he move to take up the things we threw him ashore. At length I landed went up, and embraced him; and presented him with such articles as I had about me, which at once dissipated his fear. Presently after, we were joined by the two women, the gentlemen that were with me, and some of the seamen. After this we spent an hour in chit-chat, little understood on either side, in which the youngest of the two women bore by far the greatest share. This occasioned one of the seamen to say, that women did not want tongue in any part of the world . . . Night approaching, obliged us to take leave of them; when the youngest of the two women, whose volubility of tongue exceeded everything I ever met with, gave us a dance; but the man viewed us with great attention.

*While the* Resolution *was moored in Dusky Sound, Fiordland, Captain Cook, accompanied by three others, rowed around an inlet and saw a well-built Maori*

*Maru and daughters.*

*man and two young women standing on a rocky point, each armed with long spears. It was the first encounter between these Fiordland people and Europeans. Later research suggests the man was called Maru and the girls were his daughters.*

## COOK'S MEN CLEAR BUSH AT DUSKY SOUND

*1773*

George Forster

We felled tall timber trees . . . our sawyers cut them into planks, or we split them into billets for fuel. By the side of a murmuring rivulet, whose passage into the sea we facilitated, a long range of casks, which had been prepared by our coopers for the purpose, stood ready to be filled with water. Here ascended the steam of a large cauldron, in which we brewed from neglected indigenous plants, a salutary and palatable potion, for the use of our labourers. In the offing, some of the crew appeared providing a meal of delicious fish for the refreshment of their fellows. Our caulkers and riggers were stationed on the sides and masts of the vessel, and their occupation gave life to the scene, and struck the ear with various noises, whilst the anvil on the hill resounded with the strokes of the weighty hammer. Already the polite arts began to flourish in this new settlement; the various tribes of animals and vegetables, which dwelt in the unfrequented woods, were imitated by an artist and his noviciate; and the romantic prospects of this shaggy country lived on in the canvas in the glowing tints of nature, who was amazed to see herself so closely copied.

Nor had science disdained to visit us in this solitary spot: an observatory arose in the centre of our works, filled with the most accurate instruments, where the attentive eye of the astronomer contemplated the motions of celestial bodies.

*About an acre of bush was cleared from Astronomers Point, enabling Captain Cook's astronomer to make exact observations on its geographical position. Botanists still visit Astronomers Point to measure the regenerating bush.*

## 'I DON'T LIKE TO BE SHOT AT LIKE A BIRD'

*Dusky Sound, 19 December 1795*

### First Officer John Murry

*Mr Alms [a passenger]*: You hear me Mr Waine? I now desire you to ask my pardon before Mr Murry, or give me satisfaction in another manner this instant.

*Mr Waine*: I will not! I cannot think of fighting a man who has been used to practise a Pistol. I don't like to be shot at like a bird.

*Mr Alms*: That's nonsense Sir, here are two pistolls, take your choice of them, load them yourself, you shall have every advantage I can offer, but as you have refused to make attonement for the offence, You must fight me.

*Mr Waine*: I cannot.

*Mr Alms*: Then Sir You are a Coward, a Dastardly Coward! Mr Murry you hear what I say. I call Mr Waine a Coward, who would dare affront a gentleman, and refuse him satisfaction. Mr W. you are a Coward, I shall publish this in India.

*Mr Waine*: Well!, if you call me a Coward I shall act accordingly.

(He then left the Cabin.)

Since then the Gentlemen have not spoken to each other.

*The dilapidated* Endeavour *(no relation), en route from Port Jackson to Bengal, called at Dusky Sound for a bit of sealing. On board were an unruly mix of over 100 runaway convicts, freed convicts, deserters, sailors, officers, passengers, lascars and sepoys and an exasperated captain. Waine, a first officer, swore at the passenger Alms and Murry was a witness to the disagreement.*

## FIRST CATTLE AND HORSES LANDED AT BAY OF ISLANDS

*24 December 1814*

### John Nicholas

On the arrival of the boats with the cattle, they [the Maori] appeared perfectly bewildered with amazement, not knowing what to conclude respecting such extraordinary looking animals. Cows or horses they had never seen before and, diverted now from everything else, they regarded them as stupendous prodigies. However, their astonishment was soon turned into alarm and confusion, for one of the cows that was wild and unmanageable, being impatient of restraint, rushed in among them and caused such violent terror through the whole assemblage that, imagining some preternatural monster had been let loose to destroy them, they all immediately took themselves to flight.

But this cause of their panic being removed, they did not hesitate to return, and Mr Marsden, mounting the horse, rode up and down the beach, exciting their wonder in tenfold degree. To see a man seated on the back of such an animal they thought the strangest thing in nature, and following him with staring eyes, they believed at the moment that he was more than mortal. Though Duaterra, on his return from his former visit to Port Jackson had described to his countrymen the nature and use of the horse, his account appeared to them so preposterous that it only excited their ridicule. Having no name in his language for this animal, he thought that 'corraddee', their term for dog, would be the best designation he could adopt; but as they could not elevate their ideas of it to the same height as his description they believed not a single word he said. On telling them he had seen large 'corraddees' carry men and women about on land canoes (meaning carriages) they would put their fingers in their ears to prevent themselves from listening to him, and desire him very indignantly not to tell so many lies. A few of them, however, more curious than the rest, to prove his veracity, would mount upon the backs of their pigs, saying they must be more fit for the purpose of riding than the 'corraddees'; and endeavouring to gallop them about in the style of European horsemanship, they quickly tumbled into the dirt, and became quite incredulous as their sceptical companions. This was, therefore, a day of triumph to Duaterra, as it afforded him an opportunity of convincing them by ocular demonstration of the truth of his statement.

*Settlers' spelling of Maori words and names was very haphazard until the first dictionaries and translation of the Bible became available in the 1830s. These days we spell 'Duaterra' as 'Ruatara' and 'corradee' as 'kuri'.*

## FIRST CHRISTIAN SERVICE AT
## BAY OF ISLANDS          *25 December 1814*

## Rev. Samuel Marsden

On Sunday morning when I was upon deck I saw the English flag flying, which was a pleasing sight in New Zealand. I considered it the signal for the dawn of civilization, liberty, and religion in that dark and benighted land. I never viewed the British colours with more gratification, and flattered myself they would never be removed till the natives of that island enjoyed all the happiness of British subjects.

About ten o'clock we prepared to go ashore and publish the glad tidings of the Gospel for the first time. I was under no apprehensions for the safety of the vessel, and therefore ordered all on board to go on shore to attend Divine service, except the master and one man. When we landed we found Korokoro, Duaterra [Ruatara] and Shungee [Hongi] dressed in regimentals which Governor Macquarie had given them, with their men drawn up ready to march into the enclosure to attend Divine service. They had their swords by their sides and a switch in their hands. We entered the enclosure and were placed in the seats on each side of the pulpit. Korokoro marched his men on and placed them on my right hand in the rear of the Europeans and Duaterra placed his men on the left. The inhabitants of the town with the women and children and a number of other chiefs formed a circle round the whole. A very solemn silence prevailed—the sight was really impressive. I got up and began the service with singing the Old Hundred Psalm, and felt my very soul melt within me when I viewed my congregation and considered the state we were in.

After reading the service, during which the natives stood up and sat down at the signal given by the motion of Korokoro's switch which was regulated by the movements of the Europeans, it being Christmas Day, I preached from the second chapter of St Luke's Gospel, the tenth verse: 'Behold I bring you tidings of great joy'. The natives told Duaterra they could not understand what I meant. He replied they were not to mind that now for they would understand by and by, and that he would explain my meaning as far as he could . . . In the above manner the Gospel was introduced into New Zealand and I fervently pray that the glory of it may never depart from its inhabitants till time shall be no more.

*Rev. Samuel Marsden.*

When the service was over we returned on board much gratified with the reception we had met with, and we could not but feel the strongest persuasion that the time was at hand when the Glory of the Lord would be revealed to these poor benighted heathens and that those [missionaries] who were to remain on the island had strong reason to believe that their labours would be crowned and blessed with success. In the evening I administered the Holy Sacrament on board the *Active* in remembrance of Our Saviour's birth and what He had done and suffered for us.

*A stone cross now marks the spot where Marsden first preached. Korokoro, Ruatara and Hongi were christianised chiefs who had travelled widely and spent years with Marsden in Australia.*

## ESCAPED CONVICTS RECAPTURED

*Bay of Islands, 1814*

### John Nicholas

Two men, whose feeble and emaciated bodies, sinking with famine, bespoke the very last extremes of human misery, came on board, and surrendered themselves to be taken back to Port Jackson, having more the appearance of human spectres than of material beings composed of flesh and blood. These unfortunate wretches were recognised by the missionaries as two convicts who had made their escape from the *Active*, in her last voyage to this island . . . Having contrived to get away from the ship, they ran into the woods, with the view of depending for their support on the casual hospitality of the savage natives, as they had been disappointed in returning to that country whose protection they had forfeited.

But in their expectations of a friendly reception among the New Zealanders, they were very much deceived; and their hideous state of nudity, having only the remains of an old mat tied round the waist, which served but to make their misery more apparent, and the death-like paleness that each of them displayed in his ghastly countenance, afforded the plainest evidence of the sufferings they had endured. For this state of deplorable wretchedness they were, however, very ill-prepared, considering the sedentary positions in which they had been engaged before their mal-practices had banished them from England; one having been a tailor in London, and the other a shoemaker . . . The fugitives not being willing to work, but flattering themselves with the idea that, as white men, and Europeans, they would be looked up to by the rude natives as beings of a superior order; and living by the industry of others, could spend their time in exalted laziness, while even their chiefs would come to offer their profound respect; had by such vain expectations only deceived themselves, and made their miseries more certain . . . The chiefs told them very plainly, that if they worked but little, they should have but little to eat, *ittee ittee workee workee, ittee ittee kiki*; and not choosing to accommodate themselves to active exertion, and dreading, from the temper of the natives, who had been provoked by their unseemly arrogance, that they might be inclined to put them to death, and make a meal of their bodies; they thought it best to withdraw from the place, and retiring to a solitary cave, lived there by themselves, subsisting on the fern-root and whatever else they could procure.

But while they remained here, the same alarming terrors of being attacked and murdered were continually before them; and rather than be subject any longer to such a state of terrible suspense, they preferred coming out of their seclusion, and throwing themselves on the protection of Tupee, the brother of Tarra, who possessed sufficient authority with the natives to defend them from the violence they apprehended. The chief received them with much kindness, and did not hesitate to guarantee their safety; but stipulated at the same time that they should not be idle. Tupee used to take the fugitives with him to work at a farm

he had in a remote part of the interior, and they were ready to acknow-
ledge, that his treatment to them in these excursions was always humane
and liberal. The tailor, however, fared much better than his companion;
for, having very luckily brought a pair of scissors with him in his flight,
he made himself generally useful to the natives, by acting as hair-cutter
to the whole tribe; a service which, though it could not obliterate his
offence, raised him in their estimation considerably above his fellow-
convict, and procured him very often some partial indulgences.

But these wretched men, on getting on board, did not seem to have
experienced the least difference of treatment, for both were equally
miserable in the figure they presented; and I sincerely wished at the time,
that every youthful profligate in London and elsewhere, had an
opportunity of seeing them.

*John Nicholas accompanied Samuel Marsden on this visit to Northland.*

## UTU AT STEWART ISLAND                                    *1827*

## John Boultbee

After Pete [Horomana Patu] and his party had been a few days here,
they set off for Towiwi's Settlement to carry the tidings of his death, and
to go thro' the usual ceremonies on the occasion. My love of novelty
induced me to accompany them; our party consisted of 4 men, 8 women,
and 2 or 3 young girls; the distance we had to go was about 20 miles,
part of the way led through the woods, and part along Sandy beaches.
The men had their muskets, as they always make it a point to carry
them when on a journey. I was much pleased with the trip, the scenery
was so pleasantly varied; from sandy beaches, to projecting head-lands,
which we crossed to save distance; and towards the interior, rising hills,
vallies of flax, tops of mountains etc. all conspiring to render the walk
anything but tedious. On the way we sometimes rested to drink Etootoo.
We crossed a rapid fresh water river in a small canoe that was kept here
for the convenience of passengers—we then walked along an extensive
pebbly beach, on which was a mound of earth and stones. Pete told us
this was the place where a man had been cooked! On enquiry I was
informed that this person was one Koura, who had been guilty, with

another, of the murder of an old woman, who they met in the bush; besides this, they had done other outrages. The murder was found out shortly afterwards, and the son of the deceased joined with 4 or 5 others, of whom Pete was one, determined to be revenged for her death. Accordingly they went purposely from Pahee to Towiwi's village, where they found one of the party in his house, they killed him without any difficulty as he offered no resistance. Koura however was not so easily overcome: he saw them approach and knowing the cause of their coming he armed himself with a long spear and ran to the open beach to have the greater advantage. When the 5 men came near him, he played his part so dexterously that he speared 2 of his opponents to the ground, and was making a rush on the third when Pete came behind him and struck him down with a blow of a tomahawk. He fell on his face and expired instantly. Pete said they were half an hour before they could despatch him; when the rest had glutted their revenge by eating a piece of him; Pete tried to eat a bit of his hand, but was not able, and vomited it up again! I saw the head of Koura some time after at Ruaboka, it was adorned with feathers, the hair remained set, and the whole of the face as when alive, except that in place of the eyes, bright shells filled in their sockets; the teeth were visible.

*John Boultbee, a young Englishman employed as a sealer by a Sydney firm, spent an adventurous time in Fiordland before working on Stewart Island. Pahia was the most western settlement in Foveaux Strait, but no trace of it now remains.*

## MASSACRE AT AKAROA         *1830*

### Ihaia Pouhawaiki

We sailed from Kapiti in Captain Stewart's brig. There were one hundred and seventy men, under the command of Te Rauparaha, Te Rangi hae ata, Te Hiko, Tungia, Mokau, Te mai he kia, and others. On reaching Akaroa harbour we carefully concealed ourselves in the hold, while Captain Stewart refused to hold any communication with the shore until Te Mai hara nui arrived. For seven days and nights we waited for that chief, who was away at Waiwera, superintending the preparation of a cargo of scraped flax for one of his European customers. Captain Stewart sent repeated messages to him to hasten his coming, and on the eighth day he arrived, accompanied by his wife, Te Whe, and his little daughter, Nga roi Mata. He was cordially welcomed on reaching the deck by the captain, who took him below to the cabin. He was hardly seated before a door opened, and Te Rauparaha entered, accompanied by several of

*Te Rauparaha*

his companions, who at once seized Te Mai hara nui, and taunted him with his simplicity in permitting himself to be so readily entrapped. After the seizure of Te Mai hara nui, the shore canoes were encouraged to approach the vessel, but as soon as the occupants came on board they were led to the hatchway and thrown down the hold . . . Canoes continued to come off for many hours, as there was no suspicion of foul play, it being a very usual thing for Maoris to remain for some time on board the traders that frequented the port. On the second day after Te Mai hara nui's capture, Te Rauparaha attacked Takapuneke very early in the morning. The place was unfortified and undefended. About one hundred persons were killed, and fifty taken on board as prisoners. After the destruction of the kainga, the vessel sailed away for Kapiti. During the voyage Te Mai hara nui smothered his little daughter, Nga roi Mata, appropriately named The Tears, lest she should become the wife of one of his enemies. His captors were very much enraged with him for doing so, and fearing he might commit suicide, and escape the punishment in store for him, they secured his hands, and then fastened him by a hook placed under his chin to the cross beams of the hold. The torture occasioned exquisite suffering, which was watched with satisfaction by his vindictive enemies. On reaching Kapiti, Te Mai hara nui was handed over to the widows of the chiefs killed at Kaiapoi, who put him to death by slow and nameless tortures.

*To avenge the death of some of his chiefs at the hands of Ngai Tahu in Kaiapoi, Te Rauparaha hired Captain Stewart to ship him south to Akaroa. Ihaia Pouhawaiki accompanied Te Rauparaha on his expedition. Te Mai hara nui was put to death with red-hot irons.*

## THE SPIRIT CALLS                                                  *1830s*

### Frederick Edward Maning—'A Pakeha Maori'

These priests or *tohunga* would, and do to this hour, undertake to call up the spirit of any dead person, if paid for the same. I have seen many of these exhibitions, but one instance will suffice as an example.

A young chief, who had been very popular and greatly respected in his tribe, had been killed in battle, and, at the request of several of his nearest friends, the *tohunga* had promised on a certain night to call up his spirit to speak to them, and answer certain questions they wished to put. The priest was to come to the village of the relations, and the interview was to take place in a large house common to all the population . . . Now it is necessary to remark that this young chief was a man in advance of his times and people in many respects. He was the first in his tribe who could read and write; and, among other unusual things for a native to do, he kept a register of deaths and a journal of any remarkable events that happened in the tribe.

Now the book was lost. No one could find it, although his friends had searched unceasingly for it, as it contained many matters of interest, and also they wished to preserve it for his sake . . .

We were all seated on the rush-strewn floor, about thirty persons. The door was shut; the fire had burnt down leaving nothing but glowing charcoal. The room was oppressively hot. The light was little better than darkness, and the part of the room in which the *tohunga* sat was now in perfect gloom.

Suddenly, without the slightest warning, a voice came out of the darkness. 'Salutation! Salutation to you all! Salutation! Salutation to you, my tribe-family, I salute you! Friends, I salute you! Friend, my *pakeha* friend, I salute you! . . .'

A cry expressive of affection and despair, such as was not good to hear, came from the sister of the dead chief, a fine, stately, and really handsome women of about five-and-twenty. She was rushing, with both arms extended, into the dark, in the direction whence the voice came. She was instantly seized around the waist and restrained by her brother by main force, still moaning and fainting, she lay still on the ground. At the same instant another female voice was heard from a young girl who was held by the wrists by two young men, her brothers.

'Is it you! Is it you? Truly is it you? Au! Au! They hold me, they restrain me; wonder not that I have not followed you, they restrain me, they watch me, but I go to you. The sun shall not rise, the sun shall not rise, the sun shall not rise, au! au!' Here she fell insensible on the rush floor, and with the sister were carried out . . .

'We cannot find your book,' said I; 'where have you concealed it?'

The answer instantly came. 'I concealed it between the *tohunga* of my house and the thatch, straight over you as you go in the door.' Here the brother rushed out; all was silence till his return. In five minutes he came back *with the book in his hand* . . .

An idea now struck me that I could expose the imposture without showing any palpable disbelief.

'What have you written in that book?' said I.

'A great many things.'

'Tell me some of them.'

'Which of them?'

'Any of them.'

'You are seeking for some information; what do you want to know? I will tell you.' Then suddenly, 'Farewell, O tribe! Farewell, my family I go!'

Here a general and impressive cry of 'Farewell' arose from everyone in the house.

'Farewell,' again cried the spirit, *from beneath the ground!*

'Farewell,' again, *from high in air!*

'Farewell,' once more came moaning through the distant darkness of the night.

'Farewell!'

I was for a moment stunned. The deception was perfect. There was a dead silence—at last. 'A ventriloquist,' said I; 'or—*or perhaps*—the devil.'

I was fagged and confused. It was past midnight; the company broke up, and I went to a house where a bed had been prepared for me. I wished to be quiet and alone; but it was fated there should be little quiet that night. I was just falling asleep, after having thought for some time on the extraordinary scenes I had witnessed, when I heard the report of a musket at some little distance, followed by the shouting of men and the screams of women. Out I rushed. I had a presentiment of some horrible catastrophe. Men were running by, hastily armed . . . A house had been set on fire to make a light. Before another house close at hand, a dense circle of human beings was formed. I pushed my way through, and then saw, by the bright light of the flaming house, a scene which is still fresh with me: there in the verandah of the house was an old grey-bearded man; he knelt upon one knee, and on the other he supported the dead body of the young girl who had said she would follow the spirit to spiritland. The delicate-looking body from the waist upwards was bare and bloody; the old man's right arm was under the neck, the lower part of his long grey beard was dabbled in blood, his left hand was twisting his matted hair; he did not weep, he *howled*, and the sound was that of a heathen despair, knowing no hope. The young girl had secretly procured a loaded musket, tied a loop for her foot to the trigger, placed the muzzle to her tender breast, and blown herself to shatters. And the old man was her father, and a *tohunga*. A calm low voice now spoke close beside me.

'She has followed her *rangatira*,' it said. I looked round and saw the famous *tohunga* of the night.

*As a young man, Frederick Maning moved and worked among the Maori and was known to the Auckland gentry as a 'wild man from the woods'. He became a successful timber trader, then, in 1863, a judge in the Native Land Court. Later in life he came to detest anything connected with Maori.*

## 'I DO NOT KNOW THAT I EVER CRIED IN PARTING FROM A GIRL BEFORE'  *1834*

### Edward Markham

*April 1st.* I went to Hoe mi-neigh with Manning and Poynton. I was away three nights. I went up a fine river say 25 miles, at last came to a Parr, we were well received, had Pork and Potatoes and sat up late answering questions. I slept in a place built of Wood weather boarded 6 feet by 4, a good Pig Stye. When gone to bed I found the Chief had sent a Wayheinee pi to sleep with me, and I was good humoured and took Compassion on the Lady. Next morning to my surprise I found Eleven Casks of Gun Powder. This was the Hotel de Ville and Public Store, but being a Rangatara they had given it me. There was a large fire burning all Night within three yards of it, and people looking in with pipes in their Mouths . . .

My room is finished, got in all right. Arungher Mar came and took up her quarters with me, and proved that her Heart was as good as her Face and Figure. She lived with me till I went to the Bay of Islands. I do not know that I ever cried in parting from a Girl before except one in Paris; from this time Arungher went out shooting with me, holding the Gun in her hand and Venus in her lap and sat at the bottom of the Boat whilst I steered. When in the Woods she looked out for the (Coo Coupers) or Pigeons, and had a sharp eye. She always had the fat to dress her fine long Hair with, and I taught her to dress it with Parisian Fashion. She never left me, told me every thing and watched over every thing of mine, as if they belonged to her own tribe. I have sent her presents from Sydney. A Wine glass of Grog makes her Showrangy. She was as good a Washerwoman as could be, and was as clean herself as any European Woman could be. She washed from head to foot with Soap every night before going to bed, her dress was 4 slop Shirts, black silk handkerchiefs, 3 red Shirts altered into Panny gots or Petticoats, a Blanket or Cacahow. Her hair always well dressed, and she killed Venus's fleas. I gave her a Pup to keep for 'Auld lang syne'. She could say all the Church prayers by heart, play a good game of drafts, and swam like a Fish. I have seen her swim to Moutitie and back and she saved my life when engaged with Amittie by bringing me my Pistol and flourishing a Tom a hawk over his head . . .

*June 30th.* I took leave of Koko or Coco, gave the goats to Kelly pots, pans and Tubs &c. Parker and Manning said they would go up to the Whyhoe River with me. I engaged Otterigo to go across the Country with me as Interpreter as he knows many of them; Arungher went with me to Way-hoe . . . [They slept] the Night at dutch Sams, the boat builder, so as to arrive at high Water at the head of the Whyhoe River. It rained all night; the Centre of the Islands is high wooded land. In the morning had such an affecting Scene to witness and through poor Arungher crying and hair all flowing, Cutting herself with shells, and bleeding all over, when the Boat was ready. I could not help shedding a few tears for my unsophisticated Friend. She took her Cacahow off and threw it over me, sitting and crying and not to be comforted. I had a great mind to take her with me, as I expected to be only three weeks in the Bay of Islands, and meant to visit the Church Missionaries, I thought that I should be better without her, So poor Girl I left her, may she be happy! I gave her my Sheets, 3 Blankets and a new Gown, and she cut her Sharks Tooth and gave it to me, the Greatest Compliment a Girl can pay her 'Tamee or Husband'. We have not met since; I have sent her some things from Sydney.

*Thirty-three-year-old Englishman Edward Markham relished his adventures in Northland.*

## VISITING WAIMATE                    *23 December 1835*

### Charles Darwin

At a place called Waimate, about fifteen miles from the Bay of Islands, and midway between the eastern and western coasts, the missionaries have purchased some land for agricultural purposes. I had been introduced to the Rev. W. Williams, who, upon my expressing a wish, invited me to pay him a visit there. Mr Bushby, the British resident, offered to take me in his boat by a creek, where I should see a pretty waterfall, and by which means my walk would be shortened. He likewise procured me a guide. Upon asking a neighbouring chief to recommend a man, the chief himself offered to go; but his ignorance of the value of money was so complete, that at first he asked me how many pounds I would give him, but afterwards was well contented with two dollars. When I showed the chief a small bundle, which I wanted carried, it became absolutely necessary for him to take a slave. These feelings of pride are beginning to wear away; but formerly a leading man would sooner have died, than undergone the indignity of carrying the smallest burden. My companion was a light active man, dressed in a dirty blanket, and with his face completely tattooed. He had formerly been a great warrior.

As the boat was shoving off, a second chief stepped into her, who only wanted the amusement of the passage up and down the creek. I never saw a more horrid and ferocious expression than this man had. This chief had been a notorious murderer, and was an arrant coward to boot. At the point where the boat landed, Mr Bushby accompanied me a few hundred yards on the road: I could not help admiring the cool impudence of the hoary old villain, whom we left lying in the boat, when he shouted to Mr Bushby, 'Do not you stay long, I shall be tired of waiting here.'

We now commenced our walk. The road lay along a well-beaten path, bordered along each side by tall fern, which covers the whole country . . . Although the scenery is nowhere beautiful, and only occasionally pretty, I enjoyed my walk. I should have enjoyed it more, if my companion, the chief, had not possessed extraordinary conversational powers. I knew only three words; 'good', 'bad', and 'yes' and with these I answered all his remarks, without of course having understood one word he said. This, however, was quite sufficient: I was a good listener, an agreeable person, and he never ceased talking to me.

*Charles Darwin.*

At length we reached Waimate. After having passed over so many miles of an uninhabited useless country, the sudden appearance of an English farm-house, and its well-dressed fields, placed there as by an enchanter's wand, was exceedingly pleasant. Mr Williams not being at home, I received in Mr Davies' house a cordial welcome. After drinking tea with his family party, we took a stroll about the farm. At Waimate there are three large houses, where the missionary gentlemen Messrs Williams, Davies and Clarke, reside; and near them are the huts of the native labourers. On an adjoining slope, fine crops of barley and wheat were standing in full ear; and in another part, fields of potatoes and clover. But I cannot attempt to describe all I saw; there were large gardens; with every fruit and vegetable that England produces; and many belonging to a warmer clime. I may instance asparagus, kidney beans, cucumbers, rhubarb, apples, pears, figs, peaches, apricots, grapes, olives, gooseberries, currants, hops, gorse for fences, and English oaks; also many kinds of flowers. Around the farmyard were stables, a thrashing barn with its winnowing machine, a blacksmith's forge, and on the ground ploughshares and other tools: in the middle was that happy mixture of pigs and poultry, lying comfortably together, as in every English farm-yard. At the distance of a few hundred yards, where the water of a little rill had been dammed up into a pool, there was a large and substantial water-mill.

All this is very surprising, when it is considered that five years ago nothing but fern flourished here.

*Four years out from Britain in the survey ship* Beagle, *the young Charles Darwin was feeling very homesick. He spent 10 days in Northland and was not impressed with what he saw. On leaving New Zealand he records: 'I look back to one bright spot, and that is Waimate, with its Christian inhabitants.'*

## HARPOONING WHALES OFF
## BANKS PENINSULA                                       *1838*

## Surgeon Felix Maynard

At one bound the captain sprang to the bow of the boat, and, brandishing the lance, cried: 'Ready, lads, ready!'

The harpooner took the steering oar and, according to his commands, the sailors pulled or back-watered, pulled or back-watered again.

The mother whale did not seem startled at our proximity: she frolicked, turned herself about and raised the little calf, tired with following her, upon her fin.

Captain Jay, his lance poised, waited the favourable moment to strike. The moment came, and the lance transfixed, not the whale, but the calf.

I thought at first that the captain had aimed badly, but soon I comprehended his skill and wisdom. He was aware that the first blow from the lance would not kill the mother, and that she would then fly to a distance and be lost to us; but, by killing the nursling she would be detained immovable, no matter what might be her fate; as mother she would allow herself to be killed on the spot rather than abandon her calf. That is precisely what happened. Captain Jay was able to strike at his leisure, one, two, three, ten blows. The monster floundered, spouted blood, *flurried*, and died, without moving any further away than it had been made fast by the most solid of harpoons. How admirably the power of maternal love dominates the instinct for self-preservation.

Thus at last I was able to say I had both seen and touched a living whale, and this in the very height of the combat. So close had I been to it that I was even covered in blood.

We planted a guidon of ownership in the back of the dead whale and returned on board to prepare the apparatus for raising it, while one of the men climbed the summit of Olimaroa cliff to give the signal agreed upon, by means of a flag especially erected there, for the boats to return to the *Asia*.

Part of the day was employed in towing the whale in and hoisting it by the tackle. The Maoris came in crowds to lend our men a hand, and by nightfall the work was accomplished. Scarcely was the last morsel of fat on deck than the native canoes darted towards the floating carcase,

*Whaler ship.* [Scrimshaw]

which they towed to the strand. It was then a spectacle at once comical and disgusting to see the mob of men, naked and armed with knives, some hanging above the animal's flanks and others buried within its half-open side, slashing off its flesh in every direction, and choosing enormous steaks, which the women placed on the grass in the sun.

That evening the fires of the rich and poor alike were alight for the cooking of these dainty morsels. The feast began at first with cries of joy and songs improvised in honour of the whalers, while the next day the more thrifty housewives hung from the posts of their koumaras the pieces of meat to be reserved for times of scarcity.

*The whale was harpooned off Cape Cachelot, Banks Peninsula. On returning to France, Felix Maynard, surgeon on the French whaler* Asia, *persuaded his friend, Alexandre Dumas, to help write up these exploits.*

## A Fair Exchange in Lyttelton Harbour

*1838*

### Surgeon Felix Maynard

*Felix Maynard had to amputate the harpoonist Taillevent's leg below the knee. He fitted him with a peg leg made from the handle of the very axe which had injured him in the first place.*

[Taillevent] . . . was very gloomy during the first day on his wooden leg and looked forward to a gloomy future in Le Havre. But one day he took a fancy to expose to the air and sunshine the clothes [and trinkets] contained in his box on the very day that the ladies of the village had come to visit the gallants on board.

While Taillevent was thus pitying himself regarding past prodigality, as he made the sunlight flash from those facets of coloured glass in the trinkets, one of those ladies, the great coquette of Oeteta, the legitimate and none too austere wife of the *tayo* of the *Asia*, flung covetous glances at the sailor's trumpery wares, and held out her hand to receive a pair of ear-rings, a ring, or a watch chain.

'She is not fastidious, Madame Kar-kar the fair; they will buy these Havre trinkets from you; take care!'

Madame Kar-kar was not a woman to recoil before a refusal; the passion for barter is powerfully developed among the peoples of Oceania, and especially among the females of those lands. she proposed to exchange her ear-rings with the harpooner for a pair of those contained in the box.

I made Taillevent a sign to agree without haggling, and to give Madame Kar-kar the best he had. With full confidence in me he gave her some pear-shaped imitation pearls, which were worth quite five sous each. In exchange Madame Kar-kar removed her own ear-rings and gave them to him. They were simply large Spanish gold pieces, known by the name of *ounces*. (Worth about 70/- each.) As a matter of fact the islanders only employ the monies of civilized peoples as ornaments, having no knowledge of their worth. Scarcely do they become possessed of gold or silver pieces than they perforate them, thread them upon a string of flax, and thus make of them necklaces, ear-rings, or bracelets. In this way each tribe possesses an enormous capital, the produce of trading, but especially of murder and pillage.

Taillevent could not credit his good fortune. I was obliged to repeat to him twenty times that these two pieces were of purest gold, and were worth, together, a hundred and sixty-eight francs, that is to say, he had doubled his capital more than eight times.

Madame Kar-kar, for her part, went to flaunt her false pearl drops among her companions. The example was contagious; the women of Oeteta and of the other tribes on the peninsula hastened, in emulation of one another, to propose similar exchanges with Taillevent, and the copper of the trinkets turned to gold, and contributed not a little to cure the harpooner of his melancholy.

I have heard since our return that, when walking the quays at Havre,

Taillevent met again his pretty vendor with her basket before her. Remembering that she had proved to be his good angel, and bethinking him of the five or six thousand francs (£200 to £240 at the time), obtained by the exchange of false jewellery for the gold pieces of the New Zealanders, he considered it as being the natural marriage portion of the young girl. He married her, and Madame Taillevent is, to-day, the queen of the cashier's desk in a little cafe much frequented by the sailors, and especially the whalers, in port.

*The* Asia *was moored at Little Port Cooper (Oeteta), Lyttelton Harbour. The tayo was the friend, agent or purveyor accredited to each ship.*

## SIGNING OF THE TREATY OF
## WAITANGI                    *Wednesday 5 February 1840*

## William Colenso

This morning at an early hour, the Natives, who had been gathering together all day yesterday, began to move towards Waitangi, the appointed place of meeting. About 9 a.m. the Lieutenant-Governor, accompanied by the captain of the *Herald*, arrived at Waitangi; and from 9 to 10 a.m. the officers of the man-o'-war, the suite of the Governor, all the members of the Church Mission residing in or near the Bay of Islands, together with different European and American residents and settlers, kept arriving. The day was particularly fine, and the spectacle of the most animated description. On the water were to be seen the numerous canoes gliding from every direction towards the place of assembly, their respective rowers straining every nerve to gain and keep the lead, whilst their paddles kept time with the cadence of the canoe-song of the *kai-tuki* (canoe-song singer), who, standing conspicuously erect in the midst of each canoe, and often on the thwarts, animated the men by his gestures as well as his voice; the boats of the many settlers and residents living on the shores of the bay, together with those from the different ships and vessels in the anchor in the harbour; and ships and vessels decorated with the flags of their respective nations. On shore, in the centre of the delightfully-situated lawn at Waitangi, a spacious tent was erected, which was tastefully adorned with flags, &c., &c., over which

England's banner streamed proudly in the breeze; the whites, many of whom were new-comers, who seemed to be much delighted with the scene before them, were comfortably walking up and down in different little parties, socially chatting with each other *à l'Anglais*; whilst the countenances and gestures of the Natives, who were squatting grouped together according to their tribes, bore testimony to the interest they took, if not in the business, in the gaiety and life of the day.

After the several persons who had entered had been introduced, which was soon done, the Lieutenant-Governor came out to proceed to the tent, His Excellency, the captain of the *Herald*, and Mr Busby, preceded by some of the police, leading the way; on which the Roman Catholic bishop and his priest stepped briskly up close to the heels of the Governor, so shutting us out unless we chose to walk behind them. 'Brethren,' I exclaimed, 'this won't do: we must never consent to this position.'

'No,' rejoined the Rev. R. Taylor; 'I'll never follow Rome.'

Speeches and debate took up most of the day, with most chiefs at first arguing against signing the Treaty. The following day a few Maori chiefs signed the Treaty but debate continued.

*6 February*

Here Hoani Heke signed the treaty, on which several others came forward and did the same.

Whilst the treaty was being signed, Marupo, chief of the Wanaurara tribe, and Ruhe, a chief of the Ngatihineira tribe, made long speeches against the signing of the same. Both declaimed strongly in true New Zealand style, running up and down, flourishing their hands and arms, stamping with their feet, &c. Marupo was stripped naked to the loins, and continued his oratory and his gestures until he was exhausted. Both, however, of these chiefs subsequently came to the table and signed the treaty. Marupo, having made his mark (as he could neither read nor write), shook hands heartily with the Governor, and seized hold of, and much wished to put on, His Excellency's hat, which was lying on the table. After some little time Te Kamara came towards the table and affixed his sign to the parchment, stating that the Roman Catholic bishop (who had left the meeting before any of the chiefs had signed) had told him 'not to write on the paper, for if he did he would be made a slave'.

Rewa was now the only chief of note present who still refused to sign, but after some time, being persuaded by some of his Native friends as well as by members of the Church of England Mission, he came forward and signed the treaty, stating to the Governor that the Roman Catholic bishop had told him not to do so, and that he (the Roman Catholic bishop), had striven hard with him not to sign.

During the signing of the treaty a few chiefs arrived who were not present on the first day from not receiving their summoning letters in time and from the long distance they had to come—of course on foot. They, however, signed the document.

Forty-five chiefs signed the treaty at this second day of meeting. The greater part of them were from the Bay of Islands and its immediate vicinity. Among them, however, were not many chiefs of the first rank. In fact there were none present from any distance save Tamati Waka Nene and his brother Patuone, from the Hokianga district, and Kauwata, Warau, and Ngere, from the Wangaruru district.

His Excellency appeared to be in good health and spirits, and to be much interested in the scenes before him. As each chief affixed his name or sign to the treaty the Governor shook him by the hand saying (in Maori), 'He iwi tahi tatou' ('We are one people'), at which the Natives were greatly pleased.

All that were disposed having signed, the Natives gave three cheers to the Governor. His Excellency, on leaving, requested me to attend to the distributing of a bale of blankets and a cask of tobacco to the Natives, which occupied me till late, each chief who had signed the document getting two blankets and a quantity of tobacco. By dint of close and constant management the said distribution went off well without any mishap or hitch.

*William Colenso (1811–99), printer, Anglican missionary, explorer and biologist, describes the signing. He had previously translated and printed the New Testament in Maori and later Hobson's proclamation following the treaty signing. Colenso published the above account fifty years after the signing.*

## BROKEN-HEARTED AT CLOUDY BAY, OFF BLENHEIM

*about 1840*

## Te Uatorikiriki

Moe hurihuri ai taku moe ki te whare;
Kei whea te tau i aropiri ra,
I nga rangi ra o te tuatahitanga?
Ka haramai tenei, ka tauwehe,
He hanga hua noa te roimata i aku kamo;
no to mea ia ra ka whamamao
Ki Karewa ra, au rerenga hipi
Ki Poihakena, ka whakaaokapua
Te ripa tau arai ki Oropi,
Ki te makau ra e moea iho
E awhi reinga ana i raro ra.
Ka hewa au, e koro kai te ao . . . i

I sleep restlessly in my house
Where is my lover I clung to
In those early days of our courtship?
Now we have come to this, and you are gone.
Tears well up in my eyes,
Because you are far from me.
I look out beyond Karewa, to the pathways of the ships,
To Sydney, which into the mist,
Lies the far off edges of Europe.
To my lover who comes to me only in dreams.
He embraces me in spirit.
So real, I thought you were here in body.

*A song or lament probably composed by Te Uatorikiriki, a Ngati Toa woman at Te Koko a Kupe (Cloudy Bay). Her whaler husband Joseph Toms abandoned her to return to England, leaving her with two sons, George and Tom. She is said to have died of a broken heart. Other tribes also lay claim to the song.*

*Auckland waterfront, 1841.*

## AUCKLAND'S FIRST HORSE RACE      *5 January 1842*

Ensign Best

The long looked for day has at length arrived. Natives and Pachias may be seen crowding to the race course which is a pretty spot situated on the Manakau road. We had a tolerable muster of Ladies who were conveyed in carts to the area of strife. Great had been the contention among the stewards as to the proper length of the course and it was finally carried by some Scotch men who feared the expense of clearing a greater distance that the course should be a circular half mile the most preposterous thing in the world. At one o'clock the bugle sounded for Saddling for the Town Plate of £30 with entrances. Five horses entered Haidee, Bobby, Chance, New Zealander and Kitty. Heats mile and distance. 1st heat Chance and New Zealander bolted and Kitty pulled up in first half mile Haidee won easily. 2nd Heat ditto.

The next race was the Valparaiso stakes of £20 with entrances over the same distance there were four Entrances Miss Starch Cruiskeen Mavoureen & Don Juan. 1st Heat Miss Starch again won by almost a distance. A handicap race—Five to one had been given on field against Miss Starch. A race among the Mauri jockeys concluded the days sport it was the best fun in the whole day although not highly scientific. The Mauries had had their horses given them in part payment for their land only a few days before.

*6th January.* 2nd Day. The Capital running of previous day induced many to venture to the course who had not before dared to attempt a three mile walk.

The day's sport commenced with 'The Ladies Purse' of £15 with 10 added and entrances. A Handicap of £20 with entrances followed. The Soldiers, most of whom were on the course now declared that Miss Starch (my property) had run enough and should be carried home and so determined were they that I had to smuggle her off the course to prevent them carrying their threat into effect. Dr Gammie 80th Regt is the owner of Haidee so that except for the *beaten Stakes* we carried everything into the Barracks. A capital dinner at Woods Hotel concluded the '*First Auckland Races*'.

*Abel Dottin William Best was a tough, competent horseman. After guarding prisoners on Norfolk Island, Best spent a short time in New Zealand. His regiment was sent to India where he was killed in battle at the age of 29.*

## NEGOTIATING THE BULLER GORGE                    *1847*

## Thomas Brunner

*April 29th*. Hunger drove us from our quarters. Although only showery, yet the drip from the bush made us all wet through in a short time. Completed a fair day's walking, particularly so considering it was performed in the morning before breakfast of fern tree; but Ekehu, with his usual energy, secured us a supper of wekas.

*30th*. Came on another day's walking, and were still jammed in between two high ridges of black birch hills coming almost perpendicularly down to the river's edge.

*May 1st*. An awful day's journey. The hills coming down to the river's edge with perpendicular precipices at their base, yet we were compelled to ascend them; but by night we managed to reach a shingle beach on the river-bank.

*2nd*. Searching for food. Moderately fine day, with a series of showers all night, which far from added to our comfort.

*3rd, 4th, 5th*. Continual heavy rains. Nothing to live on but a few rats.

*6th*. Raining and blowing a tempest just after dusk. The fresh in the river came down in a torrent, driving us out of our shelter into the rain and wind to pass the night how we could. We however managed to throw our blanket over a pole, and there remain without fire until the daylight assisted us in improving our habitation. When shifting, the fresh came down so rapidly, that many of our things were left to the mercy of the river, my guns and boots amongst them. The gun was recovered when the fresh abated, having lodged in an overhanging bush, but our salt was destroyed.

*7th.* Found on inspection this morning about five feet of water running over our previous dwelling. Formed our blanket into a tent, and spent the day in making a fire. Towards evening the rain ceased, and we had a fine night.

*8th.* A fine day, but no prospect of moving for some days, the fresh having rendered our progress impossible, and the hill in front too perpendicular to ascend.

*9th.* Moderately fine. The natives went eel fishing in the evening and returned with enough for two meals, and a promise that with a fine morning they would try and make some onward progress.

*10th.* Alas! this morning, instead of proving fine, was the commencement of a violent tempest, and the rain poured down in torrents all day.

*11th.* About two o'clock this morning the river again rose most rapidly; and about four o'clock it found its way over its banks, and into our tent. We were again obliged to brave the storm, and, throwing our blankets over our shoulders, perch ourselves on a tree, and await daylight, when we found means to ascend a few feet higher, and build a new house, but we had no firewood.

*12th.* Heavy rain all day.

*13th.* A series of heavy showers all day.

*14th.* The wind had changed into a better quarter, and we had a drier day, but we could find no provisions, and had only four ounces per day. The natives when very hungry wanted to kill my dog Rover, but I refused, stating, as my reason, that I wished to keep the dog for our last resource. The *katote*, a very indifferent species of tree fern, was found here, but we had not the proper means of cooking it. It requires the application of great heat, and must be allowed to remain in the oven

*Thomas Brunner.*

at least twelve hours, when it will be found a palatable, but far from satisfying dish.

*15th.* Moderately fine: and we were resolved, should the morrow prove fine, to break through our rule of holding the Sabbath, and proceed somewhere in search of food.

*Sunday 16th.* You must never calculate a day ahead of you on this river. After a fine night we had today a thorough wet day.

*17th.* Heavy rain all day.

*18th.* A fine day.

*19th.* Although the day appeared far from fine, yet we mounted our loads on our half-starved backs, and managed to proceed a short distance, hoping to push past our precipice, before which we had been detained ten days, all but starved; but the rain again caught us, and we passed a most miserable night. Heavy rain accompanied with thunder. We killed a robin, which served as the bait for an eel, which Ekehu caught, and gave us for supper.

*20th.* Another deluge of rain compelled us to erect a shelter, although half famished, and await the conclusion of these gales.

*21st.* The weather slightly moderating.

*22nd.* A bitterly cold day. We however managed to accomplish a short day's walk, at last surmounting the precipice which had so long detained us, and slept without shelter: the rain however gave us a wetting in the night.

*23rd.* Hunger again compelled us to shift our quarters in search of food, but finding none, I was compelled, though very reluctantly, to give my consent to killing my dog Rover. The flesh of a dog is very palatable, tasting something between mutton and pork. It is too richly flavoured to eat by itself.

*24th.* Last night we were again visited with a deluge of rain, which completely covered the surface of the earth, so that we had to sit all night ancle deep in water. With the daylight, we all set to work to erect a shelter, which we sadly wanted. We could find no thatch, so we made a roof of small straight birch poles. The soles of my first boots forsook me and I had to take a new pair.

*25th, 26th.* Heavy rain.

*27th.* A slight improvement in the weather, but our dog nearly consumed, and we could find no other eatable: the weather too cold for eels, and birds not seen in the black birch woods.

*28th.* A bitterly cold day . . .

*Thomas Brunner, a surveyor and explorer, set about walking from Nelson to Milford Sound with two Maori guides and their wives. They never reached their distant goal, turning back south of the Fox Glacier and returning to Nelson after 572 arduous days on foot. It is generally agreed that Brunner's journey was the greatest and most strenuous ever undertaken in New Zealand, subsisting as he did mainly on fern roots, eels, rats and wekas. As a surveyor, Brunner laid out the towns of Nelson, Westport and Greymouth.*

## FIRST OPERATION UNDER GENERAL ANAESTHETIC IN WELLINGTON *September 1847*

### *Port Nicholson Spectator* Reporter

On Monday Dr Fitzgerald, Dr Monteith and Mr Marriott, the ingenious constructor of the inhaling apparatus used on the occasion, proceeded to the gaol to try the efficacy of the new discovery on one of the prisoners who wanted to have a tooth extracted. The apparatus was applied to the patient's mouth and after inhaling for some time without effect Mr Marriott altered the instrument, when the desired effect immediately followed, the patient falling into a state of insensibility. The forceps were then applied but the tooth being decayed, the side of it fell in from the pressure and the effect of the ether immediately went off. Dr Fitzgerald said that if the tooth had not broken or with a properly fitting claw the tooth would have been extracted without pain.

The same day at the Colonial Hospital Dr Fitzgerald, assisted by Dr Monteith, removed a large tumour extending from the top of the left shoulder across the back to the right shoulder blade from a native chief of Waikanae who had come to Dr Fitzgerald for that purpose. Several of the natives of Pipitea Pa were present. Mr Marriott applied the inhaling apparatus to the patient, an old man, who soon went off into the usual state and Dr Fitzgerald commenced operation. The patient was insensible until after the third incision, but quickly recovered from the effect of the ether which was not reapplied. The tumour was very large being about 3 lb in weight.

As this, the first instance of the application of the new discovery in this settlement and the apparatus for inhaling was constructed merely from the descriptions which have appeared in the English papers, a good deal of caution was observed in each case, particularly in the latter for fear of an unfavourable effect on the native mind in the event of a failure of the experiment. Sufficient success, however, has attended the trial to warrant greater confidence in a repetition of the experiment.

*J.P. Fitzgerald (1815–97) became the first superintendent of Wellington Hospital, then of a hospital in South Africa.*

## QUEEN'S BIRTHDAY BALL ABOARD THE *MEANDER*, WELLINGTON HARBOUR  24 April 1850

## Charlotte Godley

We had the most lovely night for the ball . . . Mr Bulkeley came to tea and to go with us; we were asked for 'Dancing at nine' on a magnificent *printed* card, and presented ourselves soon after 9.30, when we found everyone arrived and in superb ball-dresses, apparently just unpacked from London, specially Mrs Eyre. We were, I think, all surprised at the general effect of the ball, it was so very good. The dancing was in three rooms, communicating with folding doors, the verandah outside, which is very large, enclosed as a relief to the room for walking about and flirtation when possible; but, as the Brigade-Major's wife, Mrs O'Connell, told me the other day, 'there were only six young ladies here and two of them are old', and the married ladies *all* dance, and as far as I can judge, don't flirt. Beyond the verandah, a space was enclosed for the band of the 65th, and that from the *Meander*, which relieved each other, and played capitally. I hear that there was a very good supper, but cannot speak to it, as we came home just as everyone else was squeezing into it. It was a *sit down* supper, at least for all the ladies; some of the gentlemen had to wait till the first detachment had done. But that is not surprising, as there were 180 people there. The *Meander's* flags assisted not a little in decorating the rooms, which were really quite pretty, with flowers artistically twined round the pillars on the verandah. At the top of the room was a sofa on which Mrs Eyre sat, without rising to receive anyone, bowing to some, and shaking hands with the more illustrious (such as ourselves!). There were about three Maori ladies (in what we should call morning dresses) there, and twice as many gentlemen, but they did not

53 ∎

dance. Not so the officers of the *Meander*, who were all heart and soul in it from Captain Keppel, who seems the most good-natured of men, down to his little nephew, the incipient middy. The next morning they were all off, and the harbour looking quite dull without them.

*Charlotte Godley, wife of the founder of the Canterbury Settlement, John Robert Godley, wrote many letters to her mother in England. The following letter describes a less happy occasion.*

## A Drowning in Lyttelton Harbour     1 July 1851

### Charlotte Godley

We have had, since I wrote, a very sad accident here, which has thrown a great damp over everything. I told you of Mr Ward having gone over to live in Quail Island, and he used to come over, two or three days a week, to bring his butter to market, and do his business at the Bank, as Churchwarden etc., for he was Trustee for all kinds of things, and looked up to by everyone for his innumerable good qualities. We made up a party to go there one day, and see the island, and were to cook our own dinner on the beach. Mr Wortley was to take us over in his little boat, which just held myself, Arthur and Powles; Mrs Fitzgerald and her little brother, and Mr Wortley and Mr Mounsell to row us, and a clothes basket of food. It was Frances' birthday, which I wanted to keep, and they were all in favour of keeping the day (though it turned out cold and rough), so we went over, and were to get Mr Ward to come over for the rest of the party, in his larger boat, which he said he would do any day. When we arrived there, we heard he was not at home. He had gone over for firewood, with his next brother to the land up the harbour, several miles from here, and said he would be back to dinner on the Monday, and this was Tuesday, and they had no news of them. The youngest brother, who is a very nice young boy of sixteen, came to meet us, and said they were very uneasy, and they were very glad to take our boat and go and see after them.

We were very little alarmed, for people are constantly missing here a day or two. Our dinner-party was rather small and it was very cold, but sat under shelter near our fire, and got a few shells on the beach, and then began to wonder they did not come back. It was very rough for our little boat; the wind too against us going home; and I who never like going in one if I can help it, was getting a little unhappy about ourselves, when just as it was getting dark, they came, the poor boy crying, and the men who were extremely fond of their master, almost as bad. They had found nothing but the boat thrown on the beach, bottom upwards, and the oars, one near, and one half a mile off, and the firewood strewed about. It had evidently been upset; one cannot account for the fact that though both could swim, besides having the boat to cling to, yet that neither should be saved, yet so it was. I brought Hamilton, the younger brother, home with us, borrowing the larger boat which we were the first to use after the accident; and I was thankful to feel myself safe on shore, for it was quite a rough evening.

Poor Mr Ward will be terribly missed, both here and at home; he was the eldest son, and had been for a short time at the Irish Bar; he was a good man of business, very sensible and very much liked by everyone. He used to sing with the Glee Club, and church practisings, dance with the young ladies, talk sensibly, or laugh and smoke with the gentlemen; work with the labourers, and was always good-natured and full of spirits. You have no idea of how much everyone feels his loss.

*Charlotte Godleys letters give a penetrating insight into life in the early settler community.*

## FROLICKING NAKED IN THE SNOW
## MAKATU VILLAGE, RUAHINE MOUNTAINS    24 October 1851

### William Colenso

Passed another wretchedly cold day, in which I have scarcely known warmth—even in a small degree. The natives, however, of the place appear to be almost insensible to cold, the majority of them being poorly clad, each in a single loose shoulder mat and yet they go sauntering about the village in the snow, barefoot and barelegged and barebreeched! of course or sit down talking in an open shed, with scarcely any fire, having half of their bodies uncovered. In this respect they differ greatly from the New Zealanders in general (the Lowlanders), who are mostly very impatient of cold. I also noticed some little children who, leaving their garments (each having only a loose harsh mat) in their huts, came out and frolicked naked about the village! regardless of the snow and sleet; nor did they return to their houses and garments until I had a second time ordered them to do so. Poor creatures, at this season they were all living on fern root, which the children were incessantly roasting and hammering; yet they were all very healthy. Indeed the great difference in this respect between the low-lying and sea-coast villages (which I had lately visited) and those of this mountainous district was really surprising; there, in every place, some one had died since my last visit (some 6 months before), while *here*, during *two years*, no one had paid the debt of nature. No doubt this is partly to be attributed to the purity of the mountain air, but not wholly so. Cook's early statement of their being a remarkably healthy race, I have often proved to be true; would that the introduction of European habits and of 'civilisation' had not deprived them of that inestimable blessing.

*The missionary and naturalist William Colenso made frequent 'pastoral circuits' on foot from his base in Hawke's Bay to remote corners of the North Island, such as Waikaremoana, Taupo and the Wairarapa, often crossing snowy mountain ranges en route. On the occasion of these observations, Colenso visited Makutu village, high above the Rangitikei River, on his way to Patea.*

## COOK'S VISIT RECALLED                                   *1852*

### Chief Horeta Te Taniwha

We lived in Whitianga, and a vessel came there, and when our men saw the ship they said it was a *tupua*, a god (some unknown thing), and the people on board were strange beings. The ship came to anchor, and the boats pulled on shore. As our old men looked at the manner in which they came ashore, the rowers pulling with their backs to the bows of the boat, the old people said, 'Yes, it is so: these people are goblins; their eyes are in the back of their heads; they pull on shore with their backs to the land to which they are going.' When these goblins came on shore we (the children and women) took notice of them, but we ran away from them into the forest, and the warriors alone stayed in the presence of

*'. . . they pull on shore with their backs to the land.'*

those goblins; but, as the goblins stayed some time, and did not do any evil to our warriors, we came back, one by one, and gazed at them, and we stroked their garments with our hands and we were pleased with the whiteness of their skins and the blue of the eyes of some of them.

After the ship had been lying at anchor for some time, some of our warriors went on board, and saw many things. When they came on shore, they gave our people an account of what they had seen. This made many of us desirous to go and see the home of the goblins. I went with others; but I was a very little fellow in those days, so some of us boys went in company with the warriors. Some of my playmates were afraid, and stayed on shore. When we got on board of the ship we were welcomed by the goblins, whom our warriors answered in our language. We sat on the deck of the ship, where we were looked at by the goblins, who with their hands stroked our mats and the hair of the heads of us children; at the same time they made much gabbling noise in talking, which we thought were questions regarding our mats and sharks' teeth we wore in our ears, and the hei-tiki we wore suspended on our chests; but as we could not understand them we laughed, and they laughed also. They held some garments up and showed them to us, touching ours at the same time; so we gave our mats for their mats, to which some of our warriors said 'Ka pai', which word was repeated by some of the goblins, at which we laughed, and were joined in the laugh by the goblins.

Now some of the goblins had walking sticks which they carried about with them, and when we arrived at the bare dead trees where the shags roost at night and have their nests, the goblins lifted their walking sticks up and pointed them at the birds, and in a short time thunder was heard to crash and a flash of lightning was seen, and a shag fell from the trees; and we children were terrified, and fled, and rushed into the forest and left the goblins all alone. They laughed and waved their hands to us, and in a short time, the bravest of us went back to where the goblins were, and handled the bird, and saw it was dead. But what killed it? . . .

I and my two boy-companions did not walk about on board the ship—we were afraid lest we should be bewitched by the goblins; and we sat still and looked at everything at the home of these goblins. When the chief goblin had been away in that part of the ship which he occupied, he came up on deck again to where I and my boy-companions were, and patted our heads with his hand, and he put his hand out towards me and spoke to us at the same time, holding a nail out towards us. My companions were afraid, and sat in silence; but I laughed, and he gave the nail to me. I took it in my hand and said 'Ka pai' ('very good'), and he repeated my words, and again patted our heads with his hand, and went away. My companions said, 'This is the leader of the ship, which is proved by his kindness to us; and also he is very fond of children. A noble man—one of noble birth—cannot be lost in a crowd.' I took my nail, and kept it with great care, and carried it wherever I went, and made it fit to the point of my spear, and also used it to make holes in the side-boards of canoes, to bind them on to the canoe. I kept this nail till one day I was in a canoe and she capsized in the sea, and my god (the nail) was lost to me.

*Horeta Te Taniwha, one-time leader of the Hauraki and Coromandel tribes, recalls Cook's visit to Mercury Bay 83 years earlier.*

## MACKENZIE'S DOG IN COURT                                                                 *1855*

### *Pioneer* Reporter

I fell right into the Mackenzie trial. It was a peepshow for the province: the tiny Lyttelton Courthouse was like a sardine tin. In front was Jock Mackenzie, stolid as a brick and dumb as an oyster. The judge called on him to plead and the case proceeded. One by one the witnesses rounded off the whole story of the stolen mob and Mackenzie's flight.

'Bring in the dog,' called out the judge.

I saw Mackenzie start and gnaw his fingers a moment, as the crowd stared at the slim, timid little black beast, that had outwitted grey old shepherds with the dumb crambo tricks Mac had taught her. She slipped her chain coming in, and in another minute the slim, sad-eyed thing was scratching and whining at the woodwork, trying to get to Jock.

And Jock—the dog's eyes had made a baby of him, six-footer that he was. The tears ran down and lost themselves in his red beard as he said over and over, 'Eh, lassie! Poor lassie. They've got you too!'

Well, I felt smaller than matchwood that minute. There, on the one hand, was all civilisation with its thumb turned down; on the other, this neolithic survival of a man and his soft-eyed dog bearing it all!

'That is enough; remove the dog,' said the judge.

'Leave the dog to me; she was mine, bought with my own money; she was doing no harm to nobody, and she was a good friend to me that has no other. Leave me the poor beastie! I'll make your roads; I'll break your stones; I'll call myself thief; but let her stay. She'll work for me, will never lift sheep more, only let me keep her.'

The judge's words dropped like frost. The keeping of the dog did not rest with him, he said, nor did Mackenzie deserve mercy after his attempt to deceive the Court.

The sentence was five years penal servitude.

*In March 1855, Jock Mackenzie was arrested for stealing a thousand sheep in South Canterbury. He twice escaped custody before being brought to trial in Lyttelton. Mackenzie was goaled and his 'low-set slut, with tanned muzzle and feet' was sold to a farmer, but, because she was accustomed to Mackenzie working her in Gaelic, the dog would work for no one else. After a year in custody, Mackenzie was pardoned and disappeared from public view.*

## German Hospitality near Motueka                 *1859*

### Julius von Haast

. . . we had a cheerful typical German guest-room before us. All round were tables and benches, at which guests were sitting: clouds of blue smoke from pipes and cigars filled the air; and the daughters of the host, red-cheeked, with true flaxen hair and forget-me-not blue eyes, served the company. It all reminded us of Home, and we thought we had found ourselves in Germany in the Antipodes.

A Black Forest clock, with regular tic-tac began to play 'Ueb immer Treu und redlichkeit' and 'Lieber Mond, du gehst so stille' [two German

*Julius von Haast.*

folk songs] and although several teeth were broken, we listened with delight. A thousand recollections of youth, long dormant, awakened. I thought of the time when I sat on the nurse's knees, learning by heart the former song for my father's birthday, and later when I read in my first lesson-book with bated breath and burning cheeks of Cook's voyages and his sojourn among the cannibals. My most ardent wish was to journey across the ocean and to see the wonders of the South Seas and the cannibals that inhabited them. If many a hope of that fair time has foundered, that wish at least has been fulfilled. I have for months at a time lived with these cannibals, slept under the same roof, eaten out of the same dish with them. I have found them hospitable and helpful, honourable and true, and could not sufficiently admire the blessings that Christendom and civilization have conferred upon this intelligent race. No wonder that, in spite of the noisy company round me, my thoughts, oblivious of what was passing around me, reverted to those vanished times, until my friend's voice called me back to the present.

In the conversation that ensured with the guests, although they had been seventeen years in an English colony, their love for their Fatherland was still warm. Even in the kitchen they remained true to the old customs, for, for our evening meal they placed before us a true German dish, ham pancakes, that smiled to us as a friend not seen ever so long.

*While investigating the Aorere gold-fields, Julius von Haast, a 37-year-old newly appointed government geologist, spent the night at the inn at Sarau, a settlement between Motueka and Nelson, with 26 German families. Haast made many scientific discoveries in New Zealand and later became the director of the Canterbury Museum.*

## CARBINE AND REVOLVER ATTACK SOUTH OF AUCKLAND                14 December 1863

Captain William Jackson

I started on Friday, the 11th inst., at 1.15 p.m., with a force of my company of Forest Rangers on an expedition towards the Wairoa River [in the Hunuas, east of Papakura]. I continued our march until 6.15 p.m., when finding we had overrun the track, I camped the night. On Sunday, Dec 13th, I broke camp at 5.30 a.m. and turned back to re-examine the path, and found tracks diverging to the left. I then posted some men to look out for smoke, which we soon discovered rising out of the ranges. We went very quietly towards it, and by using great caution succeeded in surprising the enemy about 8.30 a.m. We had got between their sentry and their camp.

When about twelve or fifteen yards from the enemy, I halted my men on an eminence, to give them breath, and gave orders that they should at first attack the enemy with their carbines, and then rush them with their revolvers. The Maoris were then cleaning their guns. The surprise was complete. After our carbines were discharged, the enemy apparently expecting we had only empty pieces, turned upon us with their guns and tomahawks, &c., but the revolvers soon sent them to the right-about. Several of the enemy who were wounded by the discharge of the carbines were assisted away by the women, who were very busy removing arms, dead, and wounded. I saw two or three natives hit who were immediately helped away by women. I had directed my men not to fire at the women, and I am happy to say they did not, though it is very possible that some of the women and children may have got hurt in the affray, but I only know of one instance, a woman I believe was wounded in the leg by a stray shot. The affair lasted only four or five minutes. I saw three dead men taken off, and four of their dead were left in our hands. Two of the natives, when surrounded, endeavoured to stab my men, one using a bowie knife and the other a large carving knife, but the revolver made short work of them. One native at great risk returned and attempted to carry away a small tin box, but a bullet made him drop it and run off . . . I estimate the number of the enemy to have been over 40 men. One of the natives, before he died, told me there were 28, and on being asked again said there were 28 double, holding up his two fingers. He also said his tribe was Ngatipaoa. He would not tell his own name, but said the man next to him was a chief named Matariki. The scene of the engagement was in the ranges, about five miles north of Paparata . . . The enemy appeared to have plenty of provisions; we found a good deal of tea and sugar and some flour; there was an abundance of fern-root, three or four iron pots had meat in them, and a good quantity of pork was hanging up. In the box which the native tried to rescue, mentioned above, there were three flags, one, a large red flag on which was embroidered a white cross and stars and the word 'Aotearoa' in white letters. It is made of silk and is neat and handsome. Another flag is a large red pendant with a white cross, the remaining flag is a handkerchief, of the Union Jack pattern. The other spoils are a double-barrelled shotgun, a large horse pistol, and a smaller pistol, three or four cartridge boxes, a great deal of property which belonged to settlers, such as scarlet hangings, fancy window blinds, small workboxes &c., some papers belonging to Mr Richardson of Wairoa, and a coat belonging to Mr Johnson of the same place, several articles which had been stolen by the natives from Mr McDonald at the time Trust's children were murdered, near Howick. I therefore conclude these natives were of the party who committed those murders. One of my men has two small packets of hair, I think European. They are evidently relics. He will give them up to anyone who may claim them. We could not bring away much of the 'loot', as we were heavily loaded with our arms, blankets &c., but I think I brought away sufficient to prove the character of the party we fell in with. We destroyed several packages and tins of gunpowder, and threw a great number of bullets in the creek.

I have great pleasure in reporting that my men behaved with great coolness and courage. There was no firing at random. I am anxious to bring to your special notice the brave and cool conduct of Ensign Westrupp, who was foremost in the attack, and made every shot of his revolver tell; also Private John Smith who had a severe hand to hand struggle with a powerful native.—I have, &c.,

WM JACKSON

Captain Command Forest Rangers

*This was one of the early actions of the New Zealand Wars. The Forest Rangers were a small band of mobile, irregular, guerilla troops who later played a decisive role in waging war against the Maori in Auckland, the Waikato, Bay of Plenty, Taranaki and Poverty Bay. There were 27 men in Jackson's No. 1 Company, including two black Jamaicans. The 'neat and handsome' flag taken here was displayed for many years in the Auckland Public Library.*

## THE LONELY SHEPHERD                    *Clarence Valley, 1864*

## Robert Palmer

My Dear Friend you must not think that I had forgotten my old Bamford friends because i did not write to you before I can assure you that I have often thought of you although so far away. I was very glad to see your letter that you sent to my mother I should have answered it before but I had not seen mother for 8 years until last July when I went to see her and she showed me your letter She could not read it her self as her sight is getting very bad and the ink had faded on the paige so she could not answer it before I wrote to you in July last but my litter was very short and I now have no newse to tell you so I will give you an account of the life I have led since I came out here.

When i first came out I engaged for 12 months as a Stockkeeper for £18 pr year at a place called the Wairau distant 120 miles from Nelson and there was very few people liveing there then. The next year I was in engaged as a shepherd at £25 pr year i had to live alone and my work was to range about over the mountains with my dog and gun i staied in the Wairau as shepherd for seven years then as i had got used to liveing along the inhabertants was getting to thick for me so there was a new place found a long way inland it was between two high ranges of mountains one range is 12000 feet high and the other is 8000 feet high they have snow on all year round and in the winter no one can cross over them. A Gentilman asked me if i would go to live in this place and I told him I would for good wages so he offered me £100 pr year and rations. So I started with 1600 sheep from Wairau on the 2 of April 1859 and arrived at my gourneys end on the 22nd of the same month I had 5 men went with me to help drive the sheep and horses as I had to take Flour, tea and Sugar enough to last me six months. the men staid with me 5 days to help me to build a hut with long grass and then when that was done then they bid me good by lo and left me to my fate for the winter and i never saw any one until the 9 of now. it was when i was all alone in the long winter days and nights that I used to think of old bramford and every one that i knew there. i staid in that place for 3 years untill i was out one day and got caurt in a very heavy snow Storm and had to stop all night in the snow it was 4 feet deep it very nearly killed me I had to go to Nelson and was there 4 months under the docters so I gave up my place turn once then i got the situation that i am in now as manager of a sheep Station my wages is £100 pr year and everything found me and two horses to ride as i was tired of liveing alone and so far away from any town.

*Palmer spent three lonely years in the Clarence Valley, Marlborough, shepherding for the future premier, Joseph Ward. A year after writing this letter, Palmer was found dead beside his horse in front of the homestead.*

## WAIKATO BATTLE                                  *2 April 1864*

### Brigadier-General George J. Carey

I decided on surrounding the place and adopting the more slow but sure method of approaching the position by sap [a trench].

About noon I ordered Captain Betty, Royal Artillery, to have a six-pounder Armstrong gun carried into the sap, an entrance having been made. It opened fire on the enemy's work, destroying the palisading, making a considerable breach and silencing in a great measure the fire of the enemy on the men engaged at the head of the sap.

*Brigadier-General Carey and Chief Rewi Maniapoto.*

As it was known that women and children were in the pa, the enemy was called upon to surrender previous to the concentrated fire of the Armstrong gun and hand grenades on their work. They were told that their lives would be spared, and if they declined they were requested at least to have compassion on their women and children, and send them out. They replied that they would not do so, but would fight to the last. The pa was then carried.

. . . I regret to say that in the pursuit some three or four women were killed unavoidably, probably owing to the similarity of dress of both men and women, and their hair being cut equally short, rendering it impossible to distinguish one from the other at a distance.

At an early hour this morning I caused diligent search to be made for the killed and wounded of the enemy. Their losses were considerable amounting to 101 killed, besides 18 to 20 reported by native persons as buried in the pa; 26 wounded and taken prisoners, and 7 unwounded taken prisoner.

The casualties on our side—167 killed and 52 wounded, of which I enclose a return—are, I regret to say, severe.

GEORGE J. CAREY

Brigadier-General

*In a desperate stand against colonists appropriating their land, 300 Kingite Maori* men and women, led by Rewi Maniapoto, fortified a pa at the village of Orakau, near Kihikihi. They feared that, if captured, they would be imprisoned for life on a coal-hulk anchored off Auckland.

## LAMENT FOR THE DISPOSSESSED          *Taupo, 1860s*

Rengiamoa

### E Pa To Hau

E pa to hau, he wini raro, he homai aroha i
Kia tangi atu au I konei, he aroha ki te iwi
Ka momotu ki tawhiti, ki Paerau. Ko wai e kite atu?
Kei hea aku hoa i mua ra, i te tonuitanga i?
Ka hara-mai tenei, ka tauwehe, ka raungaiti au i.

E ua e te ua, e taheke kow i runga ra e.
Ko au ki raro nei riringi ai te ua i aku kamo.
Moe mai, e Wano, i 'Tirau, te pae ki te whenua
I te wa tutata ki te kainga koua hurihia.
Tenei matou kei runga kei te toka ki Taupo,
Ka paea ki te one ki Waihi, ki taku matua nui
Ko te whare koiwi ki Tongariro, e moea iho nei.
Hoki mai e Roto ke te puia nui ki Tokaanu,
Ki te wai tuku kiri o te iwi e aroha nei au i.

### The Wind Blowing Softly

The wind blowing softly from the north brings longing,
And I weep. My longing for my people
Gone far off to Paerau. Who can find them there,
Where are my friends of those prosperous times?
It has come to this, we are separated and I am desolate.

Rain down rain, pour down from above.
Here below you, I shower rain from my eyes.
Wano, sleep on at 'Tirau, the barrier that hides
The land near the home we have abandoned.
Here we are on the rock at Taupo,

Stranded on the shore at Waihi with my great father
In his burial place on Tongariro, whom I see in dreams.
Within, I return to the great hot springs at Tokaanu,
The bathing waters of the people for whom I long.

*In the 1860s, government troops drove large numbers of Ngati Apakura people off their Waikato lands. The dispossessed tribe sought refuge on the western shore of Lake Taupo. A high-born woman named Rangiamoa laments the loss of her home and her kinsmen, and acknowledges the mana of the Taupo people who shelter the refugees. Maori believed the wind carried messages. This song became famous and is still widely sung.*

## 'MY CHILDREN HAS HAD TO GO BARE FUTED'

*Wairarapa, 3 March 1865*

### Jane Oates

Dear sister you say that it is 8 yers since we saw each other and thare is a grate change since that for I have had to sufer hardships since then. My children has had to go bare futed, and I have beene that I have not had a shue that wold stay on my foot, and Oates as sould the cloes of his back to the nateves for weate . . . and I ham living in a werey of split slabs and bark naled to the nicks to keepe the wind out. It is a miserable place in winter—not fit to lie in. It is no wonder hat me being hill living in such a place as this, but wat can we do for we have lade out all the money we could get for land so that we may live comfortable so that we have not got money to put up a hous. The bedsted that I li on is sowed logs with slabs naled to them. I have got too chares—one that Richard and his farther made—and a rocking chare, and the rest is stools to sit on. But now we have got plenty of sheepe and cattel and corn, and now I hope brother is able to send me the money that dear farther left for me and then we will try to have a hous to liv in. I think if my brother could see wat a place I live in he would send me sum money soon and be glad to think that he has got me out of this.

*Jane Oates writes to her sister after eight years on her husband's farm at Peach Grove, Taratahi Plains, Wairarapa.*

## 'I WAS TREATED IN A COLD, CRUEL AND UNKIND MANNER'

*Canterbury, October 1865*

# Augusta McNeill

Oh! I was treated in a cold, cruel and unkind manner by Mrs Kesteven and some of her grown-up daughters . . . after driving two long days in a Bullock-dray heaped with all kinds of rubbish I arrived (much fatigued) at my journey's end. Almost all the road had been trackless and treeless; the house was a small, miserable looking, broken down thing situated on the river bed of the Waimakariri, everything about the house and its environs was wretched and comfortless to a degree. I was received by Mrs Kesteven, a large, coarse, cross-looking woman. She introduced me to my six pupils, the eldest sixteen years old; they were like wild, untamed colts, but as pupils none could be better, they were most anxious to learn and got on amazingly. Mrs Kesteven frequently told me that she thought they were making rapid progress but notwith-standing this Mrs Kesteven was dreadfully rude, unkind, yes, even downright cruel to me, especially if she saw me looking ill. I was only engaged to teach five hours a day but I found I was expected to teach eight and a half hours and, although there were six daughters above twelve years of age, I was expected to clean out the School hut, also to fetch sticks and light the fire etc. I had to scrub floors, wipe up dishes, etc. etc. and do all kinds of menial work and after all I was accused of not doing enough and not sewing sufficiently for the family . . . every evening was spent in playing the piano from 6.30 to 9.30 for the amusement of the children or Mrs Kesteven and every moment stolen from that time was spent in fancy work for Mrs Kesteven.

*Augusta McNeill, an English governess, writes to Miss Lewin in England. Augusta was paid at a rate of £40 a year but the work was so arduous that she left after a short time and found more congenial work teaching three children at Governors Bay where her employer was 'kind, considerate and friendly'.*

## PARSON CALLS ON KANIERE GOLD MINERS 1866

### Archdeacon Henry Harper

I looked down on a group of tents, one a biggish one, from which came laughter and the sound of revelry, whilst the inevitable miner's dog announced the arrival of a stranger. The path was so steep I had to run down, and just as I reached the bottom, out came from the tent a big, young fellow, in flannel shirt, bare armed, with a can of beer in his hands, quite a couple of quarts, which he held up before me, as he straddled across the path. 'Have a drink?' he asked. 'Yes,' I said, 'I'm hot and thirsty,' and I took a moderate draft. Instantly a bout of uproarious burst of laughter in the tent; the flap of it drawn back, and a lot of merry faces, apparently poking fun at me. 'I want to introduce myself,' I said. 'I'm going to have a service tomorrow across the river; I hope you will come.' There was a general response: 'We'll be there, and give you a show . . .' Then a good deal of talk and more merriment, which I didn't understand, until on Sunday, after the service, one of them stayed to talk. I'm going to come regularly. Do you know what brought them today? We were in the tent, drinking beer, and someone sang out, "Look, there's a parson coming: never saw one here before; I'll go and offer him a drink, and I'll lay you a fiver he won't take it."' The bet was taken by several, and that chap lost his money.

*Most accounts of the Westland gold miners dwell on their drunkenness, gambling and fighting, but Henry Harper was favourably impressed.*

## THE STRATFORD FIRE STORM 1868

### Edward Gilshnan

*9 January.* . . . thank God, my eyesight has returned, although everything I look at now is very blurred and hazy. For two days I was blind, and did not think I should ever get right again. Dear old boy, I have had just about the roughest time of it that ever I had in my life, and Alice had it just as bad. When I first noticed the fire it was just behind my house, in the green bush, and it was coming on in a broad sheet of flame, which seemed to me about ten chains wide, but the way the wind was blowing, it seems as if it would miss my place; so I ran round to my next neighbour to see if I could be of any assistance, and I sent his wife and children round to our house, and I helped him a bit, and while I was doing that the fire came right through our clearing, and when I tried to get home, I found I couldn't. My neighbour and I had cut a trench round his house to keep the fire off, and we laid down in that until we could stand it no more, so we both made a rush for it, to get on the road, and although we started for my place, I never thought to reach it alive, for the fire and smoke that I had to run through was something fearful; and when at last I reached home, I sank down exhausted, although the fire was burning right up to the very house. Alice had a double duty—to draw water for keeping the fire back and to look after a lot of helpless children and a more helpless woman. After a bit I recovered, and did what I could; but with our exertions we saved the house and dairy, although the whole of the out-buildings are gone, besides some tools. The stock-yard and cow-shed went first. I began to get alarmed then. Then the fire came along to the pigstye, so I rushed in and smashed in the end of the stye, so as to let out the two pigs I had in there to fatten. The pigs as soon as they got liberty, madly rushed into the fire and got burnt to death. Then came the fire up to the dairy, and it took both mine and Alice's level best to save the place, for it the dairy had been burnt we could not have saved the house, and if the house has been burnt there would not have been a soul alive to tell the tale; for it was only by getting to leeward of the house that we could live at all.

There were sixteen hands, all told, in the house, so you can form an idea of what would have happened in case the house caught fire, for if such a thing had happened, the only thing to do would be for me to have collared a child under each arm, and Alice the same, and, in trying to get away, would either have been burnt to death in the fire or suffocated in the smoke . . . My neighbour had a mare tied up to his fence, in case he should have to ride away, but the mare got roasted to death.

*A long drought culminated in big devastating fires breaking out in many parts of New Zealand in December 1867. One started on the forested western slopes of Mount Egmont and swept towards Stratford. Edward Gilshnan, who farmed down Waingongoro Road described his ordeal to his brother Harry.*

## VISITING THE KARORI LUNATIC ASYLUM                                    *1871*

## Dr France

*Wed. 20 September: Parliamentary committee members question Dr France, the visiting surgeon.*

Do the patients get out; leave the asylum? No there is no arrangement for their going away.

Do they never leave the asylum? No.

Have you any yard for exercise? They go out of a building into a paddock containing about five acres. There are two enclosed yards attached to the rear of the buildings. There is a front garden of about a quarter of an acre in which they walk about.

I saw a man walking about in the yard barefooted and his feet were quite blue and covered in chilblains? Originally that man was dangerous in this way. When visitors were there he would suddenly become violent and kick them, and would sometimes break his boots to pieces. The peculiar colour was caused by exposure, and was what is called pigmentary. It was not from chilblains, for his feet were that colour in the warmest weather, and you see this with sailors' feet. He was a sailor, and the fact of the matter is he would not have boots on.

Female patients were also walking upon the bare floor and had no covering on their feet? Some will kick their shoes off and destroy them.

The women are not most refractory? One is very violent, she has been there for ten years.

Do the female patients ever get out? The females get out in the front, in the garden more particularly. I had a croquet ground prepared and a bagatelle table, but the men have the best of amusements at present; they have a pack of cards and a set of draughts . . .

If the site were nearer the town the inhabitants would take some interest in the Asylum? Nobody ever goes to Karori, and people never talk about it except from hearsay.

I looked in the book for visitors, and saw very few names since I was there two years ago? At present the roads are passable, but last winter they were impassable in places.

Do you allow the patients out of control occasionally? We have no means of doing so.

How do you mean no means? No means of letting them out excepting as cured.

If their friends gave a guarantee? They have no friends, they are paupers.

*Dr France had visited the asylum as least twice a week for the previous 10 years. As a result of this enquiry the asylum was closed and the buildings converted to a school, later to become Karori Normal School.*

## COACHING THROUGH OTAGO                                           *1872*

### Anthony Trollope

On the fifth day—the worst of all, for the snow fell incessantly, the wretched horses could not drag us through the mud, so that I and the gentleman with me were forced to walk, and the twelve miles we accomplished took us five hours,—we reached the town of Tuapika, whence we were assured there would run a well-appointed coach to Dunedin . . . We had come through Dunstan alias Clyde, through Teeviot alias Roxburgh, through Beaumont which had another name which I have forgotten, and at last reached Tuapika alias Lawrence. The rivers and districts have been served in the same way, and as the different names are used miscellaneously, the difficulty which travellers always feel as to new localities is considerably enhanced. At Tuapika we found an excellent inn, and a very good dinner. In spite of the weather I went round the town, and visited the Athenaeum or reading room. In all these towns there are libraries, and the books are strongly bound and well thumbed. Carlyle, Macauley, and Dickens are certainly better known to small communities in New Zealand than they are to similar congregations of men and women at home. I should have liked Tuapika had it not snowed so bitterly on me when I was there.

On the following day we got on board the well-appointed coach at six in the morning. It certainly was a well-appointed coach, and was driven by a good coachman as ever sat upon a box; but the first stage, which took us altogether six hours, was not memorable for good fortune. There was a lower new road and an upper old road. The former was supposed to be impracticable because of the last night's snow, and the

*Anthony Trollope.*

man decided on taking the hills. As far as I could see we were traversing a mountain-side without any track; but there was a track for of a sudden, as we turned a corner, we found ourselves in a cutting, and we found also the cutting was blocked with snow. The coach could not be turned, and the horses had plunged in so far that we could with difficulty extricate them from the traces and pole-straps. The driver, however, decided on carrying on. Shovels were procured, and for two hours we all worked up to our hips in snow, and did at last get the coach through the cutting. But it was not practicable to drive the horses down the hill we had ascended, and we therefore took them out and brought it down by hand,—an operation that at any rate kept us warm. We had hardly settled into our seats after this performance, before one of the wheelers slipped into a miner's water-run, and pulled the other horse under the pole atop of him. The under horse was, at it were, packed into the gully and buried, with his brother over him, like a tombstone. So we went to work again with the shovels, and dug out first one animal and then the other. We were wet through, and therefore a good deal the worse for our task, but the horses did not seem to mind it. At last we reached the town of Tokomariro, alias Milton, where comforts of all kinds awaited us. In the first place there was a made road into Dunedin, and a well-horsed coach to take us. We had descended below the level on which the snows were lying. My wife found a kind hostess who took her to a fire and comforted her with dry stockings, and I got some dinner and brandy-

and-water. About eight in the evening we reached Dunedin, alive, in fair spirits,—but very tired, and more ready than ever to agree with that up-country inn-keeper who had thought but little of the wisdom of one who came travelling by winter in Otago.

*The English novelist Anthony Trollope and his wife landed at Invercargill and made their way to Queenstown before coaching towards Dunedin. When Trollope returned to England, his publisher paid him £1300 for the story of his travels in Australia and New Zealand, more than twice the money he was paid for his successful novel* Barchester Towers.

## LIFEBOAT ADRIFT OFF SOUTH AFRICA                1874

## Second Mate Henry McDonald

I was aroused from sleep by the cry 'Fire!' Rushing on deck I found dense clouds of smoke were issuing from the fore peak. The bo'son's locker, full of oakum, rope, varnish, and paint, was ablaze. The fire engine was rigged, and the fore-part of the ship was deluged with water. They had already got her head before the wind, but presently by some extraordinary mischance, and one that was never explained, she came head to the wind; and then the smoke was driven aft in suffocating clouds. Flames burst out 'tween decks, and in an hour and a half the *Cospatrick* was doomed. Dreadful scenes followed. One boat was launched, but was immediately swamped by the crowd of demented men and women that jumped into it. The long boat caught fire; and in the end only two boats got away safely—the port and the starboard lifeboats. They stood off and, helpless to assist, watched the tragedy to the bitter end. The main and mizzen masts fell, and many of those who had crowded aft were crushed to death. Then the stem was blown out. That was the end, and the shrieks of the survivors were silenced suddenly in the roaring flames.

The condition of those who had escaped in the boats was well nigh desperate. Had they known what was in store for them doubtless most of them would have preferred a more merciful death on the burning ship. They had neither water, food, masts, nor sails; and in the starboard lifeboat they had but one oar. The two boats kept company on 20th and 21st November, but then it commenced to blow, and we got separated. I

*Edward Cotter, Thomas Lewis and Henry McDonald, the only survivors of the* Cospatrick *disaster.*

whistled and shouted when daylight came, but could see nothing of the other boat. Thirst began to tell severely on all of us. Bentley, who was steering, fell overboard and was drowned. Three men became mad that day and died. We threw the bodies overboard.

*Monday, 22nd.* Strong gale, with heavy seas running; five deaths; cut a couple for the blood and liver.

On the 24th four men died. On the 25th we were reduced to eight, and three of them were out of their minds. Early on the morning of the 26th a boat passed close to us. She was not more than fifty yards away. We hailed her but got no answer. I think she must have heard us. One more died that day. We threw one overboard but were too weak to lift the other. There were then five of us left—two able seamen, one ordinary, and one passenger, and myself. The passenger was out of his mind. All drank sea water. We were dozing when the madman bit my foot. I woke up. We then saw a ship bearing down upon us. It proved to be the *British Sceptre* from Calcutta to Dundee. We were taken on board and treated very kindly. I got very bad on her. I was very nigh death's door. We had not recovered when we got to St Helena. I had dysentery. They handed us brandy and we were in such a state that we should have drunk all of it.

We made 540 miles in those eight days. The disaster occurred in 37:15 S lat., 12:25 E long. This was at midday on the 18th. I knew that we had kept the same longitude all the time. We knew we were to the northward of the Cape. It was heart-rending to see the women when the first boat went down. They were about eighty in number. The ship's davits bent down with the weight of them. They went down with one shriek.

*The* Cospatrick *(1220 tons) sailed from London with 473 people on board. Of these, only the quartermaster, a lad, and McDonald survived. The burning and sinking of the* Cospatrick *'sent a thrill of horror throughout the Empire', especially Auckland, her port of destination.*

## COLLECTING POTATOES NEAR WHAKAREWAREWA 1870S

## Makeriti

How well I remember my young days when I lived at Whakarewarewa with my koroua Maihi te Kakauparaoa and my kuia Marara and sister, those two fine old people of the old order who lived their good and simple life, not knowing a word of English. We lived mostly at Whakarewarewa during the winter season, going to Parekarangi now and then to get potatoes and other foods, as nothing was grown at Whakarewarewa owing to the heat of the ground. We had a rua kai (food pit) on the site where the government now have a so-called model pa, for we owned the land then.

The two baskets of potatoes brought from Parekarangi would be emptied into the storage pit, and my kuia would take a supply on to the kainga which was not far away, for our immediate use. Sometimes after the hauhake (the digging up of the food), my mother or other relatives helped to carry the baskets of potatoes from Parekarangi to Whaka-rewarewa to be placed in the pit there, while the greater part of the mara kai (crop) was gathered and placed in a pit at Parekarangi, to be taken out from time to time as we needed them. In later years pack horses were used for fetching potatoes.

When I was older, and able to walk longer distances and not be carried on my kuia's back, I enjoyed these journeys backward and forward. The stream Puarenga had to be crossed before arriving at the kainga. This the people waded, generally knee deep, but after heavy rain, it became deeper in parts, and the current was strong. I crossed this stream on the back of my kuia till I was big enough to look after myself.

The place where we crossed was from fifteen to twenty yards wide, shallow in most parts, then deep under the steep bank on the other side. A path was made in a cutting down this steep bank.

How well I remember sitting on the taumata, the brow of the hill above this whakawhitianga (crossing), looking down on that dear old kainga and on the fine old people who occupied it, that old generation who have nearly all passed away. I close my eyes, and I am there again, sometimes alone, and sometimes with my relatives and playmate Ataraiti, companion of my childhood.

*In 1930, Makeriti, also known as Maggie Papakura, wrote this account as part of her thesis for a degree in anthropology at Oxford University, England. Sadly, Makeriti died a few days before her examiners saw her thesis, which was published posthumously as a book,* The Old-Time Maori.

## AFTERMATH OF THE S.S. TARARUA SINKING
*Southland, 29 April 1881*

## J. Rennie

We started next morning to walk along the beach to Waikawa and although the distance was only fifteen miles it took us all day to cover it. We were first engaged in coffining the bodies found, and that having been done we were asked to take charge of the work of interring the dead. When no bodies were coming ashore, we started on foot to search the beaches.

The bodies were sweltering in the sun, the day was warm, and every minute they were getting more offensive. The odour from so many was perceptible a quarter of a mile away, so we stayed and made thirty coffins.

The police worked in a way that was more than man could be expected to do, in fact we just don't know how they stood it out. I dug the first four graves in the Tararua Acre, the only tools available being a broken shovel and a spade. An old man, resident of the district, who saw the difficulty the searchers were in through the large numbers of bodies that were ashore, volunteered to dig graves. He unfortunately broke the already broken shovel. Well, the old man mounted his horse and rode to Fortrose, where he got shovels and brought them back to Waipapa.

The searchers have had to put up with great hardships, but have at least had blankets. The police have not been so fortunate and deserve all the praise and consideration for what were really sufferings, for in addition to the ghastly nature of their duties, they had to work and often sleep in their wet clothes.

We both went down to Waipapa without thought of fee or reward, but we couldn't go through the same scenes again for £100 a week. No one could possibly imagine the terrible sights those who had to bury the dead had to look upon. Powerful men in the police party used to such sights, turned sick, and few of those who worked amongst the bodies were able to eat any appreciable quantity of food. The food was very inferior and lobscouse cooked in a pot that was never cleaned formed almost the only meal.

We gave the settlers 23s. to bake some plain cake as a relief to the men from the monotonous diet. The cake was faithfully made and brought 14 miles to us.

*The Union Steamship Company's vessel* Tararua, *en route from Dunedin to Hobart, ran aground at night in very heavy seas and broke up with the loss of 131 crew and passengers. Only 20 people survived this, the worst disaster on New Zealand's coast. This account is from Mr J. Rennie's statement to the* Tararua *Disaster Committee in Invercargill, two weeks after the wrecking at Waipapa Point, Southland.*

## 'CRY FOR ME'                                    *1882*

Hiroki

H.M. Prison
New Plymouth
June 5th 1882

I write this letter of love and affection to you my wife Whaka Pahui, and my children, to my daughter, and my son, how are you all I have got word from the Government to me that I am to be hung for my shooting John McLean. I did not shoot him without reason. I had a reason for so doing, for surveying my land, for killing my pigs. I did not keep it a secret from all my people, my deed in killing John McLean. On the 2nd day of June I told the Gaol Authorities that was guard over me, they have sent my Confession to the Government. I would have told what I have to say if I was asked by the Magistrate at the last sitting of the court. I have no more to say about it to you. My best respects to you, and your Sister, and Brother, and to your Uncle and Grandfather, and Grandmother and all your relations, think of me, cry for me, my best respects to you all from me Hiroki to you.

Hiroki

*In August 1878, surveyors arrived on horseback near Waverley to map Maori land before it was to be confiscated and turned over to European settlers. Some of the surveyors amused themselves by killing local pigs, including some of Hiroki's animals. The aggrieved Hiroki shot John McLean, the surveyor's cook, then made off and was hidden at Parihaki village until arrested three years later. Hiroki was hanged in New Plymouth gaol the day after writing this letter.*

## 'MY TIME IS VERY FULL'                    *Nelson, 1884*

## Anne Richmond

*Oct 4.* Father has come back at last about 3 weeks ago & very glad we were. He has not been well since till quite lately. He is painting an oil painting of Mount Egmont nearly the same as that belonging to the 'client' of Mr Shaen's, you know. It is to go to Melbourne when finished. Maurice spends a great deal of time now at the public tennis-ground, as do Uncle Arthur, Tu & Mr Fell, and we cannot get them home in time for tea, now that the daylight lasts so long.

Father is talking a great deal of making use at last of our land in the North Island, south of Auckland, at the Waikato: there are hundreds of acres, which would be good for sheep as it is good grass ground, & Father I believe would like to get someone to set a farm etc. going there and send the two boys to learn farming with this 'not impossible he', but at present this is only one of many plans for their future.

My time is very full, I have made it too full on purpose or I would mope for what I can't have. Dolla & I are all right: we try to read a good deal & I have my beloved Greek . . . if I do no Greek in the day I feel sad. Dolla has painted flowers a good many; but the last few weeks not anything. She made an attempt at a portrait of Mabel, who however does not lend herself for such a thing, she is kind in not minding sitting, but she never tries to look anything but fish eyed during the operation; so this effort has been a failure. I sat one afternoon, but it takes so much time, as I may not sew or read of course at the same time. We are reading J. Macarthy's *History of our own times*. To myself I am reading *Wilhelm Meister* too, and find it most curious & interesting. Ruth can hardly tear herself from gardening to do anything. She does not go out much, won't go to dances etc. which is rather a pity, as we want to not appear too horrid.

*Oct 7*. Tomorrow evening I am at last going to hear a dear violin again decently played, for a new gentleman who plays has come to Nelson & is going to the Fells tomorrow. The piano there—a new Steinway—is delicious, very sweet and full toned, I am very happy there is such a one in the family.

*Anne Richmond writes to her friend Annie Shaen. Her father, John Crowe Richmond, was a well-known artist and able administrator, engineer and journalist.*

## SISTER JOSEPH GIVEN HER INSTRUCTIONS
*Meanee, 1885*

## Father Soulas

Dear Sister,
You will be pleased to learn that the gospel seed has borne fruit during my absence. The Maoris tell me that they have at least three hundred now attending the Catholic prayers. In a big meeting down at Ranana, a pa which is completely Protestant, there were only fifteen Maoris lately turning up to sing those droning psalms that you know of, while everybody else turned up to the Catholic prayers. May God be blessed!

All the big red prayer-books have run out; they are in demand everywhere. So instead of one hundred, bring three hundred of them.

As soon as your parcels are ready, send them.

I was thinking about your dispensary, and here's what I have decided. First of all, as regards your bag of herbs and other things like rosemary, sage, etc., the best thing to do is to bring everything, even what's at Pakipaki, because you won't be going back this year.

As for jars, bottles . . . best to bring all your bottled remedies, and also bring empty bottles, the ones you dispense your medicines in, because here you won't find any little bottles in the pa.

Here's my plan. I'll set it out for you so you can see what you have to do.

What should you bring? That's a serious question. God alone could give you a right answer to that one. For my part, you must bring everything, so, cauldrons, pots, distilling apparatus, evaporator, bottles, jars, drugs, herbs, in short, everything you have got.

Pack everything carefully lest something get lost. You know old boxes are for sale at Neal and Close's. Ask Fr Reignier if Joseph can help you. When it comes to making boxes, Cyprien knows how to do it better.

Pack everything of mine except the following; in general, anything to do with the horse, except you can bring the spur, the one at Pakipaki, and my best whip; it's in the corner of the wardrobe or near the *washing stand*. Bring my new horse blanket, too, for the nights; it's in my bedroom, and then you can bring back my old one from Pakipaki, and put it in my bedroom at Meanee. Let Brother Basile know about this.

It'd be a good idea to go to Pakipaki, and take from there what belongs to you—blankets, sheets, linen, clothes . . . you can leave the cooking pots, but bring the knife for opening *tins*, also your harmonium which is out there already. Bring slates, school books and my alphabet letters . . . All our books at Pakipaki, also the ones at Meanee, even the dictionary of great men, they're all to take the road to Wanganui. Don't forget my papers. There are some of them in the right hand draw at Pakipaki, the others, including your will, are at Father Séon's box at Meanee, the others on my table. Don't forget my cassocks and other things in my cupboard above Fr Michel's bedroom; the key is on my mantelpiece behind the homoeopathy box. However, leave some rosary beads, crosses, statuettes, and holy medals at Meanee and Pakipaki, but pack up most of them.

*Mother Aubert's herbal products were distributed by Sharland & Co. Sales helped to maintain a school.*

*Sister Joseph, who took her vows in France, worked in Auckland, then nursed at a Marist Mission in Meanee, Hawke's Bay, for nearly 20 years before her superior, the zealous Father Soulas, newly arrived from France, sent her up the Wanganui River to the Maori settlement of Jerusalem. Sister Joseph (as she was known then) was at the time 48 years old. Later she moved to Wellington, established the Home of Compassion and, as Mother Aubert, was appointed Mother Superior.*

---

## TRAPPED UNDER TARAWERA ASH                    *10 June 1886*

## Amelia Haszard

*During the Mount Tarawera eruption Amelia took shelter in the Wairoa schoolhouse, 14 km from the mountain's crater. When stones started falling on the building, Amelia gathered her children, Mona, Adolphus and Edna, around the chair she was sitting in . . .*

I wriggled the chair backwards towards the chiffonier. Just then a large beam fell down from the roof, striking my husband, and falling at one end at the spot where I had been sitting. The other end crashed down on the chiffonier, rested with agonising weight on my leg, and pinned me in a crouching position on my chair. The roar and the din was awful at the time, and I couldn't move . . .

Mona . . . cried to me to give her more room, as I was pressing her against the beam, but the load of the volcanic mud pouring down on me prevented me from being able to render any assistance, and the child was crushed and smothered in my arms, and died . . .

My little boy, who had been standing by me, said, 'We can't live, can we?' and I replied, 'No, dear, we will die together. He then said, 'Jesus will come and take us.' and I never heard his voice again. While the debris and mud were falling in, one of my little girls gave a glad cry of 'Papa' and spoke no more. All through the night, the roar of the volcano, the sound of the falling mud, and the heat of the flames continued. I could not move or make anyone hear, and but for the corrugated iron of the building I am sure I should have been burnt.

Edna, I think, died shortly after Adolphus, as she said 'Oh my head!' as the mud was beating down on her, and she spoke no more. During my entombment I thought a search party would come to search the room. I 'cooed' to the first people I heard about the place. Mr Blythe and the others got me out, on hearing my call, after being entombed for seven? six? hours.

*Later, Amelia's brother-in-law Arthur dug her out of the collapsed building and helped carry her away on an improvised litter.*

## PELICAN UP THE WANGANUI RIVER          *8 July 1889*

### S.H. Drew

Sir James Hector,
Director,
Dominion Museum,
Wellington.

Dear Sir James,
The bird shot 60 miles up Wanganui River is a pelican.

There is no doubt about it being shot there. The Maori who brought it to me states that a pakeha shot it, and hung it up. The pigs got at it and spoilt it. Some of the Maoris took one part, others other parts, this sent is all there is left. I send it to you for you to see that it is quite genuine.

Please return it by return mail so that I can preserve it and add it to my collection.

Yours in haste,
S.H. Drew.

*S.H. Drew was a Wanganui watchmaker and collector of natural objects. Subsequently, pelicans have been seen in New Zealand on three occasions— stragglers from Australia.*

## WORK IN THE BAKEHOUSE                    *Dunedin, 1890*

### 'Mr X'

I am an apprentice to a pastrycook, and work at ——'s. I was working at Hopkins' at the same business, but was not there a bound apprentice. At Hopkins we generally started at 7 a.m. and worked straight on. We had no fixed meal-hour, and after dinner we again worked on till 7, 8, or 9 o'clock. On Saturdays one lot started at 5 o'clock in the morning, and they knocked off at 2 o'clock in the afternoon. The other half came on at 7 o'clock in the morning, and worked till half-past eleven or twelve o'clock on Saturday night. I was at pastry-work, cleaning tins and odd jobs. I was there about nine months, and was past sixteen when I went there, and passed my seventeenth birthday when I was there. We never got allowances for overtime. I had 12s. a week when I left, and I started at 8s. a week. He was to give me 7s. 6d. but he raised my wages as he went on. There were five working in the bakehouse and one going messages. All worked the same hours.

The ventilation was very bad. The room was underground, and there was only one grating to it. When you went down the first flight of steps there was another small flight, about seven steps, down to another bakehouse, where there was not another 'stank'—a grating. Then there was another place where the butter would not get soft, but when the gas was burned out it was so dark you could not see your finger before you. When I went there my employer said I was to work from 7 in the morning till 7 at night, but the rest worked on and I did too. There was no over-time, except at Christmas, when I got paid two weeks and a half overtime. There were about six there younger than I was—about 15. There was no fixed times for meals, and we got our meals on the benches in the bakehouse.

There were no sanitary conveniences; you had to go outside to the station or to the saleyards. But we went on working away. We did not care to leave, and had to wait on till we went home.

*'Mr X' gave evidence to the Government's 'Sweating Commission' of 1890.*

## No Work in Hawke's Bay                                      *1893*

### James Cox

*Jan 31 Tues.* I was at the hotel at Kaitiora until about 4 p.m. then I and another came to the drainers camp at Te Aute, we are stopping here tonight but do not know yet if we can get work. They have not started work yet.

*Feb 1 Wed.* We could not get a job at the draining so left this morning and came to the Te Aute homestead where we are stopping tonight. It was only about four miles and we had to loiter on the road.

*Feb 2 Thur.* I left Te Aute with my new mate (Smith) this morning and we came to Maraekakaho about 16 miles. No work but we are stopping here. The road is a bit hilly and it is quite far enough for me.

*Feb 3 Fri.* We got two good feeds at Maraekakaho but not a good bunk, it was full of Bugs. We walked to Kereru today, Smith hoped to get on at the Woolwash. We did not get anything to do but are stopping here this evening. We came about fifteen miles today, on a hilly road, we got rather wet and had to shelter from the rain several times.

*Feb 4 Sat.* We left Andersons this morning and walked to the Woolwash. Rob Smith got a job there. I was there all day till after 4 p.m. when I came on to MacKies and am stopping here tonight. I am rather stranded as I do not know anything about this part. I did not travel far today, hardly five miles.

*Feb 5 Sun.* The manager here could not give me a job but said he should be asking a man from the Woolwash tomorrow and I might get a job in his place, so he told me to stay here today, and see in the morning. The Shepherd gave me some soap and I washed a shirt and socks. They treated me well. I have meals with the rest and a good bunk in the whare that the station hands keep in, there is only one here now. We had a fire all day or my washing would not have dried outside.

*Feb 6 Mon.* I left MacKies this morning, came to the Woolwash and got a job for a couple of days. I may get a longer job.

*Feb 11 Sat.* I put in another day today, this evening Ward told me he could not keep me any longer but I could stay until Monday. I have diarrhoea again today. I do not know why it is so.

*Feb 12 Sun.* Smith and I walked to Anderson's Wash today but the Boss was not there so I dont know if I can get a job.

*Feb 13 Mon.* I left MacKies after breakfast and walked down the creek to Anderson's Wash. I did not get a job as he was full but I had dinner and waited there till 3 p.m. I then came on to Harding but he was away and I couldn't get a job but am stopping here tonight.

*James Cox, an English migrant and casual labourer, kept a daily diary for 38 years, written in a very small hand. He spent most of this time on the road, looking for work. (See also page, 126.)*

## 'AT HOME' – GOVERNMENT HOUSE
*Wellington, July 1893*

### *New Zealand Graphic and Ladies Journal* Reporter

Lady Glasgow gave an extremely enjoyable dance at Government House on Monday evening, which was attended by over a hundred guests, among whom were about thirty officers from the Spanish warship *Nautilus*. The Captain was not present, having left the day before to visit Napier. The officers were all in uniform and added quite a brilliance to the assemblage. King's band supplied the music, the Reel Row, Pas de Quatre and other pretty modern dances being included in the programme. A light supper was served in the dining room, consisting chiefly of oysters, sandwiches, soup, cakes, wines, tea and coffee.

The house was, as usual, beautifully decorated, the staircase being a mass of greenery—chiefly bamboo and flowers, the little alcoves on

*Wellington dressmakers were kept busy creating elaborate evening gowns.*

either side being arranged as little bowers covered with greenery. The drawing room was prettily lit with shaded gas lamps and yellow shaded high standing lamps, and decorated with all the seasonal flowers, besides tall palms in draped pots and hot-house plants and ferns.

Lord and Lady Glasgow received together at the drawing room door, the Countess looking particularly well in a lovely gown of pale sage green satin, thickly brocaded with a large pattern of dark green, the bodice being trimmed with lace and green and crushed strawberry cord ornaments, and she wore her magnificent diamonds. The skirt of the gown was made very wide and slightly trained, and the sleeves, of course, very full. The Ladies Boyle wore pink cashmere frocks trimmed with white lace and tan coloured shoes and stockings; Miss Eastgate, a visitor at Government House, wore a handsome wine-coloured satin much trimmed with jet; Miss Wauchope wore a pretty white bengaline Watteau gown with Empire belt of turquoise blue velvet, the corsage softened with lace, and Miss Holroyd, pale yellow silk and lace. Capt. Hunter-Blair was in attendance, and

AMONG THE GUESTS

were Mrs Oliver, of Dunedin, in a handsome cream satin gown trimmed with gold; Mrs W.P. Reeves, a very pretty white gown with puffed sleeves; Mrs Rhodes (Christchurch), black velvet and lace; Mrs (Capt.) Russell, a handsome black watered silk with long train; Mrs Grace, black velvet and white silk striped; Mrs Dan Riddiford, white; Mrs Parfitt, pink silk trimmed with black velvet; Mrs Fell, yellow silk trimmed with wide black lace; Mrs Maurice Richmond, sage green velvet; Mrs O'Rorke, a lovely mauve satin gown, trained and softened with chiffon; Mrs Firth, black velvet with revers of pink velvet; Mrs H. Rawson, dove-coloured silk with blue velvet sleeves; Mrs W. Johnston, a lovely black and white striped brocaded silk; Mrs H. Johnston, white chiffon with puffed sleeves of lovely pale blue corduroy velvet and rosettes of terracotta and blue edging the wide skirt; Miss S. Johnston, white brocade; Miss Griffiths, a beautiful gown of pale grey or lavender silk brocaded with a darker colour, and trimmed with wide black lace and violets, and violet velvet sleeves; Miss Ralston (Rangiteiki) cream with ruby velvet sleeves; Miss Rhodes (Christchurch), a pretty pale blue silk with Watteau train, the front being beautifully embroidered with sparkling beads; Miss Heywood, heliotrope silk trimmed with bright pink figured silk; Miss M. Allan, ecru silk, the skirt trimmed with bands of black velvet; Miss Brown, a beautiful cream satin trimmed with stripes of black velvet and gold fringe . . .

*Scores more guests were listed in this leading social column, and their gowns described.*

## BACKCOUNTRY SNOW IN CANTERBURY                    *1895*

### Arthur Hope

James Pringle my neighbour at Lilybank, saw a large mob of about 4000 wethers travelling on the snow near Lilybank. He saw them camp for the night. Next morning they were frozen stiff, just as they had lain down. Pringle made some skis and practised on them before he could run the sixteen miles down to Richmond to tell us. We had then to take him back by boat to the head of Lake Tekapo and wait until he got to his house, eight miles off, and made a fire to let us know he was safe.

Twelve feet of snow fell at Richmond that winter, but it settled to six feet four inches. The stockyard there was seven feet high and only the top rails showing above the snow. Twenty-eight dogs were frozen to death in their kennels, also rabbits, horses and cattle.

In spite of the risks, the more hardy shepherds made tracks through the snow, and it is said that Jack Robertson of Richmond 'ploughed through snow to his armpits' to bring aid to the Richmond back hut.

*One of New Zealand's heaviest snowfalls overwhelmed inland Canterbury in the* winter of 1895. Fogs and frosts intensified the cold. Arthur Hope, runholder of Richmond Station, was one of 137 South Canterbury farmers who lost most of their stock that winter. Parliament passed a special Act to relieve their financial difficulties.

## MINNIE DEAN HANGED AT INVERCARGILL

*12 August 1895*

*Southland Times* Reporter

The woman Minnie Dean, convicted at the last sittings of the Supreme Court in Invercargill of the murder of a female infant named Dorothy Edith Carter, was executed in the Invercargill gaol yesterday morning. The only persons present were the convict's spiritual adviser (the Rev. G. Lindsay), the medical officer of the prison (Dr Macleod), the sheriff (Mr Martin), the gaoler (Mr Bratby), the gaol officials, and the representatives of the press. At three minutes before 8 a.m. the sheriff, in the manner provided by law, demanded of the gaoler the body of Minnie Dean for execution. The gaoler complied, and the sheriff called upon the executioner to do his duty. The procession from the cell to the scaffold was then formed.

At its head were the gaoler and the surgeon, next came the chaplain reading the burial service, next the doomed woman with a prison officer on each side, next the hangman, and last of all the sheriff. To the slow and solemn tolling of the bell they marched through the yard and ascended the steps of the scaffold, the convict walking firmly and erectly, looking around her with apparent equanimity, and at last taking her stand upon the fatal trap with marvellous composure and extraordinary self control. The hangman adjusted the rope, completed the pinioning of the woman, and the sheriff asked her if she had anything to say before she left this world. She replied 'No, I have nothing to say, except that I am innocent.' The sheriff signalled to the hangman, the latter put his hand to the lever by which the apparatus of the trap was controlled. The woman said 'Oh God, let me not suffer.' The last word was on her lips when the trap opened and a second afterwards all was over. Death was instantaneous, the neck having been broken and the spinal cord snapped.

As throwing some light on the unhappy woman's protestations of innocence it may be stated that prior to her leaving her cell she told the Rev. G. Lindsay that while admitting the jury could have come to no other verdict than they had upon the evidence, she had not been guilty of any criminal intent or forethought, although responsible for the death of the child. She claimed that she had only given the child an overdose of laudanum, and that unwittingly. Prior to leaving her cell she also said she would die like a woman and not like a coward, and expressed her thanks to the Sheriff and Mr and Mrs Bratby for the kindness and consideration with which she had been treated.

After hanging the stipulated time of one hour the body was lowered and, Dr Macleod having satisfied himself as to the actual cause of death, it was placed in a plain black cloth-covered coffin which the sheriff had in readiness.

A formal inquest was held in the afternoon before Mr J.W. Poynton, coroner, and a jury, consisting of Messrs T.M.B. Muir (Foreman), R. Blackham, W.F. Williams, W. Searle, John Kirwan, and A.J. Rankin. The following verdict was returned:—'That the said Minnie Dean was, on the 12th of August, 1895, within the common gaol at Invercargill, in due course of law, hanged by the neck until she was dead, in execution of the sentence passed upon her by Joshua Strange Williams, Esquire, a Judge of the Supreme Court of New Zealand, at a sitting of the said Supreme Court, holden at Invercargill, in the said colony, on the 21st day of June in the year aforesaid.'

The consent of the Government having been obtained, the body was delivered to representatives of the woman's husband, Charles Dean, and was taken to Winton by the afternoon train.

The scaffold used on the occasion has been stored in the Dunedin gaol for many years, it having originally been constructed for the execution of Captain Jarvey a quarter of a century ago. The hangman brought his own rope with him from the north, the same rope that was used to hang Scott in Auckland some two years ago.

This is the first case on record of a woman being hanged in New Zealand, although others have been sentenced to death. Mrs Dean is said to have written an account of her baby-farming transactions, but it will be for the Government to decide whether or not it should be published. She was an able and educated woman, and as already stated maintained a remarkably composed and serene demeanour from the date of her arrest until the final scene of the terrible tragedy. On the night before her execution she slept about three hours and a half. At 3 a.m. she rose from her bed and wrote a letter. She refused breakfast and only touched with her lips a glass of spirits with which the medical officer supplied her. Whatever her crimes may have been, however incredible her protestations of innocence, she comported herself courage-ously throughout, met her fate without flinch or falter—in short died a brave, a wonderful woman.

*Minnie Dean fostered several illegitimate babies who subsequently disappeared and she was charged with the murder of one of them. She claimed to have passed the children on to couples in Australia, but the evidence against her was overwhelming. Newly buried children's bodies and a skeleton were unearthed in her garden, and her explanation of a child who died of laudanum poisoning on a train ride to Invercargill was implausible. Dean was never called as a witness in her own defence and many still think she was unjustly condemned as 'a scapegoat sacrificed at the altar of Victorian hypocrisy'. She was the first and last woman hanged in New Zealand. (Portrait from Southland Times.)*

## THE BRUNNERTON MINE DISASTER      *27 March 1896*

Christchurch *Press* Reporters

### THE WORK OF RESCUE

*2 a.m.* The relief parties have driven into the mine about a mile and are now about ten chains from where the men were working.

Mr Seddon is on the scene at the pit's mouth, and has expressed his willingness to work a shift if wanted.

Several of those engaged in rescuing are brought out almost dead. Hundreds of woman still wait at the pit's mouth.

*3.15 a.m.* Shifts of sixteen men are now working, fighting their way foot by foot. The shifts last one hour, and the men, on being brought into the fresh air become unconscious. The ground gained is very slow, but the relief parties have got about a mile and a half into the interior of the mine.

Telegrams are being received from all parts of the colony expressing sympathy.

The hope of saving the men entombed grows fainter, as fragments of trucks are met with.

*Midday* All last night the search party continued to work with untiring zeal. Mr Seddon arrived by a special train in the evening and went to the face of the workings. His offer to work one shift was not accepted.

The scene at the pit mouth all night was one never to be forgotten, the weary faces, leaden footsteps of broken-hearted men and women meeting one on every side, and asking 'Can they be living?' or 'Poor Jack.' 'Where's my Henry?'

The air in the mine increased in foulness as the approach to the level became nearer, and it was so gaseous as to knock strong men down.

The whole populace seems unhinged. Passing along the street nothing but the piteous cries of women and children are to be heard.

At ten o'clock this morning the relief party have fought their way to the bottom level. At 4 a.m. the body of Haslin was recovered much charred. Shortly afterwards the bodies of J. Patterson and J. Watchman were brought out. Another rush to the pit's mouth was the signal for still another victim found, Paul Pellion, a Frenchman. The bodies did not seem much knocked about, and in three cases their arms were in a defensive attitude, as if the poor fellows had been trying to beat the firedamp back. The relief parties are at present engaged in working the lower part of the mine. Later on two more bodies were recovered.

The work is being increased continually but the men engaged in the work of rescue are getting very much exhausted. Fresh men are shortly expected from Kumara and Westport. It is hoped that the whole of the bodies will be recovered before night. The water is rapidly rising in the dip working, all the pumping gear having been destroyed by the explosion.

No hope is entertained of any of the men being got out alive.

## TERRIBLE EFFECTS OF THE EXPLOSION

The rescue parties at the mine continued their work all through yesterday and last night without recovering any but the bodies of Parsons, Hall, Baxter, McDonald, and Julian, till eight o'clock this morning, when the bodies of Patterson, Heslin, Watchman, and Pellion, were brought out. The rescuing men worked heroically in their endeavour to rescue those of their fellows who were entombed. The further the mine was entered the more apparent it became that the force of the explosion was even greater than was surmised. The rails, trucks, and in fact everything in the mine was very much shattered. The gas in the mine also became a great deal worse as the men further advanced, and shifts had to be shortened. There were not sufficient men for such exhaustive work, as they could not long bear up against the overpowering choke-damp, which prostrated the most robust in a very short time, and it was a very pitiful sight to see those who had been overcome by the suffocating gas once more stagger to their feet to assist to their last gasp in the rescue of their comrades. The scenes at the mouth of the pit increased in sadness, the wives, mothers, sisters, and children of those entombed staying at the mine all day and night, and giving vent to their anguish, which was too great to be borne in silence.

Several of the bodies recovered were much shattered, and one had nearly every bone broken. It was with the greatest difficulty that some were recognised. So severe was the explosion that the strong iron rails were twisted like matchwood, and iron trucks were smashed to fragments, the wheels being broken up and the axles bent and thrown in all directions. So it can be plainly seen that poor human life had not a shadow of a chance in an affair of this kind. Some of the bodies were so mutilated and torn to pieces that they had to be identified by their wearing apparel. One man was identified by the cap he wore, being that of the Salvation Army design. The belt of another was taken to several homes for recognition, and sights are being witnessed that cannot even be imagined, except by those who have the painful lot to gaze upon them.

When the Premier arrived he appointed Messrs Scott and Daniel to take full charge till Mr Cochrane (Government Mine Inspector) arrived, which was about 1 a.m. He at once proceeded to the face of the brattice work which was being pushed on as rapidly as possible, and by his calm exterior and knowledge at once established confidence. Mr Scott then returned to Black Ball, having worked like a hero since his arrival. Several times was he overcome by the after damp, but with untiring energy and pluck he again and again returned to direct operations.

Mr Lindop, manager of the Westport mine, arrived at 6 o'clock this morning, and at once proceeded to the scene of action. Mr McKenzie, M.H.R, and Mr Larsen (the Mayor) also arrived. By the *Manawatu* this evening twenty-five coal miners arrived from Westport to take part in the work of rescue and proceeded to Brunner by the 7 p.m. train. The Reefton train today brought down a large number to assist in the rescue work. Mr O'Regan, M.H.R., were amongst the number, and worked hard at the mine. The Premier and seventy-eight miners from Kumara, twenty-five from Rimu, and members of the Hokitika Fire Brigade proceeded to Brunnerton by a special train at 2 p.m. They were all attired in working clothes, and had provided themselves with tools to help in rescuing the entombed men. Mr Bishop was on the scene today, having sufficiently recovered. Mr Scott was working at the face with a body of Kumara miners at 4 p.m.

Drs Morice and McBrearty are still at the mine and have not had any rest since Thursday morning. The clergy of the various denominations stayed at the mine all day and night trying to comfort the afflicted . . .

*Later* A public meeting was held tonight to inaugurate a scheme of relief. It was decided to send lists to all bodies in New Zealand. A strong local committee was formed, and over £100 collected in the room. The town will be canvassed tomorrow. Mr Ziman sent £100, Mr T.G. McCarthy (Wellington) £50, Mrs Mills £100, and other sums from £25 downwards were received.

The rumour that the mine is on fire is contradicted by Messrs Cochrane and Bishop.

One man who was supposed to be at work in the mine on Thursday had the good fortune to 'sleep in' and went to Greymouth, thus averting a similar fate to the victims of the disaster. Several men were preparing to start work in the mine yesterday.

The local officers of the Salvation Army have been doing their utmost to soothe those who are so sorely bereaved, and have been on the scene night and day, and also at the homes of many of the miners.

Forty coffins were ordered this morning from Greymouth, and arrangements are being made for the burying of the victims to the Stillwater Cemetery in one plot, in order to allow of a national monument being placed over them.

Shipping is at a standstill both here and at Westport, owing to the accidents at both mines.

It is very painful to chronicle, among other painful occurrences, a scene where a father and three sons are victims to the explosion, viz.— John Roberts (underground manager) and his sons John, Samuel and

David. Mr Roberts, senior, leaves a wife and five children to mourn their loss. There are many other cases where two or three of one family have been entombed.

At nine o'clock the air in the mine had somewhat improved, and the work was comparatively less arduous.

Large numbers of people from the surrounding districts visited Brunnerton yesterday and last night, special trains being laid on.

The body found, supposed to be that of Joseph Scott, has been identified as Thomas Moore, jun. Owing to the charred state in which he was found it was impossible to recognise him by his features. He was identified by his brother, who recognised his boots which had recently been soled, T. Moore, sen., was also found.

The air is very good, but it is not expected that all the bodies will be got before a few days. There were too many men to work and the Kumara and Hokitika miners were sent home. Everything is now quiet.

The funerals take place on Sunday.

Three bodies are covered with sacks and debris, and it will take some hours to extract them. The gas is again getting bad.

There is still a large crowd at the pit's mouth . . .

It is now definitely ascertained that one hundred and eighty-six children have been left fatherless, and thirty-four widows. Fourteen aged and invalid persons have been deprived of their sole support. This shows the immensity of the disaster.

*The Brunnerton disaster was the worst in New Zealand's mining history.*

## VINDICATING PUBLIC PURITY          *Christchurch, 21 April 1898*

### Henry George Ell

*Mr Henry George Ell, salesman, living in Spreydon, Christchurch, is examined, under oath, about the performance of the local police.*

*Mr Taylor.* Have you had any opportunities of judging as to whether the licensing laws are enforced as they should be?—Yes.

What has been your experience?—Well, my experience, so far as Christchurch is concerned, goes back twelve years. Twelve years ago I was employed at the *Press* office chiefly at night-work, and I was not then a total abstainer, and we were in the habit of getting liquor for the men working in the establishment from hotels in the city. I have frequently gone into the City Hotel and got liquor without any hindrance whatsoever.

After 11 o'clock?—Yes; and 2 and 3 in the morning. The room in which I used to get liquor from the night porter was a room which apparently did not show any light from the street. The liquor was kept in a cupboard. I have seen as many as twelve or fourteen people sitting in there drinking.

*The Chairman.* What time?—Various hours. I have been there at 12, and at 1 o'clock.

After legal hours?—Yes.

*Mr Taylor.* You were on night duty?—I was working at night. I was some four years in the *Press* office. Unfortunately one of our men was addicted to drink, and, to stop him getting into trouble, we frequently had to go out and search for him. I went to a certain hotel in this city. I knocked on the door, and the night porter admitted me. I went inside. There was a blanket hung up across the window, and there were quite forty people in that room. There were two men behind the bar serving liquor . . .

*The Chairman.* Do you suggest any negligence on the part of the police in respect of that?—If the police had gone there, and forced their way in, they could easily have got evidence of illegal trading . . . It has occurred to me that if the constables—the Police of Christchurch—did their duty in the inspection of licensed houses with a persistency and fearlessness that our local Inspector of factories shows we should have less drunkenness occurring on the premises, and we should have less flagrant breaches of the Licensing Act. The constables could go in and see the scenes I have seen without let or hindrance. During the visits I have mentioned I have never met a constable in a hotel. They are in the streets . . .

*Mr Taylor.* Have you ever had occasion to call the attention of a police constable in Christchurch to indecent prints?—Yes.

What happened?—Some twelve months ago—it might be 14—my attention was attracted to an abominable picture exhibited in a small tobacconist's shop-window in Colombo Street. The demoralising influence of such a picture may be at once shown when I describe what it was. The letterpress description showed that it was a man in a state of

*Cathedral Square, Christchurch, 1890.*

drunkenness lying on a bed in a brothel, and a young woman in a half-naked condition escaping with his watch and chain down a trap-door. I noticed two or three young boys looking in this window, with a morbid imagination, I suppose; and it occurred to me, as a citizen, to endeavour to suppress such publications as that. I made a report to the President of the Women's Christian Temperance Union, as they had taken steps which had resulted in the conviction, some time before that, of a person selling the New York *Police Gazette*. However, no action was taken, and I then met, some week or two after this, a constable—No. 46 is his number. I asked him whether he was not aware of the fact that a prosecution had been entered against a man in Christchurch for exhibiting the New York *Police Gazette*, and a conviction secured. He said he had not been in Christchurch long and he was not aware of the fact. I said 'Of course you are aware of the fact that there is an Act for the purpose of suppressing indecent publications—pictures? He thought there was some such Act, but he seemed very much in doubt of it. 'Well,' I said, 'you know these are exhibited in windows.' I named a number of shops. I named this one in particular . . . He said, 'Yes, I have seen worse than that.' 'Well,' I said, 'it occurs to me, if you were to take steps to procure a copy of a paper—'

*The Chairman.* Was this in a newspaper?—Yes. The *Police Budget* it was called. I said, 'If you took the trouble to procure a copy, and went to the station with evidence of an indecent publication, you ought to merit some reward.' 'I am not supposed to do that. If you report anything to me, I am supposed to take note of it, report it to the sergeant-major, and I receive my instructions.' With respect to that, it occurs to me that the common-sense way would be for a constable to proceed to get evidence, where he sees it right in front of his face, and then take it, and report it with the evidence he had procured. To use the man's own words, he said, 'We are simply puppets.'

Did you take any steps yourself to vindicate public purity by proceeding against the man in respect of that exposure?—No. I think I had done sufficient by reporting it to the constable. He told me he would take a note of it and report it. I heard no more about it. Noticing little children frequently in the streets, in the company of prostitutes known to the police of Christchurch, and considering the fearful immoral atmosphere they were growing up and likely to prove detrimental to them through life, it seemed to me something ought to be done about the matter, and I stopped a constable in Manchester Street, just after leaving Gill's confectionery shop, where I had seen two prostitutes with a little boy, about five or six years of age . . .

*Mr Ell's evidence was given at a governmental enquiry into the New Zealand Police Force. Subsequently, Mr Ell was elected to Parliament and became Postmaster General.*

## OFF TO THE WAR                    *Wellington, 1899*

*Evening Post* Reporters

### FAREWELL TO THE CONTINGENT

Red-lettered in the annals of Wellington will be Saturday, 21st October, 1899. The native-born had no event in his memory which compared with the enthusiasm displayed on Saturday by our citizens towards those sons of the colony who have gone to risk life and fortune in South Africa in the interests of the Empire. When our last issue went to press—which it did at an unusually early hour, in order not to debar the *Evening Post* employees from participation in the farewelling—townsfolk and visitors were assembling in thousands the whole front of Jervois-quay. Upon the southern portion of the street a platform had been erected for the accommodation of His Excellency the Governor and party and the speakers who were to take part in the official ceremony. The whole length of footpath and roadway along Lambton-quay was crowded by half-past 2 o'clock.

### THE VOLUNTEER PARADE

At 2.30 the Volunteers, under Lieut. Col. Collins, marched on Jervois-quay, the D Battery taking up the southern position near the Star Boating Sheds and forming the barrier across the roadway. Then came the City Rifles, Guards, Civil Service and Post and Telegraph Corps, the College Rifles, the Zealandias with the visiting representatives of the East and West Coast Battalions. Of bands, there were more than had previously been heard on any parade in Wellington. Besides those of the city, there were the Napier and Palmerston North Garrison Bands, and the musicians of Pahautanui. After the soldiers had marched the length of the Quay, they divided their ranks in two, and two-deep, drove the people to each side of the road leaving a clear space for the Contingent to march down.

### ARRIVAL OF THE CONTINGENT

At this time the wharf, the decks and rigging of the vessels within sight, the windows and roofs of the buildings, and the whole of Jervois-quay was one mass of palpitating humanity. About 3 o'clock, cheers were heard from the direction of Lambton-quay, and a cry went up, 'They come!' The bands stationed along the quay had been enlivening the waiting time with the strains of martial and patriotic music, but there came a moment when emotion proved too much even for bandsmen. That moment was when the troops for the front came marching round the Post Office into Jervois-quay, to the inspiriting Garrison Band.

The scene at that moment will never be forgotten by those who had eyes to see and ears to hear. The enthusiasm was frenzied in its intensity, and even the cynic was carried out of his everyday bitterness, and had to wave perforce his hat with his fellows. 'Kerchiefs, umbrellas, canes, hats, ribbons of many colours—the waving mass was kaleidoscopic. The ten thousand heads in sight were turned towards the oncoming heroes of the hour, whilst from every throat came cheers upon cheers, punctuated with many excited exclamations. Nor were the veterans of our long-ago Maori War forgotten as they were sighted by the crowd.

## THE MULTITUDE

Various were the estimates made as to the number of people who took part in the demonstration. 'I have been in Hyde Park, London, when it was stated in the papers that 100,000 people were present, and I should say there were 40,000 with us today.' He was then gazing from the deck of a steamer in the harbour. As far as the eye could reach, from Point Jerningham in the south to Pipitea Point in the north crowds of spectators were seen. Vehicles of all sorts crowded the roadway from Point Jerningham to the Star Sheds. It is safe to say that all Wellington—fathers, mothers and children—were out; then there were the people of the suburbs and Petone, which were deserted throughout the afternoon; and added to all these were the visitors from Canterbury, Marlborough, Wairarapa, Hawkes Bay, Taranaki, and Manawatu. An attendance of forty thousand, therefore, may be said to be a fair estimate of the numbers who participated in the send-off.

*[The Governor General, The Premier, the Leader of the Opposition and the Chief Justice addressed the contingent, then the Bishop of Wellington recited a prayer and blessed the troops.]*

## CHEERING NEWS FROM THE FRONT

At this stage a copy of a cable message 'from the front,' announcing that the Boers had been beaten off at Glencoe, was read, and the news was greeted with deafening cheers, though there was an unmistakable

*Eight more contingents subsequently left New Zealand for the Boer War.*

expression of regret when it was stated that the British losses had been heavy.

The spectacle on shore was seen to best advantage from the upper decks or rigging of the big steamers at the wharf and what a sight it was!—one that may not be seen in Wellington again in a life time. When the troops moved to the place of embarkation was the moment of chief interest. From the Railway Wharf at one end to Te Aro railway station at the other the breastwork and wayside streets were one living surging mass of excited people, and in the middle of the vast parade there was the greatest press of all in the square opposite the General Post Office; extending thence down the Queen's Wharf to the gangway of the troopship. Along the wharves lay a dozen steamers, every inch of space on the decks taken up; and at the windows and on the roofs of the warehouses that fringed the streets, every place of vantage contributed its share to the crowd of sight-seers, all gazing seaward, and raising their voices in lusty cheers that made the welkin ring again.

The Salvation Army and the Fire Brigade were represented in the day's proceedings.

## WITH THE TROOPSHIP TO THE HEADS

Marine ceremonial demonstrations have been seen upon the waters of Port Nicholson in years gone by, but never the like of Saturday. Fully twenty steamships took part in the display, the marshalling being controlled by Mr A.G. Johnson, who excelled all his previous efforts afloat. He had the *Manaroa* as his flagship, and Captain M'Intyre manoeuvred the little vessel excellently.

When, immediately after the ceremony on the quay, the *Manaroa* left the wharf preliminary to the other vessels taking up their respective positions in line, the meteorological conditions were all that could be desired. A warm sun was shining, but its heat was tempered by a light breeze, the strong westerly that blew in the morning had fallen away. The order of going from the wharf to the Heads had been arranged as follows:

| PORT DIVISION | | STARBOARD DIVISION |
|---|---|---|
| *Te Anau* | *Manaroa* | *Mokoia* |
| *Takapuna* | *Waiwera* | *Rotorua* |
| *Herald* | *Tutanekai* | *Corihua* |
| *Pareora* | *Torpedo Boat* | *Opawa* |
| *Himitangi* | *Ellen Ballance* | *Pauia* |
| *Stormbird* | | *Kahu* |

As the larger vessels came away from the wharf and took up their positions their decks presented a unique spectacle, being crowded with passengers. Fully ten thousand persons were afloat upon the harbour then, and a look ashore showed the whole breastwork and wharves crowded with people. When the line which the troopship was to pass had been formed, the *Mokoia*, the outside vessel of the starboard position, was lying off Oriental Bay. Some time was spent in waiting for the troopship, the final leave-taking on the wharf delaying her departure. As nearly every vessel had a band on board, the interval was enlivened with selections, alternated with the singing of popular and national songs. Across the water at one moment came the strains of the National Anthem, then came floating the air of 'Soldiers of the Queen'. This had scarce died away when 'Rule Brittania' rang across the waves. When the

*Waiwera* finally left the wharf the Marshal's boat was lying about two miles down the harbour, and at that distance the cheers could be distinctly heard.

Once away from the wharf the troopship came steadily down the lines, and as she passed the various vessels peals of cheers and the blare of trumpets and many brass instruments greeted her. Despite the excitement of the day, and the amount of cheering already done by members of the Contingent, they responded heartily to each fresh outburst, lining the upper deck of the troopship, running from 'midship to stern, and ever and anon whooping the company's war-cry.

## GIVING THE BOERS JIP                    *Ottoshoop, 1900*

## Trooper Herbert H. Gawith

*August 16.* First day's fighting brings about the death of Captain Harvey (Manawatu 4th), trooper McDougal (Wellington 4th) and an Australian, L. Hickery, receives wounds but is still alive. A Boer took £20 out of his belt then gave him a drink of water. There are several other wounded including Lieut. Collins.

*August 17.* This afternoon our squadron was led into a trap. There were 60 of us and we were quietly marching along and were within 200 yards of the enemy when they opened fire on us from behind a kopjie. There were about 200 of them but could not shoot straight enough to hit any of our men. How we escaped is a miracle.

*August 18.* We were sent out to guard a kopjie and while I was patrolling in the morning I was fired upon while off my horse filling my waterbottle. In the afternoon we were taking it quietly when the Boers opened fire on us from 1500 yards but we soon silenced them and drove them off. C. Bartlett wounded.

*August 19.* Had a bit of shooting from the same place. Eight of us held the kopjie while the column got out of range. Retreated back to Ottoshoop.

*August 20.* Had a tough day fighting all day. Boers on a kopjie and us on the flat without any cover. Had to retire but in good order.

*August 21.* Caught the Boers nicely and gave them jip. Best bit of sport yet.

*August 22.* Everybody quiet and not a shot all day.

*August 23.* Very quiet. Boers left.

*August 24.* Very quiet nothing doing.

*August 25.* Went halfway to Mafeking for remounts. The 15th Company had a brush with the Boers.

*August 26.* Lord Methuen expected with 6000 men. Capt. Arbuthnot shot and two Australians killed, one a Lieutenant. Battle of Malmani fought between 15th and ended on the 20th, 1900. Major Davies considers that the 4th and 5th NZers have been under hotter fire than the other contingents and it was only a miracle there were not more killed at Ottoshoop or Malmani. About 20 miles from Mafeking the Dutch held it but cleared out when we came, leaving the women and children. The women are a treacherous lot and were caught signalling to the Boers so they were put into a house and a guard put over them. Most of them are dirty looking and remind me of the Maoris. As for the Boers being good shots it is all bosh. They could not hit one of us walking away at 1200 yards.

*From the diary of Herbert H. Gawith.*

---

## WELCOMING THE NEW LAUNCH AT UAWA (TOLAGA BAY), *1 January 1901*

## Eru Monita

I a Hanuere nei 1, 1901, i rere ai a *Iranui* Tima i roto o Uawa; e ahu ana te rere a te autaia nei ki uta o te awa nei o Uawa. He hari tangata tana mahi i taua ra.

Otira, me whakamarama ake i konei, ko taua ra he Nuia; he haringa mo te putanga o o tatau tinana i roto i nga aitua o te tau tawhito kua hori nei ki muri, me te putanga hoki o o tatau whenua ki roto i te ture hou kua pahi mai nei mo te iwi Maori.

Na, e hoa ma, e whakaatu ana kia rongo: he tima hou tenei hei painga mo te rohe o Ranginui-mana-nui o Te Tai Rawhiti nei, Maori, Pakeha; a, hei painga ano hoki mo te koroni katoa o Niu Tireni. Me whakamarama ake tenei wahi.

Tenei awa, a Uawa, he nui te mate o te tangata Maori, Pakeha, i nga poti tahuri, me te ruihi o nga taonga e ahu ana mai i runga tima, me nga mea e ahu atu ana i uta nei. Koia i whakaarotia ai, me tango he tima.

Huaina ana tona ingoa ko *Iranui-a-Tamatea*, tuahine o Kahungunu. Na Iranui ko Taua, i muri ko Mahaki, i muri ko Hauiti. Koia nei nga tupuna o nga iwi e noho ana i Te Tai Rawhiti nei, timata mai i Tarakeha, ki te awa o Turanganui; na Iranui katoa.

Heoi, e hoa ma, i taua ra o te Nuia, ka rere a *Iranui* ki te hari tangata ki uta o Uawa, e 20 maero te tawhiti atu i te ngutu awa o Uawa. Katahi ka utaina ki te tangata; pipiri tonu te tu a te tangata i runga, tu iho ana tetahi i runga i tetahi. Kaore i pau ki runga; ka utai[n]a ano te poti nui, te whanui o tenei poti 12 putu, e 20 putu tona roa, ka riro ma *Iranui* Tima e parete. Kaore ano i pau. Heoi, haere ana a Ngai Maua ma uta, ara ma runga hoiho; nuku atu i te 200 i haere ma uta.

Ko nga mahi o taua ra he hari, he koanga ngakau, he kai, he inu, he purei omaoma, me era atu ngahau katoa i taua ra: po iho, ao ake, he kai hakari te mahi, he waiata, me era ngahau katoa, i runga i taua ritenga ano kua tuhia i runga ake nei.

Ka rite pea taua ra ki te ra i ta ai te manawa o nga Hurai, i te kohuru a Hamana mo Mororekai ratau ko tona iwi, a, maka ana e ratau he puri. A, koia te ra o Purimi, he kai hakari e tuku ai te tahua ki tona hoa, ki tona hoa.

Kua waiho nei e Ranginui te rua o Hanuere ko te ra o Purimi, i ta ai o tatau manawa hei ra kai whakahari, tuku iho ki o matau whakatupuranga i muri nei.

Heoi ano, kia ora koutou me to tatau taonga.

na to hoa pono,

Eru Monita

On 1 January 1901, the s.s. *Iranui* sailed into Uawa. This extraordinary vessel was making its way up the Uawa River, its task that day being to transport people.

But let me explain that this was New Year's Day, and we were rejoicing because our bodies have emerged from the troubles of the old year that lies behind us—and because our lands, too, have emerged into the safety of this new law that has been passed for the Maori people.

Now my friends I will tell you about this, so you can hear. There is now a new steamboat for the benefit of the people, Maori and Pakeha, in this district of Ranginui-mana-nui on the East Coast—and for the benefit too of the entire colony of New Zealand. Let me explain this part of the story.

This river the Uawa, has given much trouble to Maori and Pakeha; boats have overturned, and goods have been lost while being brought in from the steamers or going out from the shore. That's why it was decided we had to acquire a steamboat.

She has been named Iranui-a-Tamatea after Kahungunu's sister. Iranui had Taua, later came Mahaki, and afterwards there was Hauiti— and these are the tupuna of the iwi here on the East Coast, in the region that starts at Taraheka and goes all the way to the Turanginui River. All of these iwi are descended from Iranui.

Well, my friends, on that New Year's Day *Iranui* sailed off to carry people inland into Uawa, 20 miles in from the mouth of the Uawa. The people were put on board packed tightly together, one on top of another, but still there wasn't room for everyone, and some were put on a big boat, 12 feet wide by 20 feet long, which was taken in tow by the *s.s. Iranui*. Still they couldn't all get on, so our party rode on horseback along the bank. More than 200 of us did this.

On that day we were happy, and our hearts rejoiced. People ate and drank, they ran races, there was every kind of entertainment—and this went on right through the night and into the next day. There were feasting, singing, and all sorts of entertainments, because of these events I have described above.

That day must have been like the day when the hearts of the Jews recovered after Haman had tried to murder Mordecai and his people, casting lots—and that was why the day of Purim became a time of festivity, with presents of food sent from one friend to another. And now Ranginui have established the second of January as the day of Purim, the time when our hearts will recover on a day of rejoicing—and this will be passed down to our generations to come.

So much for that. Greetings to all of you, and to our taonga.

From your good friend,

Eru Monita.

*Eru Monita wrote this letter to the Maori newspaper* Te Puke ki Hikurangi *which Margaret Orbell translated into English. The taonga (treasure) alluded to is* Te Puke ki Hikurangi.

## THE MAIL MUST GET THROUGH                    *1901*

### Herbert Bird

You were a man at sixteen then, you know. You weren't a boy. You had to be out and earning. That was the way things were. But, by jingies, it was a tough life all the same . . .

Of course the roads then were something terrible. Really, you could hardly call them roads at all. They were little better than tracks. Not metalled for the most part. Oh, I suppose the County was trying hard enough, but there was no money about at all. And there was certainly no road-building machinery. No, men and horses built the roads; picks, shovels and horses and carts. Horses used to snig logs over the rough bits to flatten them out. And when it rained, the whole darned lot turned to mud.

We would ride through to Martinborough and ride back with the mail from Featherston. As there got to be more and more mail, you took along a packhorse.

I remember when Martinborough was flooded in for seven days. No-one could get in or out. The town was completely cut off. But the mail had to go through.

I would ride out as far as I could. Then I would dismount and lead the horse as far as it was possible to take him. From there I would have to take the mail on my back, through the water and mud up to my thighs. Of course, there was only one way to cross the river—swim. Once over that you would have to walk, over slips and fallen logs, through more mud and water.

When I got to as far as they could get in from the Featherston side I would sling the mailbags down and crack a joke by saying something like: 'Sold,' or 'Here's a present for you.' A few minutes for a breather, and I would grab up the Featherston mail and go back through it all.

*Herbert Bird later graduated to become the driver of a splendid mail coach which is displayed today at Greytown's Cobblestone Museum.*

## ESCAPING BURNHAM INDUSTRIAL SCHOOL

*about 1905*

## John A. Lee

I was a police-dodging outlaw during many years of my early manhood. At any moment, on any corner, a hand might have reached out, a voice declaimed, 'John Lee, the police want you.'

I can say that as I shifted from job to job I left no trace of criminality. I burglariously entered the house of no citizen. I molested no man's property. My solitary crime was that I ran from a custody that was a sterilising hell. The offences which caused me to be sent to Burnham would in these days place me under the control of a welfare officer for a month or two. In Burnham a lad could rot until the age of twenty-one, with never a book to read, a trade to learn, with never an interview with the manager, to whom each boy was merely part of a mass. Burnham boy—there was no such thing, only Burnham boys. Staying in Burnham in seven years I would have been given no book, no newspaper, no skill, merely have been expected to eat, sleep, work, pray, and wonder what would happen when the gates fell down. I would be taught to be in some ways uncivilised.

I do not know whether it was late or early in my seventeenth year that I became a chronic fugitive from custody.

Given a ticket back to Burnham from a job at Duntroon, I had not gone north. At Oamaru, I altered my written ticket for Burnham and made it read Dunedin. As my train sped south I believed I would not be missed in the north before I reached Dunedin and I knew the police no doubt had my photo but would not hear of my absence for some time. Twilight was upon us as the train reached Dunedin. I moved to the very rear of the train because I expected police to be standing at the station entrance and one might recognise me. The moment the platform was crowded with passengers at journey's end, I alighted and rapidly made my way with my small kit to a side street.

**NEW**  **GOVERNMENT**

**ZEALAND** **RAILWAYS**

What a start there was in my home when at dark I sneaked down the lane so that other lane residents would not see me.

'Johnny,' said Mother as I opened the door.

'It's Johnny,' from my dear sister.

'It's the bairn himself.' My grandmother was first to embrace me.

Quickly I explained. Home was no place for me. At any moment the police might come to search the house. I had to leave rapidly. My brother Fred lent me a few shillings. My sister and mother gave me food to eat and cups of tea.

'Where will you go?'

'I'll go into the country and find work. I can do any sort of ordinary farm work now.'

'Don't take anyone's property.'

'Never again.'

'Go to Aunt Nellie at Gabriel's Gully,' Mother decided. 'I'll give you a letter. They'll never find you there.'

*When he was 14 years old, John A. Lee was committed to the Burnham Industrial School, outside Christchurch, for trifling offences. Thirty years later, Lee became the Undersecretary for Housing in the Labour Government (see page 166).*

---

## Richard Seddon Welcomes the All Blacks Home
*Auckland, 1906*

### *New Zealand Herald* Reporter

The Premier, who was received with loud applause and cheers, said that the present gathering was unique in its character. (Applause.) They had met to do honour to New Zealand's brave sons. (Hear, hear.) When Auckland did a thing, it did it well. (Hear, hear, and laughter.) Aucklanders had welcomed the team home on behalf of the whole of New Zealand. Whilst the footballers should be proud of the welcome received, Aucklanders should also feel proud of the way in which that day's function had been carried out. (Hear, hear.) He expressed pleasure at the cordial reception given to His Excellency the Admiral, who, he said, had known when to have the right ships in the right place at the right time. (Applause, and laughter.) Referring to the remarks made at the

*New Zealand's brave sons.*

send-off to the team at Wellington, he said that the record of the tour had proved that it did not need any advice. They had made up their minds to do honour to their country in Rugby football, and when New Zealanders made up their minds about anything—well the Boers knew what that meant. (Applause.) The result of the tour had justified all their anticipations in this respect. They had had representative teams sent Home before, and he referred to the Maori team, and the marks it had left on the football annals in the Old Country. New Zealand was proud of that team, but now that the 'All Blacks' had superseded the browns, and had put down the 'All-Whites' the Colony still had greater reason to be proud. (Applause.) When the 'All Blacks' went Home, one of the London papers said that they might be able to hold their own against an ordinary county fifteen. (Laughter.) That paper had reason sub-sequently to change its opinion. (Hear, hear.) . . . some 12,000 miles away a band of fifteen hardy sons of New Zealand were contending against the representatives of the teeming millions of the Mother Country. They, in New Zealand, were proud of their sons and if they could not be with them in the flesh, they had been with them in spirit throughout the tour. Even after the try had been given against them the New Zealanders fought an uphill game to the finish. They had accepted the decision against them in a true, sportsmanlike spirit, although in their opinion, and in that of many others, there was no defeat at all. (Cheers.) The team had stood English, Irish, and Scotch hospitality (laughter) and no doubt they decided to be generous to Wales. (Renewed laughter.) . . .

As a representative of the whole Colony, he deemed it to be an honour, as well as a duty, to be present to welcome the footballers. (Cheers.)

At the call of the Premier, three loud cheers were given to the team, and the crowd cheered individual players lustily on its own account.

*To the surprise of pundits, the 1905 All Blacks won 31 out of 32 matches on their tour of Britain.*

## ANNUAL SCHOOL PICNIC                    *about 1906*

## Alex W. Hepburn

Annual picnics were held from early days on Boxing Day, and a large crowd attended from far and near and finished up the outing by an all night dance in the school; no charge. The catering for these picnics was done on a very decent scale. About 9 a.m. people began to arrive on horses of all sorts of sizes. With them came hampers and baskets, then boys and girls on foot, with kits etc. (there was no room for them to ride in the spring carts and buggies following behind). They (the carts) were full of 'tucker'—and the old people. By this time the fire was alight, iron bars were set up on bricks left there from the year before; colonial oval boilers were filled with water from the stream. Very shortly they would be boiling, plum 'duffs' would be dumped in. It did not matter whose they were, they might not get their own back, another for peas and beans, another for tea. Now, by the time these were boiled, tablecloths would be spread everywhere in shady spots, plates, cups, saucers, knives, forks, etc., would appear by the score. Elderly women would probably be sitting down by this time at the head of their respective spreads, directing young women and young men about various tasks.

'Potatoes are ready, Mum,' calls one of the girls. Now a roast goose would come to light and 'Mum' immediately attacks the beautiful bird (she has been fattening it for weeks) with knife and fork, and it quickly loses its symmetrical lines. Something similar is happening to a turkey on the next spread, and a sucking pig with a potato in its mouth is fast losing its beautiful outline and providing an extra large amount of stuffing. A ham dwindles rapidly. Everyone gets a bit of each. Vegetables there are in plenty. The noise decreases; there are not many returns required, and the puddings are now being served. In about ten minutes everyone feels content, each one having eaten enough for a shepherd and a couple of dogs. The wash-up is over in a very short time. Someone has taken care to see there is plenty of hot water, and the young people are not allowed to go until everything is done and in order. Consequently there is a general hurry up and 'many hands make light work'.

Now the usual footraces and games of the times were indulged in—including quoits for the older men.

*An old boy recalls his Henderson School picnic on the outskirts of Auckland.*

## JUMPING THE BABY UP AND DOWN AT WAIPUNGA
*20 November 1907*

## Katherine Mansfield

Dear my mother—

I wrote you my last letter on Monday—and posted it at Pohui in the afternoon. I continue my doings. We drove on through sheep country—to Pouhi that night—past Maori 'pahs' and nothing else—and pitched our camp at the top of a bare hill above the Pohui Accommodation House—kept by a certain Mr Bodley—a great *pa*-man with 14 daughters who sit and shell peas all day! Below the hill there is a great valley—and the bush I cannot describe. It is the entrance to the Ahurakura Station—and though we were tired & hungry Millie, Mrs Webber & I dived down a bridle track—and followed the bush. The tuis really sounded like rivers running—everywhere the trees hung wreathed with clematis and rata and mistletoe. It was very cool & we washed in a creek—the sides all covered in daisies—the ferns everywhere, and eventually came to the homestead. It is a queer spot—ramshackle and hideous, but the garden is gorgeous—a Maori girl with her hair in two long braids, sat at the doorstep—shelling peas & while we were talking to her—the owner came & offered to show us the shearing sheds. You know the sheep sound like a wave of the sea—you can hardly hear yourself speak. He took us through it all—they had only two white men working—and the Maoris have a most strange bird like call as they hustle the sheep—when we came home it was quite dark & how I slept.

Next morning at five we were up & working—and really looking back on yesterday I cannot believe that I have not been to a prodigious biograph show. We drove down the Titi-o 'Kura—and the road is one series of turns—a great abyss each side of you—and ruts so deep that you rise three feet in the air—scream & descend as though learning to trot. It poured with rain early—but then the weather was very clear & light—with a fierce wind in the mountains. We got great sprays of clematis—and konini, and drove first through a bush path. But the greatest sight I have seen was the view from the top of Taranga-kuma. You draw rein at the top

*Katherine Mansfield.*

of the mountains & round you everywhere are other mountains—
bush covered—& far below in the valley little Tarawera & a silver
ribbon of river—I could do nothing but laugh—it must have been
the air—& the danger.

We reached the Tarawera Hotel in the evening—and camped
in a little bush hollow.

*Grubby*—my dear— I felt dreadful—my clothes were white with
dust—we had accomplished 8 miles of hill climbing—so after
dinner (broad beans cooked over a camp fire and tongue & cake
and tea), we prowled round and found an 'agéd agéd man' who
had the key of the mineral baths. I wrapt clean clothes in my towel
& the old man rushed home to seize a candle in a tin—He guided
us through the bush track by the river—& my dear I've never met
such a cure—I don't think he had ever possessed a tooth & he never
ceased talking—you know the effect?

The Bath House is a shed—three of us bathed in a great pool—
waist high—and we of course—in our nakeds—the water was very
hot—& like oil—most delicious. We swam—& soaped & swam &
soaked & floated—& when we came out each drank a great mug
of mineral water—luke warm and tasting like Miss Wood's eggs at
their worst stage—But you feel—inwardly & outwardly like velvet—

This morning we walked most of the journey—and in one place met a most fascinating Maori—an old splendid man. He took Mrs Webber and me to see his 'wahine' and child—It was a tropical day—the woman squatted in front of the whare—she, too, was very beautiful—strongly Maori—& when we had shaken hands she unwrapped her offspring from under two mats & held her on her knee. The child wore a little red frock & a tight bonnet—such a darling thing—I wanted it for a doll—but in a perfect bath of perspiration. Mother couldn't speak a word of English & I had a great pantomime.

Kathleen—pointing to her own teeth & then to baby's—'Ah!'
Mother—very appreciative—'Ai!'
Kathleen—pointing to the baby's long curling eyelashes 'Oh!'
Mother—most delighted 'Aii!'
And so on.

I jumped the baby up & down in the air—and it crowed with laughter & mother and father beaming—shook hands with me again—Then we drove off—waving until out of sight—all the Maoris do that—Just before pulling up for lunch we came to Waipunga falls—my first experience of great waterfalls. They are indescribably beautiful—three—one beside the other—& a ravine of bush either side. The noise is like thunder & the sun shone full on the water. I am sitting now on the bank of the river—just a few bends away—the water is flowing past—and the manuka flax & fern line the banks.

Must go on. Goodbye, dear—Tell Jeanne I saw two families of wild pigs & horses here & that we have five horses—such dear old things. They nearly ate my head through the tent last night.

I am still bitten & burnt, but oil of camper, Solomon solution, glycerine & cucumber, rose water are curing me, and I keep wrapt in a motor veil. This is *the* way to travel—it is so slow & so absolutely free, and I'm quite fond of all the people—they are Ultra-Colonial but thoroughly kind & good-hearted & generous—and always more than good to me. We sleep tonight at Rangataiki & then the plains and back blocks.

Love to everybody. I am very happy.
Your daughter
Kathleen.

*Later.* Posting at country shed. Can't buy envelopes. Had

wonderful dinner of tomatoes—Ah! he's found me an hotel envelope.

*During a trip home to New Zealand, young Katherine Mansfield (real name Kathleen) motored along the Napier–Taupo road.*

## WINNING THE NOBEL PRIZE      *1908*

## Ernest Rutherford

*To Otto Hahn in Berlin*

*29 November.* I much appreciate your kind congratulations and wishes on the award. It is of course quite unofficial but between ourselves I have no reason to doubt of its correctness. I must confess it was very unexpected and I am very startled at my metamorphosis into a chemist.

I may tell you in *strict confidence* that my wife and I are going to Stockholm via Hamburg and Copenhagen to arrive there on the 10th. We shall probably return via Berlin for the express purpose of seeing you. It would be convenient for me to get my letters forwarded to Berlin. Could they be addressed to you at your private address? If so, let me know as soon as you can the exact address. I should be glad if you would take charge of them before I arrive. We should of course also be glad if you could mention a comfortable hotel handy for looking round Berlin.

*Ernest Rutherford.*

*To his mother in Nelson*

*24 December.* I am sure that you have all been very excited to hear that the Nobel Prize for Chemistry has fallen my way. It is very acceptable both as regards honour and cash—the latter over £7000. We have just returned from our journey to Stockholm, where we had a great time—in fact, the time of our lives.

*Rutherford was a physicist and was surprised to be given the Nobel Prize for Chemistry. Rutherford never thought his discoveries would be put to any use but, in Berlin, 30 years later, his colleague and friend, Otto Hahn, first propounded the theory of the atomic bomb.*

## ADVICE TO MOTHERS                                    *1909*

## F. Truby King

The destiny of the race is in the hands of its mothers. Today our historians and politicians think in terms of regiments and tariffs and dreadnoughts; the time must come when we must think in terms of babies and motherhood. We must think in such terms, too, if we wish Great Britain to be much longer great.

The modern world needs stimulation of interest and rational, practical, sympathetic education and help in Motherhood and Mothercraft.

Going about our streets today, what is it that strikes us, if we trouble to observe and think whether we are doing justice to our race? As the crowd passes up and down the street before us, how many youths or adults of either sex could we pick out who would compare favourably, as samples of human perfection, with beautiful babies who are so common. The vast majority are out of the running altogether.

This failure to develop and grow up according to early promise causes no surprise or protest—we have got out of the way of expecting the average man or woman to have the shapely feet, good limbs, broad hips, deep chest, square shoulders, good muscles, graceful, easy carriage and aspect of radiant health and perfection which would be the prevalent type if man took as much trouble about rearing and care of his own species as he does about the rearing and care of cattle and horses.

Deformed and crippled feet, spindly calves, indifferent bodies, shallow chests, round shoulders and slouching gait, characterize the majority.

Even among the elect few, where can we find the individual who, however well he may look, would be fairly entitled to 75% of marks as an ideal specimen of manhood or womanhood if the five following points were given the place they ought to have in standards of reasonable attainable bodily perfection:

1. Well-developed jaws and sound teeth.
2. Fully-developed nose and throat, free from all restrictions and obstructions.
3. Fully-developed chest and ample breathing capacity.
4. Sound digestive organs and freedom from indigestion.
5. Shapely well-developed calves and feet, free from distortion and deformities.

Our shortcomings are obvious even to the casual observer, yet for the most part people regard the present state of matters as normal. There is no general protest against human unfitness. So long as people can manage to struggle through their daily work with the occasional patchings up by the doctor and dentist, it does not occur to them that any higher standard is to be expected. Yet, it is quite safe to say that, with few exceptions indeed, the great majority of those who drag along with indifferent health and who hardly ever feel perfectly well, strong and fit, could have grown up excellent specimens of humanity had they been properly and sensibly reared.

History has shown that the decline of the great nations and empires of the past has been ushered in by a falling off of home life, and in the unwillingness of man and wife to devote themselves to the full duties, sacrifices and responsibilities of parenthood.

The great fact which all the most highly civilized nations have to face today is, that love of home and family is on the wane. The tide is still going out as regards the most advanced Western nations.

Everyone knows about the modern 'small family' tendency. Very few realize the extreme gravity of the situation. The most urgent and pressing need of our vast Empire is ample British-born population.

In all civilized countries a smaller and smaller percentage of the new population is being derived from the best sources, and from quarters where there would be ample to provide for larger families if they were desired.

Every detail of our own falling off during the last half century in

*Bathing baby.*

respect of population and family life was illustrated in Greece and Rome, but their children, delivered over to be suckled by slaves, were better off than ours reared by hand, whether the bottle-feeding is done in the palace or the cottage or the creche.

The rapid growth and extension of creches and day nurseries for babies, however necessary and beneficent at the moment, is a further menace as regards the future. Facilities offered the mother to spend her day away from home, afford no true or permanent solution to the problem. However stupendous the obstacles that lie in the way—and they are stupendous—a solution ought to be found which will enable all children to be nursed by their mothers for at least six months. Surely some way can be found to enable the married woman to complete the cycle of motherhood honourably and faithfully, instead of making it easy for her to spoil herself and the child at the most momentous period of life for both, merely in order to supplement the husband's earnings.

What is best for the child is best for the mother and best for the race, apart altogether from the question of the fate of the individual child itself. Parenthood is after all the greatest and most enduring privilege, blessing and joy of life.

Devotion to family, clan and country (patriotism), and devotion to the broad interests of mankind (humanitarianism), are built into the same foundations. If the foundations are made sound all will be well.

*F. Truby (later Sir Truby) King founded the Plunket Society and, thanks partly to his and the Society's efforts, New Zealand's infant mortality rate fell to be the lowest in the world.*

## DRUNKS FIGHTING LIKE DOGS AT TOLAGA BAY

*22 March 1914*

### Florence Harsant

*2 a.m.* Wakened by a man rattling the door handle. Crash! He'd fallen down outside the door.

*2.05 a.m.* Another man comes, swearing volubly. Trips over the first, and tries my door in turn. I hear him trying other doors opening off the corridor.

*2.10 a.m.* He's found a spare room. Scuffling sliding noises—he's dragging his mate with him.

*3.00 a.m.* A tremendous row breaks out upstairs. I look through the window. Three men are fighting and snarling like dogs, just above my room.

*3.15 a.m.* A woman appears on the scene, screaming and shouting at the men and driving them out on to a small landing that gives access to an outside stairway. She has a broom and lays into them like an Amazon, driving them into the sodden yard below.

*6.00 a.m.* Two men go to the bathroom next door, and I hear them discussing the night's performance. The actors were apparently the landlady, her drunken husband and his two equally drunken companions. The boys next door chuckle at her appearance in curlers, a bedraggled dressing gown, and armed with a broom.

*6.40 a.m.* Have all the men dispersed? I think so. I open my door. Through the open door of my room directly opposite I see a man lying, his head on one stretcher, his feet on the other, and his body suspended between the two. His mate is curled up on the floor. I go to the sitting room—full of drunks. Make my way to the kitchen, to pay for my bed. The landlady suggests breakfast—I tell her I can't leave quickly enough. She tells me such a thing has never happened in her boardinghouse before.

Buns and a glass of milk for breakfast, from the local dairy, then I called at the saddlers to enquire about decent lodging. Fortunately the saddler's mother is a W.C.T.U. member and he brought me along to her home here.

The boardinghouse, she tells me, is notorious as a weekend rendezvous for all drunken bushmen in the district.

*Florence Harsant, a pretty, 21-year-old organiser for the Women's Christian Temperance Union, was nine months on the road on horseback setting up branches of her Union in remote North Island Maori villages. On this occasion, she had booked into a cheap boardinghouse for the night.*

---

## LANDING AT GALLIPOLI                    *Sunday 25 April 1915*

## Lieutenant H.H. Spencer Westmacott

I had hardly turned over to sleep again, when the rumble of guns made me jump out of my bunk and the two others joined me at the porthole. They were the guns of Cape Helles where the 29th Division must by now be going ashore. Day was just breaking. There was a slight mist along the shore. Save for flashes from the ship's guns we could see nothing in the half light. It was nice and cool with the promise of a glorious day. It was a little after 4.00 a.m. I said [to Lieutenants Baddeley and Allen] 'We will not rest so comfortably tonight. Let us go to sleep again,' and we did very quickly. My words were prophetic. Before another night both my friends were dead.

We were up and dressed at 7.00 a.m. and went to Holy Communion under Fielden Taylor in the saloon. Breakfast was at 8.00 a.m. We visited our men. They were all happy and well fed. We went on the top deck. The ship lay at anchor several miles off shore, which was clear to see, a rugged coastline. There were ships all round us, a magnificent sight, with bright sunlight shining upon a calm blue sea and clear sky. The high cliffs, north of Gaba Tepe, afterwards called Anzac, were straight ahead.

Yes, and there they were, real shells bursting like puffs of cotton wool against a clear blue sky at the summit of the cliffs. Pictures had always shown a simultaneous flash and smoke. We noted that the flash came first, leaving the smoke afterwards. Interesting. Someone was getting it under those bursts at that very moment. To right and left of us, a mile away in each case, our warships lay close in shore pounding away at the enemy's position, and between us and the beach, at the foot of the cliffs, a stream of destroyers, picket boats and lighters crowded with men, plied their way back and forth ceaselessly. As we watched, at about 9.00 a.m. a heavy roll of musketry from a ridge to the left of where the troops were landing grew to a roar then died away to a few occasional dropping shots. Colonel Chaytor's eye caught mine. His eye lit up and he nodded his head at me, as if to say 'Now we shan't be long'.

All fully equipped we now went below to the troop decks and inspected our men who had fallen in and were awaiting us. All ranks were in caps like the British infantry. This applied to the Australians too, being a Corps Order. We had noted with disapproval that when 3rd Auckland went ashore a few men wore hats; but their discipline was slack. Once again we checked over their equipment, satisfying ourselves that each man's water bottle was full. When we had seen the three days extra rations, the men fastened their haversacks, showed their extra hundred rounds in their breast pockets, and the usual hundred and fifty in their pouches and closed them too.

*Lieutenant Westmacott.*

We gave the order 'Charge magazines'. In went ten rounds and the cut offs were closed. I loaded my R.I.C. revolver, and there was a short silence so I said, 'We are about to go into action. We are all ready and remember that if anyone is hurt no one is to leave his place to take him to the rear. That applies to me as well as all the rest of you. The stretcher bearers are there to help the wounded. Remember also that I will allow no man to open fire, until we see something to fire at.' The leading platoon now began to climb upon the deck and the others in turn filed after them.

On deck we formed up our platoons in close order and waited. I had fifty-six other ranks, the company strength being two hundred and twenty-three. Biscuit tins full of water were placed at intervals along the deck and our orders were to drink all we could of this as our water bottles were not to be used without permission, probably not until night, and the water we drank now would abate our thirst til then. We doubted this . . . but we did as we were told. Young Cliff Barclay passed me going to his platoon of 2nd Canterbury further along the deck. He said 'We are going ashore in a minute. The lighters are coming alongside.' We wished each other good luck.

It was shortly before 10.00 a.m. Alderman said a few words to the whole company, 'We are going ashore now; but I do not think anyone is going to be killed today.' At which there were roars of sceptic laughter from his listeners. They were all in such high spirits. It was glorious to lead such men.

Alderman and some of ours filled the first lighter. My platoon were in the second and two platoons of the Canterbury regiment, whose colonel Macbean Stewart and his battalion headquarters also came and took their places forward. Critchley-Salmonson, their adjutant and I sat near them on the port side, our legs hanging over the water. Jack Anderson of divisional H.Q. who was being left on board . . . waved to me and I waved back. We were quiet enough. There was no talking at this stage. A destroyer came to take us in. The tow rope tightened. We were under way.

*From the diary of Lieutenant Westmacott, platoon commander of the 16th Waikato Company.*

## BURYING THE DEAD AT GALLIPOLI                 *24 May 1915*
## Lieutenant Colonel P.C. Fenwick

The most ghastly day. This morning I was ordered to act as delineating officer for the burial of the dead. The Turks had asked for an armistice and it had been arranged that no firing should take place between 7.30 a.m. and 4.30 p.m. today. At 6.00 a.m. I and my orderly, Crawford Watson, left with Col. Skeen and others and went along the beach toward Gaba Tepe. 50 men, carrying white flags, followed. The battleships fired till 7.10 a.m. and at 7.20 we crossed our wire entanglements on the beach. Raining heavily. I got the loan of a dead or missing man's overcoat and was all right.

We were met by some Turkish officers who arrived on horseback followed by very fine looking Turks, carrying Red Crescent and white flags. One of the officers was a German doctor. We were introduced by our interpreters and moved up the hillside in two long lines. Every hundred yards or so we stationed a man with a white flag, and opposite to him the Turks posted one of their men. We clambered through dripping bushes, with beautiful poppies and flowers, reaching the top wet through. From

*Gallipoli survivors.*

here we could see, over to our right flank, rough high hills covered with dense, waist-high scrub, and occasional patches of cultivated land. At the top of the second hill, we halted for a slight argument as to our route. The Turks wanted to keep up towards our trench, but Col. Skeen refused so we kept straight down a steep narrow cleft between. Here we heard two wounded men crying for help, and found one with a fractured leg. I gave him cyanide and borax and he touched his forehead and breast. The Turkish medico was a charming gentleman and we talked in French. Coming over the crest of the hill, I found the first New Zealander, lying on his face. Poor lad! A few yards climb brought us to a plateau, and a most awful sight was here. The Turkish dead lay so thick that it was almost impossible to pass without treading on their bodies.

The awful destructive power of high explosives was very evident. Huge holes surrounded by circles of corpses blown to pieces. One body was cut clean in half; the upper half I could not see, it was some distance away. One shell had apparently fallen and set fire to a bush, as a dead man lay charred to the bone. Everywhere one looked lay dead, swollen, black, hideous, and over all a nauseating stench that nearly made one vomit. We exchanged cigarettes with the other officers frequently and the senior Turkish medico gave me two pieces of scented wool to put in my nostrils. Further along the plateau, the distance between the trenches narrowed. We kept very carefully to the centre. The narrowest place was not 17 feet apart.

In this trench lay 4 dead Turks, head to heel, blocking it. We stopped our men. I found an officer's sword and bugle, and kicked it towards our trench and asked a corporal to deliver it to Col. Beeston when he was relieved.

In one charge 5 or 6 Turks had reached our trench and died with their heads on our sandbags. From here a long file of dead reached back to the front of the Turk's trench.

At another place a dead Turkish officer lay close to our trench face down, grasping his revolver. We passed on until we stood on a plateau at the head of Monash's valley—the Valley of Death.

From here we looked down that awful cut between the mountains. We could see the winding road, crossed by sandbag traverses to prevent the snipers killing the men as they marched up. Here we parted from the Turks. They went to the right and we descended the side of the cliff, and up again. In this manner neither side had the advantage of seeing the other's trenches. In a steep cut I found a N.Z. officer, head down. I got his identity disc.

Meantime we found 2 dead snipers and then 8 or 9 more, hidden in holes. How many lives they took before they died, no one knows. At least 50. We climbed up through deep, narrow, winding trenches, emerged on the plateau again and met the Turks. Again there was a mass of dead Turks. From here the land was flatter and we moved on through a welter of corpses.

Behind us, for at least two miles, we could see our burial parties, working furiously. In some cases the dead actually formed part of the trench wall. It was a terrible sight to see arms and legs sticking out of the sand underneath the sandbags. The final stage was opposite the extreme left flank. There was a narrow path, absolutely blocked with dead, also a swathe of men who had fallen face down as if on parade— victims of our machine guns. The brink of the precipice was thick with bushes and every few yards we found dead. Here I saw 2 N.Z. officers; one was Grant. Our journey took from 7.30 to 12.30. Col. Ryan came up here and after superintending the interment, I left, feeling dreadfully ill. I got back via the wonderful trenches of the left bank, and found Guthrie, Blair, and Findlay, who gave me tea.

Padre Bush King was here. Padre Luxford had been busy on the plateau reading hasty services over our dead. I only saw about 10 of ours but, at a very moderate estimate, I saw 2,000 dead Turks.

The Turkish officers were charming. The Germans were rude and dictatorial and accused us of digging trenches. I lost my temper (and my German) and told them the corpses were so decomposed they could not be lifted and our men were merely digging pits to put the awful things into. He was a swine, this particular German. The Turkish medico was extremely nice. We exchanged cigarettes and I said to him I hoped after the war we should smoke a cigarette—I cut short suddenly, for I was going to say 'in Constantinople', but he smiled and bowed and it was all right. I pray God I may never see such an awful sight again. I got back deadly sick and got phenacetin and brandy and lay down. I shall certainly have eternal nightmares. If this is war, I trust N.Z. will never be fool enough to forget that to avoid war one must be too strong to invite war.

*Lieutenant Colonel Fenwick's diary is in the archives of the Waiouru Army Museum.*

## DOCTORING TO THE TROOPS AT GALLIPOLI

*Monday 9 August 1915*

# Dr Te Rangi Hiroa

We took shelter behind a low ridge below one of the Turkish outposts that our men had assisted in capturing. The padre and I with stretcher-bearers climbed up the hill under what cover we could find and explored the trenches. We found a number of Maori dead and buried them with the rites of the Church. We got some greatcoats in a Turkish bivouac and they came in handy. In spite of the protection from the ridge, we had a few casualties from overs. One of our officers was drinking out of his water bottle when a bullet struck it, skidded off and lodged in his neck. My hospital corporal was also hit and made a characteristic Maori speech. He said he hoped to look after me till the war ended but . . . He wept as we sent him off on a stretcher.

I went over the crest with my orderly, asking the stretcher-bearers to follow at intervals so as not to attract fire. It was an experience popping over the ridge and knowing that one was in full view of the enemy sharpshooters. The only chance was that they were occupied with larger interests. I had no nails in my boots and the grass on the other slope of the apex was dry and slippery. As I sprinted over, I slipped, rolling head over heels down the slope, momentarily expecting to hear or feel the zip of a bullet. However, I landed safe and happy in a dry stream bed under perfect cover. We worked up the bed and came to a little terrace formed by two streams which had converged to form that by which we had ascended. The terrace was crowded with wounded men and the two stream beds, instead of flowing with water, were flowing with a steady stream of wounded men. The most piteous case was a man whose leg had been blown off just below the knee. A comrade had tied a shell dressing over the stump with puttees. The patient was pulseless and his comrade asked me in a whisper, 'Has he any chance, sir?' I shook my head. He picked up his rifle and said, 'I'll get back to where I'm needed.'

The French seventy-fives on our left had got our range perfectly. They could burst their shells so that the shrapnel sprayed the stream beds. When the shelling was on, we lay flat in our shallow terrace on the left bank of the stream watching the burst of bullets hitting the ground a few feet beyond our own feet. At times they were so close that we felt inclined to sit up so as to draw our feet closer in, but we refrained from the fear that we might get hit in the head instead. On one occasion I was dressing a wounded Ghurka when shelling commenced. I had to lie flat on the ground beside him to finish the bandaging in the best way I could.

*Te Rangi Hiroa, previously government Minister of the Maori Race, served in the New Zealand Division at Gallipoli as a medical doctor. He was twice mentioned in despatches and awarded the Distinguished Service Order (DSO). Later he became renowned as the anthropologist Sir Peter Buck. His Gallipoli experiences were related to friends in Honolulu in 1940.*

## 'HOPE SOME WORK WILL COME MY WAY SOON'

*Carterton, 1915*

### James Cox

*Oct 11 Mon.* This morning I walked to Belvedere, Carrington and Cemetery here. I took it easy since I am sixty-nine years old today and am no better off financially than I was fifty years ago.

*Oct 12 Tues.* This morning I walked to Greytown and back by Wiaroa, Dalefield and Belvedere. I loafed since.

*Nov 10 Wed.* This morning I walked to Greytown and back and loafed since I am out of the way of work again.

*Nov 15 Mon.* To Martinborough this morning to see about a job but did not take it.

*Nov 16 Tues.* I returned to Carterton this morning. I feel better for having a little change but hope some work will come my way soon.

*Cox, a casual labourer, walked tremendous distances in search of work over 25 years. He occasionally worked in flax mills, bagged chaff or potatoes, chopped wood, gardened, but never for longer than a few days in any place. He died a pauper in 1925. (See also page 85.)*

## THE FIGHTING AT PASSCHENDALE
*Belgium, 11 September 1917*

### Brigadier-General Bernard Freyberg

The morasses of mud, which paralysed the British attacks, were caused by the breakdown of the drainage system in Flanders, once the shelling by both sides had destroyed the culverts and small streams. Even the slopes of hills were reduced to the consistency of a bog, while the valleys of the Stroombeek, the Raveek and the Haanbeek became impenetrable marshes.

During the fighting, attacking companies waded knee-deep, and often up to their waists in mud before gaining their objectives, while, in many cases, whole waves disappeared, or were held captive in the mud within speaking distance of the British line, until they either died from exposure or were blown to pieces by artillery fire. It was a most wicked battle and the night after any attack, men with ladders and ropes worked away in the most appalling danger, trying to save those who were bogged.

There were no roads, just a few shellswept duckboard tracks and wheeled transport could not reach the gun positions with ammunition. Packhorses carried forward eight rounds at a time, and the slaughter of these animals, to say nothing of their leaders, threatened to cause a horse shortage. Advancing the guns in this fluid country was a problem which had to be solved; in some cases a light railway was laid on brushwood or any other available debris, and the guns were taken forward in pieces and reassembled.

Most of our men lost themselves in the dark, or became bogged, and wandered about between our lines for days. On 16 September one of our low-flying aeroplanes reported that three men in khaki had signalled from a shell-hole in no-man's-land. An officer went out in broad daylight and brought these men in, who stated . . . that, the morning after the attack, they saw a party of our men, after being disarmed and made

*British coat of arms.*

prisoner, bayoneted by the enemy. They said the men's screams were dreadful. They could do nothing because their rifles were jammed with mud and out of action.

*[A large shell exploded in the mud at Freyberg's feet, wounding him in five places; fragments went right through a lung and blew a hole in his thigh the size of his fist. This was his ninth wounding in that War.]*

We were badly shaken but managed to crawl on all-fours a distance of three hundred yards through deep mud to a first-aid post, where they bound up my chest and thigh which now rendered me immobile.

I decided to keep the fact that I had been wounded from the troops, to command the brigade from brigade battle headquarters by telephone, to send the brigade major round the troops in the assembly area and hand over the command to Colonel Dann when the objectives were captured some time during the following morning.

The approach march and assembly were difficult. It was a pitch dark night, and as the men marched down the St Julien road they were heavily shelled. After passing St Julien, where the men left the road, they had to be roped together by platoons to prevent individuals from getting lost. The artillery of both sides were harassing the forward areas; we had to prevent the enemy relief from taking place, and they to prevent us from assembling. And to add to our difficulties, it was raining as we waded in with mud over our knees. The men were just as frightened of being swallowed up in the mud as of being blown to bits by the enemy shells.

At one o'clock in the morning we received the welcome message by telephone that the assembly was complete. This was a great relief to us, and at 5.40 a.m. (20 September) the barrage opened, and the Second and Fifth Armies had launched the attack which is known in history as 'the Battle of the Menin Road'.

All our objectives were captured to plan, but not many prisoners were taken by our men. The incident of a few days before was too fresh in our minds.

*The 28-year-old Freyberg commanded a British Brigade which tried to break the German Hindenburg line east of Ypres, a ridge of high ground strengthened with concrete redoubts and bristling with machine guns.*

## No. 1 Field Punishment                                      *Belgium, 1918*

## Archibald Baxter

The whole enclosure was about an acre in extent, but enough barbed wire was used in making it to secure a fair-sized farm. A double row of barbed wire entanglements surrounded the whole enclosure. A further row ran round the two tents in front of the guard huts, and, inside that again, each tent had its own encirclement of wire. A Lieutenant of the Imperial Army and a New Zealand sergeant were in charge of the compound. Coming along the duckwalk from the gate I observed a long row of stout high poles to the right. These poles were used for the infliction of No. 1 Punishment.

Handed over to the sergeant in charge, I was searched and stripped of everything except the clothes I stood up in and my two blankets. No prisoner was allowed to have a knife or razor or any sharp instrument of any kind.

'The other men are out at work,' said the sergeant, 'but I can give you a job helping in the cook-house in the meantime.'

'I don't obey any military orders,' I said. 'It's for refusing to obey military orders that I've been sent here.'

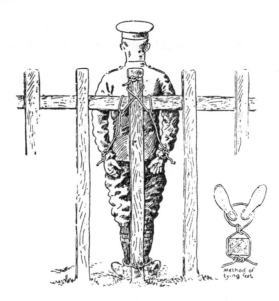

Method of tying feet

*No. 1 Field Punishment. ' . . . irons should be used when available, but straps or ropes may be used in lieu of them when necessary. Any straps or ropes used for this purpose must be of sufficient width that they inflict no bodily harm, and leave no permanent mark on the offender.' (Manual of Military Law. National Archives.)*

'Then you'll have a tough spin. You'll get No. 1 when the other men are at work and on pack drill. Better think it over.'

'There's no need for me to think it over. I'm not taking on anything.'

'Right-oh.' he said. 'Come along. I've got my orders.' He took me over to the poles which were willow stumps, six to eight inches in diameter and twice the height of a man, and placed me against one of them. I stood with my back to it and he tied me to it by the ankles, knees and wrists. He was an expert at the job, and he knew how to pull and strain the ropes till they cut into the flesh and completely stopped the circulation. When I was taken off my hands were always black with congested blood. My hands were taken round the pole, tied together and pulled well up it, straining and cramping the muscles and forcing them into an unnatural position. Most knots will slacken after a time. His never did. The slope of the post brought me in a hanging position, causing a large part of my weight to come on my arms, and I could get no proper grip with my feet on the ground, as it was worn away round the pole and my toes were consequently much lower than my heels. I was strained so tightly against the post that I was unable to move body or limbs a fraction of an inch. Earlier in the war, men undergoing this form of punishment were tied with their arms outstretched. Hence the name of crucifixion. Later, they were more often tied to a single upright, probably to avoid the likeness to a cross. But the name stuck.

A few minutes after the sergeant had left me, I began to think of the length of my sentence and it rose up before me like a mountain. The pain grew steadily worse until by the end of half-an-hour it seemed absolutely unendurable. Between my set teeth I said: 'Oh, God, this is too much. I can't bear it.' But I could not allow myself the relief of groaning as I did not want to give the guards the satisfaction of hearing me. The mental effect was almost as frightful as the physical. I felt as though I was going mad. That I should be stuck up on a pole suffering the frightful torture, a human scarecrow for men to stare at and wonder at, seemed part of some impossible nightmare that could not possibly continue. At the very worst strength came to me and I knew I would not surrender. The battle was won. And though the suffering increased rather than decreased as the days wore on, I never had to fight it again.

The poles were in full view of passers-by in the road. By turning my head a little—the only movement I could make—I could see them as they came from one direction towards the gate. Then they passed out of my line of vision. Peasants came by in carts and on foot, people from the small towns round about, Belgians, I suppose. The civilian population, one and all, went past with averted heads, never looking in my direction, as long, at least, as I could see them. But the men in uniform, whether on foot or not, always looked.

*Baxter, an Otago farmer and conscientious objector, would not fight in the First World War. He was, nevertheless, forcibly conscripted into the army and, in an attempt to break his spirit, the New Zealand Expeditionary Force subjected Baxter to two hours of No. 1 Punishment a day for 28 days at 'Mud Huts' Field Camp near Dickebusch, Belgium. Archibald later fathered the poet James K. Baxter.*

## 'I RESPECTFULLY BEG TO APPEAL'  *1918*

# Captain Alfred Jonas

*Letter to the Minister of Defence. June 10, 1918*

On May 15, 1918 I was arrested in Whakatane, brought to Wellington and then taken to Somes Island internment camp. Sir, I sincerely hope that you will consider my case and appoint an enquiry. As I do not know that I have committed a crime against the British Empire or the New Zealand Government. As I have looked for protection of the British Empire since I was 17 years of age. Sir, I have a wife, four boys and a girl at school, all dependent on me. Thanking you in anticipation, Alfred Jonas.

*Letter to Minister of Defence. July 26, 1918*

I respectfully beg to appeal against the decision of the Defence Headquarters that I am to remain in internment until the termination of the war. I would ask you to consider fully that I have the personal guarantees of four well-known and respected citizens who, in addition to vouching for my character are prepared to give a *cash* bond each of £50 that I will keep the parole conditions. I have been a loyal citizen of this country since 1880 and have never come into conflict with the law at any time. I am prepared to live quietly at my house and keep away from wharves and shipping. . . . Alfred Jonas

*Alfred Jonas was born in Denmark in 1863, went to sea at age 12 and jumped ship in Auckland at the age of 18. He became a naturalised New Zealander and a respected sea captain, running coastal ships out of Auckland for 34 years. In 1917, war fever ran high in New Zealand and rumours circulated about Captain Jonas' possible connection with Germans. The War Cabinet decided that he was a security risk. Jonas remained in internment on Somes Island until the end of the war when he was transferred for a time to an internment camp at Featherston. He emerged from that camp a sick and broken man. Three of Jonas' sons served in the wartime navy, two of them killed in action against the Germans.*

## WAR'S END AND INFLUENZA STRIKES — *Stratford, 1918*

### Dr Doris Gordon

The joy bells of peace with Turkey rang out when we had probably twelve to twenty severe cases of influenza in our region of ten thousand people. But no one had the authority to stride down the street shouting 'do not forgather, do not celebrate—death is round the corner'.

So collectively we celebrated, and danced in the Town Hall on a warm November night, and within twenty-four hours nearly a third of the revellers were rigoring. Amongst the stricken was my only medical colleague in the area. He telephoned: 'I've got it. I'm only a hundred point five, and with aspirin and quinine I think I can carry on by day. Will you do my night work?' That night the blast of dual telephone calls began.

One call was to a woman with a temperature of 104, coming into premature labour. She was in a smallish room of a three-roomed house. Her case looked grim . . . I decided to give her priority and watch through her labour, letting other calls accumulate. As two drunk men, still celebrating peace with Turkey, sprawled in the only sitting room, I found it preferable to sit all the time beside the slightly delirious patient . . .

*[Dr Gordon contracted influenza from this patient and was forced to go home to bed.]*

While I was still abed, the joy bells for the truce with Germany rang out. For years I'd lived and prayed for this moment and now it found me pickled in toxins, aspirins and quinine. In the next bedroom was my sister-in-law equally ill with gastric influenza. I staggered into her room and pitched myself on to the foot of her bed—I had just enough humour left to think what a queer pair of jubilant soldiers' wives we looked—and croaked, 'Dot, that's *peace*, and they are not killed yet!'

Unfortunately many moderately infected cases got out of bed on that Armistice Day; for youth in full flush of adolescent enthusiasm could not remain in bed for an ache and a cough when Stratford's Broadway was *en fête*. As a result many mild cases developed complications, and as the disease leapt from case to case it enhanced its virulence until many people were stricken from the outset with lethal infection which turned them first dusky blue then petechial purple.

When I resumed work, finding even the doctor's bag a trial to carry, I had the whole district on my hands, a more virulent type of disease, civil panic and total disorganisation of services.

Terrified relatives camped in my car drive ready to pounce the second I returned and to compel me to go to their homes next. This procession of demanding relatives went on all night. Doing some seven or eight visits before breakfast, I would find that the people had prevailed upon the telephone exchange officials to ascertain in which street my car was standing. When I went out, three or four people would be standing by it demanding that I go to their homes next.

I went two miles out of town to visit the large family of a hard-working old German. It was heart-rending to go rapidly down the bedrooms of six women, all moderately ill, and be only able to spare time enough to fix their drinks and pills on bedside tables. The only two sons were in a back bedroom, one severely ill, the elder obviously dying. In the kitchen was the tall sandy-headed father, the only one upstanding.

'Well,' he said, 'how are they?'

It's contrary to medical tradition to be brutally blunt, but in November 1918 there was no time for finesse. I looked the old man straight in the eye. 'The women, I think, will all do well; your younger son, with care, will recover. I am sorry to tell you your eldest son will be dead before night.'

'My God!' The old man reeled against the table. 'Then I've killed him; for only two days ago I told him he just had to get up and help me milk the cows!'

On the third day after Dr Paget left I spent most of my time verifying that the victims of Armistice Day celebrations were pulseless and signing their death certificates.

At 9 p.m. I was in the home of a master painter whose only two children had both got out of bed and walked round two blocks to witness the Broadway celebrations. I verified that the elder son was dead, went into the kitchen to sign the certificate, and was startled to find the undertaker there tape in hand; and I literally shivered when he suggested I also sign the death certificate for the other lad who was undoubtably just about to die.

It seemed ghoulish to sign while there was a flickering pulse, but the undertaker was as hard pressed as I was. Authority had ordered funerals to take back streets and to *hurry*. Funeral processions were banned and often relatives had to help the over-worked grave-diggers. As I stepped off the verandah of the painter's house, a dog howled mournfully and I nearly leapt out of my skin.

In my car I nearly broke down, but instead drove to the Mayor and demanded he use his authority to recall Dr Paget for the duration of the epidemic. The military authorities by now had realized the gravity of the disaster which had overtaken the civil community. Dr Paget came back with a military car and driver. The old doctor established his own sort of military law within six hours.

*Doris Gordon was Taranaki's first woman doctor, working out of Stratford. The fatal strain of influenza struck Auckland city first. Two days later, the infection reached remote Stratford. After the Second World War, Dr Gordon became the Director of Maternity and Child Welfare Services of New Zealand.*

## THE SPORTING LIFE      *Palmerston North, 23 November 1919*

## Herbert Watson

Dear Dan,

Yours of 23rd reached me during the week. The main reason for my last is that I have promised a cup for the men's singles at the P.N. Lawn Tennis Club, and with the price of silver going up so rapidly I want to get one as soon as possible. So I hope Marion got to work at once. I want you to do a small commission for me. I was playing fair golf at the beginning of the season and as you may remember won the medal competition the first time I completed with an 89, playing round with a short-headed brassie, a push click and a putter. Then I got rheumatic and did no good till the end of the season. On the last competition day (Bogey) I did so without the semblance of a fluke. I was 9 up on Bogey but had not taken out a card. If I had taken one I should not have the face to put in such a score. But the odd thing was that I had left the old club at home and had played with a long-headed driver, a spoon and mid-iron and the same putter as before. In 1910/11, when I was playing pretty well, I relied chiefly on my mid-iron, which was a beauty I had imported from America. It was stolen from my locker & I always thought McEwan the professional was the culprit. The one I am playing with now is a 'Maxwell' iron with a flange at the bottom. The 'Maxwell' clubs are well-known and used to be obtainable anywhere. The one I have is enormously heavy and I think I should do better with a lighter one. I know they are made lighter for the ex Hon. Sec. of the Isle of Wight G.C., with whom I played a lot of games in England, used to play with one and a good deal lighter than mine. That is what I want viz: A Maxwell mid-iron but not the heaviest pattern. We were in ChCh for the Cup Week and also your mother and Ngaire there. We went down in the *Mararoa* the same trip. I did not turn a hair thanks to having got rid of my 'inside fat' by strenuous squash playing—but Mollie & Sophie were very ill. Viv was sick for the first time in ten years. Next morning Sir F. Bell was the colour of putty. We had splendid weather in ChCh and the racing was very enjoyable. Mascot had a very easy win in the Canty Cup. She looked very fit and well. Motuihi is only a second-rate sprinter on present form. Going's horses did very badly. The Martians did very well, the NZ Cup, Canterbury Cup, Derby and Oaks going to some of his progeny. The consequence was that his yearlings were in great demand. The top-priced colt went to the Williams (who is standing for Bay of Plenty) at 1150 gs and the top-priced filly for 700 gs but Triv was the chief buyer and got some that should do great things if looks and breeding go for anything. He also bought the highest-priced Boniform for 600 gs. The Martians were mostly put in at 300 gs. The stock of other horses was much harder to sell. If McDonald of Wairarapa had not supported the Kilbroneys they would have done badly—I don't like them. Too purified—the Solferinos were mostly squibs. Jim Reed came to the rescue or they would have had a bad sale. Ian Deans offered three by Clemenceux. Two were sold at 21 and 27 gs & I think will prove great bargains. The half sister to Kilian fetched 310 gs but I can't remember who bought her. A three-year-old half-sister of Menelaus and Nones was knocked down for 85 gs the previous day. I was not there and would certainly have gone to 100 gs for her. Sorry to hear that Philippa has gone wrong but I have known several children who had a squint and were eventually cured so I shall expect her to do the same. I have had no lawn tennis yet having strained a muscle at the back of my thigh which I injured when running between wickets in a cricket

*Anyone for tennis?*

match in France in June '17. Sophie is playing a good deal and I have seen Going at the courts. He plays a good placing game of the 'patball' type. The club here is strong now, quite twenty fair players among the men, though no outstanding players. The ladies are weak, but Mrs Bett (nee Olive Gore) should strengthen the team. Smith got back about a week ago. You remember that he and I couldn't agree on the respective merits of Buster and Rags and that we agreed to decide the question at the P.N. Show. Both were entered but, owing to shearing, Ian, who was then taking care of Rags, couldn't send him and Buster took every first prize for which he was eligible and the medal for the best Aust. terrier in show. Rags went to Wanganui and took all the available firsts and special for best in the show. So we are no nearer a decision. They are not a bit alike and if he is right mine is wrong & vice versa? But whether right or wrong I like Buster's type much the best. I am looking for a wife for him but can't find one that I like. The primping at the show this year was first rate. Dan got the Challenge Cup and also the Qualified Hunters' with old 'Dugold' who went wonderfully well and with lots of dash in the hands of Dan's new whip, a half caste named Smith, who also steered the second in each event. Mickey Dee was not placed and is evidently done. Poor old Randall Pratt went out suddenly nine days ago. I understand that he did not suffer much. He and Arthur Russell were the oldest members of the Club, both having joined in 1883. Harry Cooper had pulled himself together and is not quite as bloated. Abrahams and Williams Ltd are increasing their capital to £500 000—Did you get your Vauxhall car and if so was the price £1200 as agreed upon? Mollie and Sophie are at present working hard with a stall for the rotten Catholic Church Bazaar. The priests seem to have got hold of Millie all right and are squeezing her to some effect. But I am glad to say they do not come to the house, at any rate when I am at home. Today is the first day since we came home that it is not blowing a gale so I am going to golf. We are talking of laying out an entirely new course here, fit for the championship and Clements has drawn up a plan with the play parallel to the ridges instead of across them except at one hole, and getting rid of the very bad 1st, 6th & 8th altogether. Love to Meta.

Yours Herbert N. Watson

*Letter to D.H. Riddiford, then in England.*

## GROWING UP IN LYALL BAY                          *1920*

Barbara Chorlton

*January*
*Fri 14.* It is raining. My father bought me a diary and mother and himself

*April*
*Mon. 28.* Went to Princess saw *Red Lantern.* tepid baths night.
*Tues. 29.* Stayed home. Tony went to museum.
*Wed. 30.* Went to gans got new sandels cake and tea Lindsays
*Thur. 31.* Got new pram. Took baby out in pram.

*May*
*Fri. 1.* April fool. I April fool twice. Took out baby.
*Sat. 2.* Tony gone to baths with Harry.
*Sun. 3.* Olive came to home. Tony didn't go to church prayed with us.
*Mon. 4.* Auntie Eeva was here for dinner. Bluebird slept with me. mother didn't. Went home gone to Avenue today.

*Tues. 5*. I went to Wilton's Bush with nuns. Nature saw AI in car with me.

*Wed. 6*. Played marbles

*Sat. 9. Kings Charter*. Stayed at Rosines.

*Sun. 10*. Went out with Auntie Enid Oriental Bay. Went to Mass.

*Mon. 11*. Went to school

*Tues. 12*. Went to school

*Wed. 13*. Went to school

*Thur. 14*. Went to school. Started knitting french.

*Fri. 15*. Went to school

*Sat. 16*. Took baby out. Tony and RF went to pictures. Owen Moore.

*Sun. 17*. Went and played with Olive and Maureen. Took baby out. To church.

*This was the first of Barbara Chorlton's diaries, kept when she was ten years old. Barbara subsequently wrote diaries for decades. (See also her entry for 1928, page 155).*

---

## THE PRINCE OF WALES WELCOMED TO DUNEDIN
*20 May 1920*

### *Otago Daily Times* Reporter

Never before in the history of Dunedin has a better arranged or more loyally enthusiastic children's demonstration been held than that which took place at Tahuna Park yesterday morning, when the school children of Otago assembled en masse to acclaim their future King. It was a wonderful gathering and worthy in every way of the important occasion which it marked in the minds of all who took part in it.

Although the ceremonial had been carefully rehearsed there was an air of spontaneity about the whole proceedings which was most refreshing and imparted a pleasing touch of naturalness to everything that was done. The effect was further heightened by the fact that the marching and the various movements that were carried out were simply a representation of the ordinary physical work which is daily carried out in the schools. The scholars too, were for the most part, dressed in their ordinary clothes, but they also wore as distinguishing marks the colours of the respective schools. A great many of the girls of course appeared in white dresses and this contributed to a very pleasing general effect. The steadiness of the children on parade and their splendid behaviour during the whole course of the proceedings commanded admiration alike from the general public, and this approval was expressed on not a few occasions by the warmly appreciated outbursts of applause which recognised some especially neatly executed movement. The children's part in the celebration marking the Prince's visit to Dunedin undoubtably achieved a wonderful degree of success and it was merely stating the obvious to say that vivid recollections of the occasion will be retained during the rest of their lives by all the young folk who participated.

The Prince takes a special delight in meeting the children of the Empire and, wherever he has gone the demonstrations arranged by the young folk have been an outstanding feature of the rejoicings. There is a peculiar appropriateness in bringing the children as closely as possible into contact with their future King, for no better means can be devised of fostering that spirit of loyalty to the throne, which is one of the most powerful factors in strengthening the bonds of Empire and in the welding together in one common bond, the colonies and the Motherland.

The Prince, accompanied by Admiral Halsey, advanced to the front of the dais, the St Kilda Band playing six bars of the National Anthem, and the Royal Standard being broken out on the breeze. The Dunedin Highland Pipe Band was also in attendance. The children presented a magnificent spectacle as they stood up smartly to attention and the Prince acknowledged the greeting by raising his hat.

An interesting ceremony which followed was the presentation to the Prince of a beautiful greenstone and silver inkstand, mounted on a pedestal of Maori carving and also a handsomely-bound copy of the Peace Booklet. The presenting party consisted of eighteen girls chosen by ballot from the city and suburban primary, secondary and private schools, and dressed in pure white, they made an exceedingly pretty sight as they advanced between the two divisions and approached the dais where they halted in front of the Royal Standard and curtsied to the ground. Miss Rita Boyd, of Columba College, and Miss Doreen Hayward, of the Normal School, then ascended the dais and made the actual presentations. His Royal Highness accepted the various gifts with a brief and cordial acknowledgement. The Prince next proceeded to inspect the lines of assembled scholars, a task he performed with great thoroughness and to the accompaniment of a constant clicking of camera stops. As he stepped from the dais Messrs. A.P. Roydhouse, J. Rennie (musical director), and Colonel Mcdonald were presented and the various line commanders were also presented as the Prince made his tour of inspection. During his tour around the ground the Prince was loudly cheered by the different sections of the crowd. During the actual inspection the ranks preserved the greatest steadiness and orderliness and the Prince made many flattering comments on what he termed 'the soldierly bearing of the children'.

Before leaving the ground the Prince warmly congratulated Mr Clark on the fine appearance of the children and their accurate marching. 'I am very delighted with your charming display,' he said. 'It has been most excellent in every way. I will be glad if you will congratulate all those concerned and tell them that I am very grateful to them. Will you see that all the children have a special holiday granted to them this term to show how much I appreciate what they have done? That is my personal request.'

*Edward, Prince of Wales, visited New Zealand to thank our troops for their part in the Great War. He was greeted with tremendous adulation throughout the country. Dunedin was one of his last stops on the tour.*

## TEA WITH THE MAYOR OF WANGANUI                1920

### D'Arcy Cresswell

I am a returned soldier, 24 years of age, and reside with my parents in Timaru, in the South Island. I have done no work since I returned from the war. I came to Wanganui on Monday, the 10th inst., and met Mackay on that day. I met him at dinner at Chevanne's Hotel, with my cousin, at Mr Mackay's invitation. Nothing abnormal happened at dinner. I spoke to Mackay between the time I had dinner with him on Monday night and entering his office on Saturday morning, and returned to Wanganui the following evening, the 15th inst. My cousin and myself went to the Hawera races on Tuesday the 11th inst., and returned to Wanganui the following evening. I met Mackay on Thursday and asked him to come to dinner at the Rutland Hotel that night with my cousin and myself. Mackay kept the appointment and we had dinner at the hotel. Nothing took place while we were at the hotel, and I had not said anything to Mackay that would offend him. On the Thursday evening Mackay invited me to go to the Art Gallery with him on the Friday afternoon. I accepted as I wanted to know more about Mr Mackay. On the Friday afternoon about 4 p.m., I met Mackay at his office in Ridgeway street. Then we went to the Wanganui Club, in Hill street, and had a cup of tea. From there we went to the Art Gallery. We went to Mackay's office in Ridgway street, and while there I discovered a certain disgusting feature of Mackay's character. He also showed me several photographs of nude women. I purposely encouraged him to display the qualities in his nature which I had expected. On making this discovery I told him that I had led him on on purpose to make sure of his dirty intentions, and I told him, also, amongst a lot of other candid things, that he must resign the mayoralty at once. He then pleaded mercy and asked me to think over it for the night and come and see him next morning and let him know my decision. I stayed at Rutland Hotel on Friday night, as I was going to a dance in the Druids' Hall that evening. During the night I decided he should resign the mayoralty in a week's time. At my suggestion and partly at my dictation, Mackay wrote a letter to my cousin, and I saw it posted in the morning. As arranged I called on him at 9.30 a.m. at his office in Ridgeway street on the Saturday and the whole morning was spent by him pleading with me, on account of his wife and family, not to force him to resign. I however, was quite determined that he should resign, even though he threatened to commit suicide. I did not believe that he had the courage, and I did not believe him when he said that his wife was dependent on the £300 he got for being mayor. I was very anxious to be just and to do nothing cruel to his family. He told me he was suffering from a complaint which made it impossible for him to control his passions, and he said his doctor could satisfy me in that respect. He rang up his doctor on two or three occasions but each time the doctor was out. After useless talking and long silences, he asked me to come round to the club and try to reconsider my decision over a cup of tea. As I could not stand being in his office much longer, and was very knocked up, I consented, and we went. Here he became very earnest about his decision to commit suicide and the absolute impossibility of resigning the mayoralty. Nothing more happened here than had happened in his office. I think I was very foolish not to have left him, but I was anxious to be quite just to him. I should say here that I promised to say nothing about what I discovered if he would resign at the end of the week. I did not want to judge him, but I was determined that he had no business to be Mayor. Back in his office again, I being very tired, took a more determined stand about it and threatened that if he didn't immediately give me a letter promising to resign at the end of the week I would at once wire to my Dad in Timaru to come up, as it was getting too much of a strain on me alone. He seemed so terribly upset that I extended the time to a fortnight, and then he implored me for a month's time, and spoke a lot about his wife and family. I was quite firm about a fortnight, and he then asked for a few minutes alone to clear his head or something of the sort, and went into an anteroom, where a girl worked. He was away a few minutes and then came back and said: 'Cresswell, give me a month and I will sign a letter straight away.' At that time I was getting very tired, so I said: 'All right. I will give you a month from today.' Then he came over to his table and wrote a letter promising to resign his mayoralty a month from that date, and he put it into a large envelope. We then arranged that it should be addressed to me at the General Post Office and registered, and I promised to let it lie at the Post Office until the month was up, so he put it in his pocket and we walked towards a door marked A, Mr Mackay leading the way. Before reaching the door Mackay suddenly turned round, and I found that he had a revolver pointing at my chest. We were only a foot or two apart. I think that he said 'This is for you,' but I am not sure. Then he fired almost immediately, before I could recover from my amazement, and I felt the bullet enter my right breast and I fell down. He stood where he was and looked down at me, and then came over and thrust the revolver into my right hand. Immediately I got the revolver I rose to my feet and kept him covered. He looked very surprised and wild and then ran through a door marked B. I followed him and when I reached the door I found that it was either locked or else he was holding on to the handle. I did not wait to see but ran into Mackay's office, to the window facing Ridgway street and threw a chair through it to bring assistance, and when I had smashed the window I called out to some chaps in the street to come up. Then evidently Mackay, hearing my calls for help, and thinking that he couldn't escape, came back and asked me to shoot him, and then he rushed me and I kept the revolver pointed clear and pulled the shots off. The next thing I can remember I was running down the stairs and telling someone that Mackay had shot me and I heard Mackay say over the stairs that he had shot me by accident. I don't remember much more. I was wearing the clothes produced when shot.

Accused said: Sergeant, I have shot a young man through the chest and I believe he will die. When the Prince was here I was carrying an automatic revolver. I was showing it to a young man Cresswell, and demonstrating it, when it accidentally went off and shot him.

*Charles Mackay, for 15 years Mayor of Wanganui, eventually pleaded guilty to the charge of attempted murder and was sentenced to 15 years' gaol. D'Arcy Cresswell, a witness at his trial, became one of New Zealand's leading poets.*

## ARRIVING IN NEW ZEALAND                    *25 March 1921*

## Walter Brockie

Dear Mother,

I arrived at Colon 6th March, and despatched a letter there which I hope you get all right. On the whole the voyage across the Atlantic was very uneventful except for a glimpse of the West Indian Islands. We only passed three small steamers, and during the first week cold winds and rough seas made sailing rather unpleasant. We sighted the isthmus of Panama shortly after breakfast last Sunday, and soon the smoke of steamers and the tall framework pillars of a wireless indicated the town and harbour of Colon . . .

On Wednesday, two days journey from Panama, we sighted the Galapagos Islands. From then on we saw nothing but sea and sky. The weather was fine and very much cooler than I had expected. On crossing the equator a nice breeze was blowing and it was very pleasant on deck.

Everything went on as usual on the boat. Fancy dress parades, concerts, whist-drives, dancing and sports were all arranged, so we had plenty of amusement. An international tug-of-war was won by the Scotchmen. Jim was pulling in this, so had his share of the honours.

About seven days before we landed in New Zealand (I am writing this from Dunedin now) we stopped at Pitcairn Island, and were met by a party of the islanders in a small boat bringing fruit. When the boat came near our ship the Islanders began to sing a hymn. They appeared to have very good voices, and a fine volume of sound came across the water. All the fruit they brought was a present to the passengers on board, and consisted of bananas and pineapples. There were other things given as souvenirs, such as fans and polished coconut shells with painted flowers on them, but I wasn't lucky enough to get any. Nor did they lose anything by their presents because a lot of the passengers threw over numerous and varied assortment of clothing, and the captain lowered a sheep carcasse and a bag of flour, so they went away as they came, singing 'Till we meet'.

We arrived in Wellington on Wednesday the 20th March after a voyage of 40 days, so we weren't very long. Jim and I immediately sought digs and along with another two chaps got a room in the suburbs. We had intended going up country right away but Jim had been bothered by a cold and a touch of influenza during the last week of the voyage he wasn't feeling just up to it, so we changed our minds and got the boat for Christchurch and from there by train to Dunedin (We got this journey free from the Shaw Savill Coy).

Arrived in Dunedin we made for Jim's friend's place, viz Jim Walker, and he had a very welcome reception from both him and his wife. We arrived here on Friday night so we have been here three days. They are very hospitable.

Mr and Mrs Currie from Mosgiel visited us on Saturday night and we had a fine crack. She is getting on fine and appears to be doing well out here. I have had a busy time in the garden this after-noon, cutting grass, trimming edges, and cutting ivy, getting my hand in as it were.

Jim Walker, who works on the railway, says he may be able to have a job for us there by the end of the week so we might fall in right away.

Tell Mrs Currie that we delivered parcels all right and that Mrs Edgar was very pleased with her skirt length. Jim is improving, and will be all right in a day or two so we may start work together next week. Hoping all are well.
Love to all
Your loving son
Walter

*Three years after being released from a Turkish prisoner-of-war camp, Walter Brockie left Scotland for New Zealand on an assisted passage on R.M.S.* Waimana.

## JUVENILE DELINQUENCY IN REEFTON          *early 1920s*

# Redmond Phillips

'You were a long time in the Stewards' room.'

'Yes. That was on account of the Muldoon Handicap. We had some pretty rough riding today: it's getting worse, I think. And the usual disagreements . . . The other stewards wanted to penalise Billy Winters but I said quite emphatically "No, it wasn't Winters, it was Jorgensen on Omaha." Interference as clear as day.'

'That's right!' Alford jumped in excitedly. 'Jorgensen took the whip to him . . .'

'He what?' My father put down his knife and fork.

'Jorgensen took the whip to him and then kicked Billy's foot out of the stirrup.'

Icy silence followed this revelation, then: 'Could we have that again?'

Alford drew back from the yawning chasm. 'I mean . . . I was told . . . on good authority. Well, Alec and Bob . . .'

'You were out on the Waitahu Road with the school harriers.'

'Oh, yes Dad.'

My father's brow darkened with suspicion. 'Was your informant a fellow harrier, might I ask?'

'Not exactly a harrier, no.'

'You weren't harrying around the boundary road at the back of the course, by any chance?' He rose, pulled back the bentwood chair and threw down his napkin with a gesture of sudden rage.

'It was the trail, you see,' said Alford, usually a truthful boy and weak on invention, but now, alarmed by his parent's sudden ferocity, his imagination took wing. 'The trail, you see. We followed the trail down the Waitahu Road all right, then through the dairy factory yards . . . poo, the smell . . . around the old cemetery, then followed the creek bed as far as the traffic bridge, but the Council men wouldn't let us over because they were laying down some asphalt, so McMaster said: "That's it, boys. We can't cross the bridge, we've lost the trail, so all we can do is nip across Heaphy's orchard and take the short cut . . ."'

' . . . down the boundary road to the back of the racecourse.' My father's neatly clipped moustache wriggled with sarcasm.

'Yes, the back of the racecourse.'

*'Leave this to me, Bessie!'*

'In time for the Muldoon.'

Alford did not reply and for a long time there was silence in the room.

'I could have sworn I saw Alan McMaster coming away from the Tote,' my mother said. 'He was in running shoes. Yes, now I come to think of it, running shoes. He's not what you'd call a dressy little man at the best of times so I thought nothing of it. But he was wearing running shoes alright.'

There was a small infamy in the air.

'What time was this, Bessie?'

'Mrs Auld and I had just come back from afternoon tea. That was after the Big Race.' She alluded to the Inangahua Cup, but no one called it that. 'It must have been about a quarter to four. Just before the Muldoon Handicap.'

My father resumed his seat, glowered, and was silent. We thought the storm had passed, but worse was to come. 'I hate a liar', he said.

'I'm not lying!'

'Listen to me, boy. The harriers never get back from their run until five at the earliest. But being race day, what is more, Cup day, Alan McMaster decided to cut short the run and slip into the course for the last three events.' Strong on deduction, he was now putting the case for the Crown with devastating forensic skill.

'There's no charge for admission after three o'clock anyway,' my mother put in.

'We had to call off the run,' Alford pleaded. 'They wouldn't let us over the bridge.'

My father had gone from the room, his place taken by Prosecuting Counsel, who now, in his turn, had made way for the ex-president of the Inangahua Harriers' Club. 'You could have gone over the Suspension bridge, could you not, and come down the power-house road, or even have forded the river just behind the town baths. It's shallow there. Or were you frightened of losing the scent?' he added bitingly.

Alford was mute.

'You could have double-backed after you left Heaphy's orchard,' he went on, 'crossed over the railway line, taken another short cut through the Recreation Ground, run up the reservoir road, down and around the buttes, past the cattle pound and straight down to the school gates. No trouble at all.' As well as being an old harrier himself, he was also a handy man with an ordnance map and more than a match for his delinquent son. 'Instead of which'—

'I'm pretty certain it was McMaster we saw at the tote window,' said my mother pensively.

'Instead of which, with the connivance of McMaster, an inveterate racing man, wouldn't you say, Bessie?'—

My mother agreed with 'inveterate', adding that according to Mrs Auld's sister-in-law, Linda Applejohn, McMaster was as thick as thieves with the racing crowd who drank in Stallard's Hotel after hours.

A not unfamiliar figure himself in Stallards back bar in the long winter evenings, he was prepared to let this pass and pushed on relentlessly. 'McMaster used the closed bridge as an excuse, terminated the exercise and by half past three was queuing up at the Tote to place his bets, while you, left to your own resources, scrambled over the back fence and took your place up in those pine trees with the rest of the town's hoodlums and urchins.'

'That's a bit strong isn't it Tom?' My mother did not enjoy the spectacle of her husband bullying a witness, and as for hoodlums and urchins, some of them at least were the sons of her croquet-playing friends.

'Leave this to me Bessie,' he snorted. 'You have been expressly forbidden to go near the racecourse unless you are accompanied by your mother or myself. At a committee meeting the other night they were discussing these trespassers and larrikins. It's an annual problem, and I moved that the Police be instructed to patrol the area and deal with the offenders on the spot. Not very nice for me, is it, barrister and solicitor and club steward, to have my own son rounded up with the town's riff-raff. But not only have you disobeyed me, you have lied, and liars must be punished.' He breathed heavily like the skipper about to flog a seaman.

Beatings were infrequent in our household. Somewhere in a dank cupboard in the back hall, a heavy leather strap was kept for ritual chastisements. Black as liquorice or unholy relic, the finger or kneecap of a martyr gaining a potency by being withheld from public gaze and becoming visible only once or twice a year perhaps when certain solemnities had to be performed. But, usually, the threat was enough and it was always Alford who was the victim. I don't know why this was: he was a gentle, well-behaved boy, the apple of his mother's eye, but sturdy and manly too, and his companions, wild and high-spirited country boys, always included him in their escapades. They accepted thrashings cheerfully as a fact of life. Sons were expected to be beaten and fathers were expected to thrash them. It was as simple as that, but not for Alford. And not for my father. I suspect he found the stern, Victorian paternal role distasteful and my mother's natural instinct was to protect Alford, but their moral duty was firm and clear.

While we waited for my father to pronounce sentence, my mother served the pears and custard, glancing nervously at him while he deliberated. She firmly believed that boys should be whipped, not necessarily her boys, but boys in a general way, unruly, disobedient, foul-mouthed boys . . . Of course it was for the man of the house to decide these things, but in spite of her strongly-held views, she would have danced on hot coals to spare Alford the pain and humiliation of a thrashing.

The sound of a bicycle's handle-bars bumping against the wall of the back porch promised relief to the overwrought atmosphere of the kitchen. Sadie, who had been a silent witness to the altercation, flew to the window and startled us all by announcing the arrival of Constable McClaren.

'What did I tell you?' my father said grimly to a white-faced Alford. In his professional capacity he had a good deal to do with the local constabulary, but social contacts were rare. Although McClaren had come to the town some years before, he had never endeared himself to the populace. He was officious, never a man to wink the other eye at an infringement, which a West Coast copper could reasonably be expected to do. In so far as Reefton was concerned, the qualities most to be admired in a man of the law were his inattention and inertia.

After civilities had been exchanged, apologies offered and refreshments refused, Constable McClaren, rather stiffly, got down to business. 'It's a simple matter of trespass Mr Phillips,' he said after a preamble delivered with a mixture of unction and solemnity. 'Your committee knows all about it and I've just this minute come from Mr Hubert Quilley.'

At the mention of Quilley's name, my father winced.

'Up in the trees,' McClaren went on, 'a whole mob of them, a dozen lads at least, squatting on their hunkers in the lower branches and, by the look of things, I'd say they'd been there the whole afternoon. Peanut shells and lolly-papers all over the place. It's got to stop.'

'Most of the afternoon?'

'I'd say so. The fence on that part of the course is in bad repair, but that's no excuse. I mean, as I see it, it's just the same as breaking and entering. Or going in under a tent at the circus. Remember when Wirth's Circus was here last year? I put a stop to that didn't I? Some people make light of this sort of thing, but you know, and I know, it's an indictable offence.'

'I don't know about indictable,' my father said mildly.

'Where did you get money for peanuts and lollies?' my mother demanded fiercely.

My father quelled her with a wave. 'How many of them, did you say?'

'A dozen at least. Half the town, four to a tree. The McDonald twins were the ring-leaders by the look of things, and your boy and young Humphries seemed to be making the book.'

'Making the book?' This revelation of depraved (and unfamiliar) practices left my mother aghast. 'What book, Tom? Making what book?'

'They were betting, Bessie.' Then, turning to the Constable he said wearily, 'All right, McClaren, what do you want me to do about it?'

'I don't have to tell you what to do about it Mr Phillips, do I, you being the boy's father and a barrister and a solicitor. No, I don't have to tell you. That's just what I said to Archie McDonald. And that's what I'll be saying to young Humphries' Dad. But if you ask me, I'd say it was a matter for the Juvenile Court.'

'We don't happen to have a Juvenile Court,' my father reminded him.

'More's the pity,' said the Constable and, with a sour smile, he took his leave, retrieved his bicycle and pedalled off shakily up the rough track to the Humphries' farm.

'Well, what about that?' My father, drained, in a state of moral shock, could only gesture feebly in the direction of my brother, a gesture that relegated him to Dante's abyss, the innermost circle. The thick leather strap, stiff as a crow-bar, hovered over the supper-table as ominous as Banquo's ghost. 'Most of the afternoon, eh?'

Alarmed and indignant, Alford jumped to his feet. 'No, no,' he protested, 'we got there just after the Muldoon Handicap. Late. I told you. The field came right under where we were sitting and we saw Jorgensen take the whip to Billy Winters and kick his foot out of the stirrup and . . . '

'I don't want to hear another word of this, not another word. Do you hear?'

The silence of the tomb descended and minutes went by. The farm clock ticked away rheumatically, coals turned over in the fuel stove and a light rain began to spatter the window panes.

'You remembered to bring in the washing?' my mother enquired of my sister in a strained, sotto voice.

Bereft of speech, Sadie nodded her head.

At last my father cleared his throat. 'Jockey Jorgensen took the whip to Billy Winters and kicked his foot out of the stirrup. Is that what you're saying?'

'Oh, Tom, give it a rest, you're not in Court now.'

'Hold on, Bessie. He kicked his foot out of the stirrup, eh?'

'Yes, and he used his whip on him hard. Bash, bash, bash.'

'Bash, bash, bash?'

'Yes,' said Alford.

'Hmmmmm.' Another silence, but this time longer, even more profound.

My mother would have liked to clear the table and move into the sitting-room and she fidgeted. There was nothing in the world she enjoyed more than to toast herself in front of a log fire on a wet spring night, but that would have to wait. The tension continued to mount as my father sat with his head sunk on his chest as if struggling with his daemon, or, alternatively, praying inwardly for guidance, then broke as, with grim resolution, he got to his feet and strode out into the hall, not, as we expected, to the cupboard where the instrument of torture hung, but to the wall-telephone. Two brisk rings and he was through to Myra Jenkins, the exchange operator.

'I haven't got Mr Quilley's home number at hand, Myra,' we heard him say, 'but would you mind putting me through please?'

My mother leaned out of her chair and prodded the door further ajar, the better to hear this conversation.

Minutes went by, it seemed, while Myra, a slow mover but indefatigably obliging, used all the resources of the exchange to trace the errant Quilley. My father began to whistle a doleful little tune and was almost into the middle strain of 'Keep the Home Fires Burning' before Myra got back to him. 'No luck?' he enquired. Then, confidentially, 'You could try Stallard's back bar. You've rung there? No, no, don't do that. Don't do that Myra. All right, I think he must still be at the clubrooms. Don't bother. Thank you very much, Myra.'

He hung up, and offering no explanation whatever for this turn of events, almost at once got out his bicycle and, after announcing that he would be at the club-rooms, pedalled off into the night.

The matter of the Norfolk pines was never referred to again except that on the following Monday a brief announcement appeared on the sports page of the *Inangahua Times* to the effect that, following the Muldoon Handicap protest, the Racing Committee's ruling had been reversed as a result of fresh evidence supplied by Mr. Thos Phillips, barrister and solicitor, and that Cedric Jorgensen, Omaha's rider, would be suspended for three months.

My brother went unpunished and, although no specific reference was made to the deplorable events of Cup Day, he was warned that if he didn't choose his companions with more discretion in the future, he would be getting a bad reputation for himself.

*Redmond Phillips was born in 1912 and brought up in Reefton. He became a radio script writer in Australia and, after 1948, a stage and screen actor in Britain. In retirement, he recalled 'the people on the verandah'—his family—with nostalgia and deep affection.*

## THE BOMBAY FOOTBALL CLUB

*13 April 1922*

## William Massey

Prime Minister's Office
Wellington

Dear Sir,

I am in receipt of your letter of the 10th inst., informing me that I have been re-elected Patron of the Bombay Football Club for the coming season. Will you please convey to the members of your club an expression of my thanks and appreciation of the courtesy extended to me, and my acceptance with pleasure of the Office. I am enclosing herewith a cheque for one guinea as a small contribution towards the funds, and take this opportunity of wishing the Club every success during the ensuing season.

Yours faithfully
W. Massey

J.R. Evans Esq,
Honorary Secretary
Bombay Football Club
P.O. Box 7
BOMBAY

## FIGHTING THE BLACK MARLIN OFF THE BAY OF ISLANDS

*1920S*

## Zane Grey

'They're waving on the Captain's boat.'

'Sure enough,' I said. 'Guess he must have a strike or have seen a fish.'

But when Bill appeared waving the red flag most energetically I knew something was up. It took us only a moment or two to race over to the other boat, another one for me to leap aboard her, and another one to run aft to the Captain.

153

His face was beaming. He held his rod low. The line ran slowly and freely off his reel.

'Got a black Marlin strike for you,' he said with a smile. 'He hit the bait, then went off easy . . . take the rod!'

I was almost paralyzed for the moment, in the grip of amazement at his incredible generosity and the irresistible temptation. How could I resist? 'Good Heavens!' was all I could mumble as I took his rod and plumped into his seat. What a splendid, wonderful act of sportsman-ship—and friendliness!

'Has he showed?' I asked breathlessly.

'Bill saw him,' replied Captain.

'Hell of a Buster!' ejaculated Bill.

Whereupon with chills and thrills up my spine, I took a turn at the dragwheel and shut down with both gloved hands on the line. It grew tight. The rod curved. The strain lifted me. Out there a crash of water preceded by a whirling splash. Then a short, blunt beak, like the small end of a baseball-bat, stuck up followed by the black-and-silver head of an enormous black Marlin.

He led us out to sea, and in two miles he flung his immense, gleam-ing body into the air ten times. Naturally this spectacular performance worked havoc on my emotions. Every time I saw him I grew more demented. No child ever desired anything more than I that beautiful black Marlin! It was an obsession. I wanted him, yet gloried in his size, his beauty, his spirit, his power. I wanted him to be free, yet I wanted more to capture him. There was something so inexpressibly wild and grand in his leaps. He was full of grace, austere, as rhythmic as music, and every line of him seemed to express unquenchable spirit. He would die fighting for his freedom.

Whenever he showed himself that way I squared my shoulders and felt the muscles of Hercules.

*Zane Gray was a wealthy, glamorous, American sportsman whose books brought New Zealand big game fishing to the world's attention.*

## SCHOOL HOLIDAYS UP COUNTRY            *1928*

## Barbara Chorlton

*January*

*Mon. 23.* Came up to Wangaehu. Mr T. away only Brooks and George here. Lovely to be here again. The grass is dry. Brooks looks very delicate after operation.

*Tue. 24.* Haymaked all day & finished stack. Great.

*Wed. 25.* Paper Brook's room. I helped in afto. I like David a bit & his brogue very much. I dislike his friend.

*Thu. 26.* I finished room & cleaned up house. washed my hair & wrote to Peggy—Dear old Peg. Mr Turner returned. Finished *The Morals of Marcus Aurelius.*

*Fri. 27.* Went to Wanganui. Went to Fennels. Got myself in a fix. Hadn't intended to stay there but circumstances forced me to. Jolly pest. They are all in same as ever. Rosie and I end to end in small bed. didn't sleep well.

*Sat. 28.* Matric results out. see if we have passed. discover I'm still very selfish. Beat the other girls. Eustace is as soft as ever. Albert still as mad. Mrs T. is very good-hearted & I like her and Rosie very much (went to pictures).

*Sun. 29.* Went mass. Had corking fruit salad. Messed around all the afto and sang in the evening. They are a very musical family but shout a bit.

*Mon. 30.* Returned to Fennel's though they are very nice people they are inclined to be a bit eccentric. Awful train journey from Wanganui to Wangaehu. Glad to be home.

*Tue. 31.* Had corking bath and went over to see Brooks milking. The river is lovely and quiet. It appears to me to go on and on like the everlasting.

*February*

*Wed. 1.* Dave and his friend came down & I retired.

*Thur. 2.* Read nearly all day. very lazy day.

*Fri. 3.* Worked in day but too hot to do anything very strenuous. Went down to Mrs Cray's

*Sat. 4.* Very very sorry to leave. Caught train. Had awful train journey down. Dusty and dirty wasn't the name for what I felt like. All the same with me. Tony's matric results awfully good. I know he has beaten me hollow.

*Eighteen-year-old Barbara Chorlton lived with her parents in Wellington and holidayed north of Wanganui. She became an enthusiastic tramper who wrote up details of all her trips. During the Second World War Barbara served in the WRENS in Egypt and England, returning later to live at Makara. (See also her entry for 1920, page 138)*

---

## FIRST TRANS-TASMAN FLIGHT    *Wigram, 11 September 1928*

## Squadron Leader Kingsford Smith

Description of machine

| | |
|---|---|
| Class of plane | FOKKER TRI-MOTOR TYPE F7 |
| Engines | 3 Wright Whirlwinds—each 220 HP |
| HP | Mason Revolutions 1800 |
| Wing spread | 71 feet 8$^{1}/_{2}$ inches |
| Weight empty | 6000 lbs |
| Carrying capacity | 6000 lbs on this flight |
| Personnel | Squadron Leader C.E. Kingsford Smith MC AFC RAAF Born Brisbane 9/2/1887 Co-commander |
| | Flight Lieutenant C.T.P. Ulm AFC RAAF Born Melbourne 18/10/1897 Co-commander |
| | Mr H.A. Litchfield. Navigator. Born Peak Hill |

NSW. 24/6/1901

Mr T.H. McWilliams. Wireless Operator. Born
Thames NZ 16/6/1897

|  |  |
|---|---|
| Place of departure: | No. 3 Squadron RAAF Aerodrome. Richmond NSW. |
| Time of departure: | Sydney Time 5.31 p.m. date 10/9/1928 NZ Time    2.01 p.m. |
| Place of arrival: | Wigram aerodrome Christchurch New Zealand |
| Time of arrival: | 9.26 a.m. NZ Time Date 11/9/1928 |
| Distance travelled: | 1660 land miles |
| Time occupied: | 14 hours 25 minutes |
| Average speed: | 119 miles per hour |
| Petrol consumption: | 380 gallons |
| Weather conditions: | Particularly adverse—cloudy and stormy—strong NW winds |

*Vast crowds were on hand to welcome this flight at Wigram. Details of the flight were written on the back of a map and calendar and signed by Kingsford Smith.*

## ESCAPING THE MURCHISON EARTHQUAKE
*Monday 17 June 1929*

## Vita Harney

I heard a dreadful roar and yelled to the children, 'Come to me.' Thank God, they moved as one man. I was able to collect them, scrum formation, in the doorway between school and porch. Then we caught it—blackboards, books and bottles flew in every direction.

I was afraid the chimney (brick) would fall, but it's the only one in the whole district left. After 5 minutes I thought we'd better get, so formed threes and marched my company to the road. Brave bairns—no panic. White faces but no tears and implicit obedience. We happened to be on the only safe piece of road for some distance. 2 chains away, on either side, the road was cracking and heaving like a thing alive. The trees in the bush were cracking, mud pools bubbling up in the playground and the school swaying as if crazy. Soon we were joined by a frantic woman with 3 tots and a babe in arms. I went back into the school to get her a chair and had to crawl . . .

As soon as the beach people came for their bairns I was faced with the problem of seeing them safely home. It was a nightmare—had to lift them over several huge fissures—the road quivering all the way, and we just passed one place when a tree fell across the road. We found the residents collected in an open field. Some had food so we boiled the billy and had a meal . . . All decided to camp that night in the Hall, the only building that escaped injury.

We camped 10 days in the hall (with food and blankets retrieved from a nearby homestead). The continuous rain and slips caused our river to run a banker for days and we were in danger of flood.

*Vita Harney was the schoolteacher at Oparara, near Karamea. The earthquake, 7.8 on the Richter scale, produced explosive noises like artillery fire, and a booming sound heard as far away as Taranaki. Seventeen people were killed in the quake. Karamea was cut off for a fortnight and aftershocks continued for six months.*

## AHURIRI LAGOON TURNS TO DRY LAND                                 1931

## Ruth Park

On a still hot morning, February 3, an extraordinary phenomenon occurred. The tide went out and didn't come in. This was not a spectacular event. The sea did not roll up like a scroll, like the sky in Revelations. It quietly withdrew. Fraser the beard [a small dog] and I were fooling around in the shallows in the dinghy at the time, and I felt this withdrawal abruptly, as though the water had been yanked away from underneath. We bumped and dragged on the stony bottom.

'Crumbs, what's going on?'

People began to run down to the beach, Captain Toms from the store, a couple of stationhands, Aunt Wendela flapping her hands and calling us back in.

Panicky fish were everywhere, flipping over the wet stones, trying to wiggle under them. Little fingerlings, bright as new tin, flip flop, scutter, gape and gasp.

I saw things I had never seen before—the sharp incline fifty metres off low water mark, and then the seagrass-covered sandy plateau, flat as a plate, lying as far as the eye can see. The seagrass was all combed one way, as though the retreating water had tried to take it with it. The air glittered with leaping fish, red snapper, dogfish, mullet, and clouds of sprats that had taken to the air in their hysteria. Afar, a huge ray lifted first one wing and then the other in a mad shuffle towards the water.

The beard slipped out of my arms, and went off at a fast waddle across the seagrass. It had fixed its unseen eye on something waggling around, scooping sand from under a rock, throwing up a long flexible arm in its hurry to find a hiding place.

I had never seen a live squid, but I knew this was one, and I took off after the beard. The little dog, which had never made a stand in its life, was probably curious. But perhaps like its owner, it had lost its head altogether.

The squid, half-deflated, a canvas bag of a body, and momentarily disclosed a large black and white eye. Its tentacles quickly pretended to be a bunch of seaweed.

'Wam! Wam! Wam!' shrieked the beard and a sound as of chattering teeth came from my cousin in the dinghy.

'Go on, get out of there!' I shouted at the dog. My feet were being sucked into the sand to the ankles. But who can guess the length of a squid's arms? It caught me and the beard in the same melting movement, one arm corkscrewing up my leg like a frond of ivy, and the beard being whipped in a frenzy of sand, water and hair towards the creature's body. I screamed blue murder.

Nobody tells you that to be embraced by a squid hurts. My leg felt that it was burned with acid. Meanwhile the beard was being choked. For the first time I saw its tongue, looking blue.

Panic-stricken, I hammered at the tentacle, jerking away with all my might. But all I did was lift the squid's body, now flushing yellow and pink, off the ground. It had twitched three more of its arms around the rock, and another about my ankle.

It was not a big squid, nor was it truly on the attack. A timid animal, all it wanted was to defend itself against me and the beard.

Then there was a rush, and two or three men grabbed me and pulled. Others whacked the squid with rocks. But it was Poa, one of the Maori farmers, who disposed of it, jabbing his stiffened fingers in its eyes. All I knew at the time was that the tentacles slowly relaxed their grip, like perished rubber.

*The tide went out as a consequence of the Napier earthquake, which turned the Ahuriri inlet into dry land. Napier Airport now stands on this land. Ruth Park's 'squid' was really an octopus.*

## NAPIER MORTUARY AFTER THE BIG QUAKE
1931

### *New Zealand Press Association* Reporter

One has seen heaps of mangled bodies after a minehead accident on the Rand and the sights of uncleared battlefields, but there was a pathos and horror of its own about this house of death. Every corner was occupied. The faces were covered and only revealed for those seeking to identify missing friends. The improvised drapes were not long enough to conceal all. Here were the elegant silk stockings and shoes of a fashionable girl, there the coarse moleskins and broad-toed boots of a labourer. The neatly creased trousers and carefully polished shoes (still evident though smirched and scored) of the businessman appeared side by side with the knickers of a schoolboy, or the tiny body of a child. One had to place one's feet carefully between the rows. Rigor mortis had set in and frozen the corpses in the attitude of death. Bareheaded police stood around and directed those looking for lost relatives. A sad elderly lady came in. The cloth was removed from the face of a grizzled bearded man. 'Yes, that is my dear one!' She rose from stooping and went sadly and aimlessly away.

*The Napier courthouse was temporarily converted to a morgue. Fifty bodies lay there at the end of the first day of the earthquake.*

## THE UNEMPLOYED RIOT IN
## QUEEN STREET                                       *1932*

## C.G. Scrimgeour

From across the road and the elevation of the Mission in Airedale Street, I had a grandstand view. The shabby little cottage at No. 2 was my home, and from my front door I could look directly into the door of the town hall.

The riot started at the main entrance. I don't think any member of the unemployed carried anything that could be used as a weapon. They weren't prepared for violence but they despaired of food for their families and selves, and their desperation was such that violence could easily erupt.

I wasn't close enough to pinpoint the exact outbreak. I knew the frustration of these men, I knew the hopelessness of their circumstances. I knew they were possessed of great desperation that could turn to anger, drive them to action. They'd planned no more than an orderly protest but suddenly all was violence around the main entrance and the men were coming across to get the pickets from my cottage fence to defend themselves. Desperate men with nothing to lose.

No one came to me. I went down Queen Street telling people to go home and not take any loot.

On my return to No. 2, three very anxious people were waiting to see me. They wanted to know if I could get a doctor to stitch up Jim Edwards' scalp. They'd taken Jim to the casualty department of Auckland Hospital. Jim had a towel around his head and one around his neck to hide the blood. While they were waiting, two policemen arrived and moved to the enquiry counter to examine the entries. While they were busy Jim's friends escaped attention and took him to a secret address.

'Can you get a doctor urgently?' I was asked. This was not as easily done as they thought it could be. If the police had alerted doctors, or if doctors had been asked to report, Edwards would have been arrested. I rang Harold Pettit to ask if there had been an alert and to ask if he was obliged to report an injury. Harold replied in the negative unless it was a gunshot wound.

'Would you be prepared to sew up a seriously-damaged scalp without reporting it.'

'Yes,' said Pettit. 'What's the address?'

'I can't tell you but you'll get a call in a few minutes.'

As a minister of religion I couldn't deny knowledge if the police asked me if I knew where Edwards was, and I couldn't place the doctor in the same position. Pettit knew I would see to that.

The scalp wound needed more than thirty stitches. In the following twelve months I never knew where the patient was.

*C.G. Scrimgeour was a Methodist Minister, socialist and Auckland City Missioner. As 'Uncle Scrim' he hosted* The Man in the Street—*a very popular Sunday night national radio show. Jim Edwards was the unofficial leader of the unemployed during the depression. He was later gaoled for his views and stood as the Communist candidate for Auckland Central in 1935.*

## THE DEPRESSION HITS DONEGAL FLAT
*Kaikoura, early 1930s*

### Ellen Donegal

During the Depression we had our farm freehold. We were producing nearly all of our own food and my husband was working sixteen hours a day, but still we weren't able to keep our heads above water. There was just no sale for stock. They had to cut the calve's throats when they were born and drive the sheep over the bluffs; you couldn't sell them and couldn't afford to keep them. You'd send bullocks or steers to the market and all you'd get back would be the bill for the transport. During one year of that Depression our total income was £200 and we had to pay all sorts out of that: keeping the place going, tax, unemployment tax, food for the five of us.

Of course there were lots worse off than we were. Some families around here couldn't afford to buy bread. They might have a cow and a few vegetables, maybe a few hens, but then the problem was to feed those hens; they've got to be fed well to lay well. Many families like that struggled fearfully in the Depression. The father would cut firewood and go round in a horse and cart trying to sell it. The mother would walk way down to the hospital, more than four miles away, and do a day's washing; she'd get a decent meal there in the middle of the day. We'd all pitch in and give them what we could—a sack of swedes or potatoes—

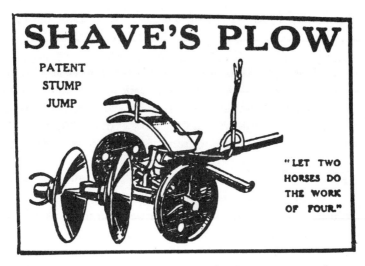

*Buying new equipment was an impossible dream for most farmers during the Depression.*

but most of us didn't have much to spare either. Their kids would run home from school at lunch-time and all they'd get was a plate of swedes or potatoes. They'd have to run home a mile for that. And then they didn't learn much at school, couldn't concentrate with no decent food in them. To this day you can see the starvation on those people. Their flesh never plumped out; it still looks hard, as if it never got the chance to expand. And those poor kids didn't even have a proper pencil or anything for school, just the butt end of a pencil they'd found somewhere.

There was sheer hunger round during that Depression, especially in towns where they couldn't grow their food. The Government announced that anyone who had a shepherd's hut or shearer's cookshop was to let people use them in return for work of some kind, and the Government would pay a nominal price for their food. One farmer near here took on nine or ten men. He picked them up from the station in his wagon. One chap fainted on the platform, through hunger. There were all sorts came— doctors, accountants, dentists—and the farmer said that for ten days he couldn't give them enough food; they just couldn't get enough. He got tired of rounding up sheep and killing them for food so he went out the back and shot a huge wild steer. That lasted them a week.

Yes, we wasted nothing in those days; hung on to anything that was reasonable. Mind you, a lot of the stuff we have today isn't really essential. In my day houses had no cupboards to speak of, just a wardrobe or two and a pantry if you were lucky. Then for many people the wardrobe was simply under a bed, or a nail on the back of the door.

Our bathroom was a tin dish on the verandah. It was always there at the back door—a tin dish, with a piece of soap and a towel hanging on a nail, for washing your hands. You'd fling the water into a ditch when you'd finished. Pollution you'd call it nowadays! Then we had an old oval galvanised bath; we used that for washing clothes as well as bathing ourselves. You'd put it in front of the fire to bath the kids, then take it into the bedroom for mum and dad. Those were the days.

I had everything I wanted. And the quiet life—the slow pace here suited me. My husband was the same—a very quiet man, from Donegal. They used to call this area Donegal Flat because there were so many Donegal people here. Donegal people, it's a habit our family have. We often married relatives, just like royalty do! At one stage there were 120 people in the area had our surname, including twenty-seven women, and they were all first cousins. Then they even started doubling up on the christian names so we'd have to give them nicknames. There'd be old David, long David, new chum David, Davey of the Rosses, Bucky David. They gave their farms Irish names—Carrickfin, Coleraine—and sang all the old songs. There's still a lot of Irish descendants here in Kaikoura and round about, but we don't stand out in any way. We're just New Zealanders.

*In 1982, Ellen Donegal recalled her life at Donegal Flat, just north of Kaikoura. At age 95 she still lived in the same country road where she had been born.*

## LABOUR VICTORY                                    *8 December 1935*

## Michael Joseph Savage

My head has not increased in size as the result of our great victory. My feet are still on Mother Earth, and my reason is sufficient to make me avoid erecting a pedestal from which to look down upon the people. Without them I'm nobody. With them I can see endless possibilities. I have only one ambition left: that is to empty the poorhouses and see the people enjoying the fruits of the earth. Whatever part I can play in bringing that about will be the only monument that I will seek. I look on that as the greatest privilege in life and the greatest monument in death. We are in deed making history.

*Michael Joseph Savage, newly elected Labour Prime Minister, writes to his niece, May Savage, in Australia. On his death, Savage got a bigger monument that he sought in the letter. The public raised £35,000 to build an imposing memorial at Fort Bastion, Orakei, Auckland.*

## THE *GULL* LANDS AT AUCKLAND AIRPORT
*16 October 1936*

### Jean Batten

Suddenly a dark blur loomed through the rain, and the *Gull* flashed past a small rocky island.

'Land!' I shouted with joy, recognizing the island as a rock just off the coast. Within a few seconds the *Gull* swept over New Plymouth, absolutely on its course . . . It was still raining heavily, and all but the base of Mount Egmont was shrouded in black cloud. My altitude was less than 500 feet as I flew over the town, and I could see people running into the streets waving a welcome.

Throttling back I glided low over the aerodrome in salute. It would be so easy to land now and be welcomed home by my countrymen, then sleep. 'No.' I thought quickly, remembering my intention before I left England—to make the first direct flight right through to Auckland, my home town.

An hour later I sighted Auckland, and, escorted by a number of machines from the Aero Club, flew over the aerodrome. The ground was black with people, and hundreds of cars were parked in long lines along the boundary.

I closed the throttle and glided down to a landing, and as the wheels of the *Gull* came to rest felt a great glow of pleasure and pride. This was really journey's end, and I had flown 14,000 miles to link England, the heart of the Empire, with the city of Auckland, New Zealand, in 11 days 45 minutes, the fastest time in history. With this flight I had realized the ultimate of my ambition, and I fervently hoped that my flight would prove a forerunner of a speedy air service from England.

*Jean Batten.*

As I taxied the *Gull* up to the large reception dais where civic author-ities and representatives of the Government and the Services waited to welcome me I was delighted to see my father, and recognized many friends among the crowd. The machine came to rest, and I switched off the engine of my faithfull *Gull* for the last time on that flight and entered up the time of my landing, which was 5.05 a.m. G.M.T.

*This fast flight from Britain to New Zealand excited world-wide interest. Jean Batten was heaped with honours for her pioneering flights to many parts of the world. Central Auckland's Jean Batten Place and Rotorua's Batten Square are named in her honour.*

## PARLIAMENTARY PROCEEDINGS    *3 December 1937*

### John A. Lee

Is it Balzac, the *Decameron*, or Parliament? A drunk in Parliament, H——. He had arranged a room of an absent MP and a round with a woman. Another Lothario beat him to the couch and locked the door.

The drunk MP parades around showing a handful of pessaries saying, 'Look, I came prepared. By God I am wild!' he has to send the lady away and out of frustration gets drunk. I've stopped his booze supply. He'll bite the leg of the table directly.

Second story. Two MPs in tower room of the old parliamentary building with two women. O——, D——. One pair uses the floor, the other the couch. Fellow on couch takes off his pants, gets busy. So busy he kicks the floor-recumbent on the head. He makes love three times, with the others in the room. D——, O—— talk about their performances, the news gets round. C—— boasts about the size of his penis. But the boys who lead a rough-and-tumble life come up fighting for a radical policy on every occasion. Another MP gets a woman in family way. Her husband bombards him with the cost of an abortion.

*John A. Lee.*

*John A. Lee, Under Secretary in charge of Building in a Labour Government, kept an occasional diary. Most of his diary records the day's political events, but occasionally Lee writes cryptically about other events. (See also page 108)*

## LIFE IS GOOD IF YOU'VE GOT THE GUTS
*Lowry Bay, Wellington, 10 December 1938*

### Archie Hull

Nothing matters a damn and I'm going flat out to make the next few days good for as long as I can. Photo to get taken today. It's got to be good. Tennis perhaps this afternoon.

Life is good if you've got the guts. Tennis at the bay.

When I came back her photo had fallen down the second time in a day.

She looks pretty fine in her tennis togs. White suits her so well and I like the way her hair is done best then. She is a rather bewitching creature. The way she sits, the way she looks and her eyes move. I suppose what attracts me so much is that she is so graceful in all her movements, her conversation seems to have an exquisite rhythm. She is so gay and sparkling and yet there is a lot of serenity that I almost worship. I envy her it so much. In her photograph it is there too, spirit of the Naiad which at once charms me in its idealisation of pure joy and simplicity and fills me with fear because I cannot understand it.

If love be always the same, I'll never get any nearer. When I feel so close I am sure she is mine completely, that Naiad-like look comes into her eyes. Just as I feel she's a complete woman in my arms she eludes my possession & I am so very empty. But I love her for all these things. It is good to store up memories of her for barren days and empty nights, when there will be only my books. The bird of time has such a little way to fly, and lo, the bird is on the wing.

But I feel it is wearing thin for her. It is hard not to cut loose before things get too beastly but I must not. This time I must fight to the finish with my back to the old wall. I've got to retreat in good order and not let it appear that it's a retreat. Christ how it hurts to hear some of the things she says but I know she does not suspect how I feel. It is all so comically funny belonging or playing at belonging to her world for a while and knowing I can never fit in properly and knowing why. I see things so clearly it is too laughable. That first day in the bush I knew our history so clearly and now it is happening. A fortnight today I will know. How I still hope in spite of things. It will be Air Force. There will be one good thing left in life to completely conquer my spirit. I feel that cold hand of fate creeping over me as I did at the end of the first capping in ChCh walking in the mist by the Avon seeing so clearly through the gloom, the wonder of the darkness and the crackling leaves and amazing stillness of the night. And up in my study afterwards looking out over the park and thinking, planning almost to dawn. And looking at Sam sleeping and falling asleep in the old chair. And last Xmas at Endeavour Inlet—the blue fish and writing to B. The Dawn with Currie, the wireless hill lights and flying. I see things so clearly on these nights. And this was the hour of knowing and she will be gone soon. It is so laughable knowing what is coming yet hoping that I don't and being unable to avert the crash. Why do I always see myself hovering over Lowry Bay bush but there is a Naiad in the shadows. Sleep will not come to me tonight. She has given my life colour and beauty for a while. Cannot hope for more. I'm glad I can be composed about it.

*Dec 11th.* Today is very windy and dull. So different from last night. The moon was just coming over the hill and shining through the edge of the bush where I left her. When I got home it was high up and the harbour from Hutt to Thorndon was all golden and smooth. I could not look at it for long. I wonder how she really feels. I think I understand but I wonder if I really do. She is so full of strange mysterious things. I wish I could fathom all her profound movements. They torture me sometimes.

*Archie Hull MSc was killed in July 1940 while completing his training as a pilot for the Royal New Zealand Air Force, aged 25.*

## CABINET HEARS BRITAIN DECLARE WAR ON GERMANY *Sunday 3 September 1939*

### Bernard Ashwin

On that night Cabinet was assembled and most of the Heads of Depts were there grouped around a radio listening for news from Daventry England. The war declaration was received first through the naval wireless about 10 pm. In the early hours of the morning there was much activity. Fraser (Deputy PM) handled the situation well and there was no confusion. Cabinet sat and Heads of Depts were called in one after the other in rapid succession and morning saw a large number of emergency powers previously prepared and first brought into force.

*Ashwin (later Sir Bernard Carl Ashwin) was Secretary to the Treasury and kept a personal diary of daily events. The New Zealand Government declared war on Germany the Tuesday following this entry (5 September). It is often claimed that we declared war against Germany before Great Britain, but Ashwin's diary gives the lie to the story.*

## HMNZS *Achilles* in Action off the River Plate

*13 December 1939*

# Jack S. Harker

Distant flashes through black smoke, and soon the whine and *whirrhhh* of 670-pound projectiles passing over head. We manoeuvre to throw her aim off and, as we watch, columns of discoloured water and smoke rear out of our curling bow-wave just right of the bridge. Red-hot metal fragments crash through armourplate, spattering the Control and tearing through the flesh of men, who cry out in mortal agony.

Neville Milburn feels a jolting stab. He slumps, hearing the loud crash and opening his mouth to exclaim, but making no sound as everything around him blurs. He drowses into an enveloping dizziness. His headphones clatter as he sinks unconscious. The other wireless operator, Frank Stennett, raises his hand to his shattered head, topples through the manhole, and lands on the rangetakers below. Milburn has now fallen through the same hatch and lies on top of him. The Sergeant of Marines, as Assistant Spotting Officer, half rises to his feet and falls forward with a moan.

Eddie Shirley is standing on a stool, his head and glasses above the Control roof for better vision as he checks our distance from *Ajax*. His legs buckle and he collapses with a cry of surprise on to the DCT deck where Guns sways, shaking his gory head over our Rate Officer. He, Nippy Watts, grabs the first-aid bag and digs out a roll of lint which Lieutenant Washbourn immediately starts to doctor himself with, leaving Nippy to administer to others in worse condition.

Sergeant Trimble has now recovered sufficiently to help as they made a pad to put on Milburn, whose neck-pulse still beats, but, as they pull him out straight, he chokes, coughs blood, and dies. Shirley lies inert, bleeding copiously from face and thigh wounds . . . the young OD coughed and slid to the deck with a steel fragment through his chest. He needed no more help, he never knew what hit him; but another man lay in immense pain with wounded thighs and a red-hot splinter embedded in his backside.

On the bridge, splinters slashed through Captain Perry's calves, bringing him down, hanging on to the binnacle. Martinson also went down with both legs smashed.

*[Harrassed and damaged, the* Graf Spee *retreated to the shelter of Montevideo harbour pursued by the smaller Allied ships.]*

We advance in single line ahead, *Ajax, Achilles, Cumberland,* battle-flags whipping taut.

Down in the mess there has been a sober supper, and when the alarm sounds we look at each other and go without a word. Our thoughts are all the same . . . 'Who will be here for breakfast?' All close up with a will, the tension has gone and we can blow off steam.

*Ajax*'s plane catapults. We sight smoke we know only too well. Everything is set and we are speeding towards her.

The Seafox signals '*Spee* appears to be preparing to scuttle'. Then '*Spee* is blowing herself up'.

We look at each other in amazement and, as the truth dawns, we laugh with relief. The Captain orders all hands on deck. We are cheering ourselves hoarse. Guncrews stand atop their turrets, each ship is black with ratings from director-top to fo'c's'le, all cheering laughing and singing as we steam towards her and sheer out; and as *Ajax* passes close she gives us three cheers with hats raised to full arm's length. An *Ajax* crewman hollers, 'Well done the Diggers!' Our loudspeakers come on and Captain Perry's voice asks us a sheer-ship with the New Zealand version, and as the switch cuts a great roar goes all over our ship.

When the echoes die, we hear the loud strains of 'Auld Lang Syne' rising and falling in harmony. As *Ajax* finishes, the whole length of *Achilles* bursts into 'Now is the Hour', harmonising with the Maoris aboard who are singing 'Po Ata Rou'. We're closing at a slower rate now, and there is a large black mushroom rising in the western sunset. *Ajax* has dropped astern to recover her aircraft; we slow down until she rejoins, still cheering, and again we respond.

*Spee* is becoming visible and the smoke is giving way to flames. We've been ordered into line ahead while drawing closer. It is now 2300 and the Germans have made a thorough job; she burns fiercely from end to end with dull explosions every few minutes. Each new detonation is greeted with renewed cheering.

*Off the mouth of the South American River Plate, the German pocket battleship* Graf Spee *defends itself against the New Zealand light cruiser* Achilles *and two British ships, the* Exeter *and the* Ajax. *Captain Langsdorf, commander of the* Graf Spee, *went down with his scuttled ship. Jack Harker was a radio operator on the* Achilles.

## FAREWELLING THE TROOPS

*1940*

## Ruth Park

In New Zealand you bore loss with bravery and reserve. You did not shout your grief and deprivation to the skies. A dignified self-effacement was regarded as a primary virtue; it was a tradition inherited from the settlers from the British Isles.

A memorable example of this quiet reserve occurred in 1940 when the First Echelon of the 2nd NZEF marched down Queen Street, Auckland, before their embarkation for Egypt. There were crowds along both sides of that long important street, almost silent crowds. I recall a patter of clapping, a stifled murmur as someone recognised a friend under the stiff, awkward khaki. The heavy rhythm of marching feet, creak of leather, a faint grunt of concerned breathing, that was all. A young girl, subject to sudden and imprudent indignations, I began to cheer. A woman next to me said sharply, 'Behave yourself!'

I would have retorted angrily had I not seen tears in her eyes.

She whispered, 'Don't you know what's going to happen to many of them? There's nothing to cheer about.'

## HUNGARIAN REFUGEE'S FIRST JOB IN NEW ZEALAND

*1940*

## George Haydn

My new boss was extremely kind. I still think of this man with great warmth and affection. He took me to a furniture factory and arranged for me to start work there. He even bought for me the tools I needed. But unfortunately, I had no training in operating the machines to use on that job. Yet my employers were marvellous. Although I was absolutely useless and destroyed a number of bits of equipment, they put up with me for about a week. However, after that time my boss said, 'I'm sorry, you just have to go.' He was very, very apologetic. I then tried other jobs. My cousin and I would both start at eight in the morning and by about twelve we were both out—fired. We would usually end up in the public library and sometimes at the pictures. Once, I got a job as an upholsterer. I think I lasted all of a day. Goodness knows how many jobs I had as a carpenter. Building the aerodrome at Whenuapai, on my first day I trod on a rusty nail, which was very lucky because for one week I could live on 'compo'. Another time I was working in a joinery factory and I chopped a little bit off my finger. Once again, I had a week living on compo. It just went on and on. At one stage, I was working on a building at Waiouru. I had to work on the roof. I was terrified of falling. Someone had to come up and help me down. On yet another occasion, my cousin and I both got jobs on the site of a military camp at Papakura. We began work on different parts of the site. At half past eleven the foreman came to tell me I was finished and I went to the pay office to collect my pay for the half day. And who was behind me but cousin Andrew who had also been fired! It was very, very easy to get jobs. There were many jobs available for experienced people. But it was also very difficult to keep the jobs.

*As a 20-year-old, George Haydn (originally Hajdn Gyorgy) fled Budapest and came to Auckland with his cousin Andrew in 1939. He had previously been a student of economics at a Hungarian university. After his unpromising start in the building trade Haydn started a successful building company (Haydn and Pollett Construction Coy) and rose to be a leader in the field, representing the building industry on a number of committees, including the Metric Advisory Board.*

## RETREAT FROM GREECE AND CRETE                 *1941*

## John Watson

He [the German army] just completely routed us. We just did not have the equipment to defend ourselves with. It was terrible. We were running away all the time. We were on the run and that's awful. From the very first day we were defeated. The German had complete control of the air, and used his Stuka bombers, which were terrifying things. On their wings they had screamers which made the most awful sound you ever heard in your life.

It was a terrifying noise. And they came down from a great height and just came straight down, and of course the air rushing through those

*German parachutists blot out the sky.*

screamers on their wings made this very eerie, ghostly noise. And they bombed and strafed us with machine-guns and that. We got driven back twenty miles or something like that and we'd stop and try and fight again with what little we had. But it was hopeless, you know. We were completely ill-equipped. Hopelessly ill-equipped. We should never have been there.

Oh, carnage of human beings. And of course the civilian population as well. It was terrible . . . little children and all were being massacred. Mostly from the air. The German was coming behind us. He was quite a long way back. We didn't have much hand-to-hand fighting of any sort in Greece . . . They didn't need to waste their troops and risk them being killed because they had us beaten in the air. Completely and utterly beaten.

It wasn't very nice. I was fairly hard and having worked on farms and that sort of thing I suppose I've seen death with animals a lot. And I'd killed a lot of animals myself and bobby calves. But I knew nothing of death with human beings. But you get hardened in war and the point is that you develop an attitude of not caring too much, unless it's a friend of yours, by the fact that it could be you next. So it's dog eat dog and man for man in many ways . . . As warfare develops you become a creature it's hard to describe. We had fairly heavy losses in Greece, in my battalion. We did lose a lot.

*[In Greece 950 New Zealanders were killed and 4000 taken prisoners. John Watson escaped to Crete, to be harassed by German planes.]*

You could just about touch them. They came down vertical and just dropped their bombs and up again. They came down very low, a thousand feet, you know.

We fought rearguard actions all the way across the island. A certain number of people would be detailed to stop behind and hold the German up while the rest of the force got further ahead. We spread out but we were not a fighting force. We were far from it. In other words he had nothing to beat. There were a lot of casualties.

*[After three days Watson and other survivors reached the coast on the opposite side of the island, near Skafia.]*

Fortunately it was the place where they were taking troops off at night. There were thousands there. There were caves in the cliffs and we used to hide in the caves, didn't want the Germans to know where we were. I was there for three nights before I got off. The waiting was shocking. Absolutely shocking. It was the last night and I think the last ship, and scrambling down the cliffs to get into the barges, I had false teeth . . . and I coughed and spat and I unfortunately coughed my teeth out going down the cliff. I fell, you see. So I said, 'Gawd, I've lost my teeth.' A mate said, 'Where?' I said, 'I don't know and I don't care.' I left them there and I got back to Egypt and I had to get new teeth. But I wasn't worried about my teeth. All I wanted to do was get off the place. Never ever thought I would. You know a lot of people didn't get off. They just had to leave them. Of course the Jerry got them the next day.

*John Watson, a 20-year-old machine-gunner in the New Zealand Expeditionary Force, was posted to the northern Greek frontier to help stem the advance of the German army. They escaped from Greece to Crete, but German parachutists drove them off the island with heavy casualties.*

## 'IT IS MY INTENTION TO COME OUT ON THURSDAY' *Koiterangi, Westland, 6 October 1941*

## Harold Fuller Cooke

Mr Stanley Graham.

Dear Sir,
re: OVERDRAFT
We wrote to you on 25th ultimo but unfortunately you have not

acknowledged its receipt or responded to any of its requests. Your account after charging up interest and Bank fee for half year ended 30th September, now stands *Debit* £183 6s. 3d. The bank is disappointed and concerned that we did not receive any share of your recent dairy bonus cheque. Under the circumstances and realising the fact that you have not paid in any cheques since December 1940, the Bank now considers that you should give security for the debt, by executing a second mortgage over the land for say £200. We would like to point out that the giving of this mortgage would in no way prejudice the anticipated sale of the property. It in most cases is helpful in that the mortgage is taken over by the proposed purchaser, which means he has to find less ready cash.

I would like to stress the fact that the Bank considers that they have been most tolerant, and now it is up to you to respond to their request. They cannot be expected to remain passive any longer.

If you are not prepared to effect the security asked for then please state so by return mail arriving Wednesday. If I do not receive a reply on Wednesday it is my intention to come out on Thursday (9th instant) arriving say about 2 p.m. with the necessary forms for your signature. Hoping that you see the reasonableness of our request and be willing to give the security asked for.

Yours Faithfully

H.F. Cooke

*Cooke managed the Bank of New South Wales in Hokitika and Stanley Graham farmed a few miles inland. After a succession of reversals, the 41-year-old Graham became very bad-tempered and developed irrational grudges against several people whom he thought were poisoning his cattle. He drew a rifle on several neighbours and passers-by. Cooke's letter 'was enough to complete Graham's journey into insanity'. Two days after receiving this letter, Graham shot four policemen and a civilian who had come to enquire after him. The following night he shot three home-guardsmen then fled into the bush. A huge manhunt was organised but Graham evaded police, army troops and home-guardsmen until 20 October when he was gunned down.*

## BOMBARDMENT AT EL ALAMEIN     *Egypt, 30 October 1942*

## Lieutenant Colonel H. Murray Reid

I looked at my watch repeatedly; time passes so slowly that I thought it had stopped. At 9.35 p.m. I looked at it for the last time, being then kept in conversation with the Brigade intelligence officer until the guns opened fire.

Bang! Bang! Bang! Merging almost immediately into a continual roar. It was 2140 hours, and the Battle of Alamein had started!

As I had waited so long for the guns and then forgotten them altogether for a few minutes, the reports gave me an awful fright, and I visibly jumped, much to the intelligence officer's amusement. I had been wondering what the barrage would sound like. Now I certainly knew. It was terrific. The whole horizon to the rear was a blaze of light, and it was nearly impossible to pick out any individual gun flash . . . the noise was unbelievable, and made ordinary speech impossible. It seemed to get right inside one's head, and to jar the very ground on which we stood. We wondered what it was like where all that steel and high explosive was bursting. It must have been plain Hell let loose.

As the creeping barrage commenced in earnest the first wave of attacking infantry went over. It was a great sight to see them going ahead with so much confidence and determination. They were well spread out, and with fixed bayonets glistening in the light of the guns must have created a panic among any of the enemy left to dispute their passage.

The officers in charge of our two sections went forward behind the first wave to locate and mark the enemy minefield. They carried small blue lights to mark the field and to serve as a guide to the following sappers.

Half an hour after the wave left the Maoris went over as the 'mopping up' battalion, their role being to deal with any opposition missed in the first wave.

*Lieutenant Colonel Reid commanded New Zealand's mine-clearing engineers. The bombardment marked a big turning point in the Second World War when, for the first time, German and Italian armies were driven back in North Africa. During the Alamein battle 163 New Zealand troops were killed, 947 wounded and 167 went missing.*

## MUTINY AT POW CAMP    *Featherston, 25 February 1943*

## Second Lieutenant Keith Robertson

I have been stationed at the POW Camp, Featherston, since November 11 1942. Since then I have moved among the prisoners freely and generally. I have been able satisfactorily to understand the speech of the Japanese there, and they have understood mine. Generally speaking the men in No. 1 compound have been very co-operative with camp authority. They have shown quite a readiness to do anything asked of them. The No. 2 compound men have been just the opposite. I attribute this obstructiveness to the fact that they are comprised mostly of naval personnel and they have given me the impression that they do not think it is quite the thing for them to be engaged in manual labour. Judging from experiences we have had recounted to us, the labour is left to the working type of Japanese and the soldiering is left to the naval and military personnel. There has been considerable feeling evident between the working section and the military prisoners. A spirit of animosity has been to some extent evident between the men of No. 1 and No. 2 compound. The fighting man considers, in my experience, that he should be treated on a different basis from the worker.

There are 46 NCOs in No. 2 compound out of a total of somewhere about 280. As far as I am aware the NCOs have not been asked to carry out manual labour. They are very jealous of their rank and their ranks are respected among themselves. They know that they are liable to assist the camp authorities in a supervisory capacity only. As far as I am aware the camp authorities have not asked them to do more than that. As far as I know there has been a general willingness on the part of the NCOs to assist the camp authorities. They seem to have experienced difficulties in producing working parties at odd times. From the point of view of acceding to personal requests they have not been very co-operative. The men of No. 2 compound enforce discipline on themselves. The naval branch of the armed service predominates in that compound. The other arms of the service are in the minority and the discipline is definitely naval; discipline, which is among themselves rigidly carried out. So that naval men in the compound give the orders and they see that they are carried out.

I saw the possibility of a clash with the camp authority taking place some day because of their strict adherence to their naval discipline. Never have I gone into No. 2 compound without there has been a considerable amount of parleying as to whether they have the men and so forth. I have heard of the existence of a certain amount of animus between the army personnel and the navy personnel. The Number One of the No. 2 compound, because of this feeling, said that in his estimation the only way to solve the problem of this antagonism was to have the various branches of the services in separate compounds.

On Thursday February 25th I went across to No. 2 compound about 1000 hrs and I found certain escorts posted outside the gate. A few minutes after my arrival Nishimura, the Japanese officer, was brought out by the unarmed guard. I then walked back towards the end of the corner of the compound and while I was making my way I heard the volley of fire. From where I stood I could see the Japanese all laying on the ground, and a few seconds later saw them putting up their hands.

Previously that morning I had been engaged on duties elsewhere in the camp and had not entered No. 2 compound at any stage until I did so immediately following the shooting. After I saw the bodies of the Japanese lying on the ground I immediately entered the compound with the idea in mind of lending assistance. This I did. One particular man called out to me. He was Adachi, the Japanese officer. He was lying on the ground some eight feet away from a hut and, calling me over to him, told me he accepted all the responsibility for the terrible happenings and, grasping my hand in his, pleaded with me to kill him.

As far as I remember them, the actual words spoken by Adachi were, 'Robaatoson San, Kore wa watakushi no sekinin desu, koroshite kudasai,' which being interpreted means, 'Mr Robertson, this is my responsibility. Please kill me.'

I have seen Adachi since that time. I visited him again in Anzac Hospital the following morning and he reiterated his sense of responsibility in the recent unfortunate happenings, and made a statement to the effect that if he did not die it would be very embarrassing for him to return to the compound. Then he asked after the health of Nishimura and sent his kind regards to the Colonel.

At Greytown Hospital the same day as the incident a young man, Iwasa, who was wounded in the shooting called me over to the bed and gripping my wrist firmly and with tears in his eyes said, 'Today it is very regrettable. I apologise.'

After the shooting, after leaving Adachi I was immediately called by two more Japanese lying together. From these I forcibly removed two knives while they pleaded with me to kill them. The men wrestled with me with what little strength they had left, in an effort to retain them. From one of the wounded men while he was still lying on the ground I took the improvised weapon produced and marked 'M' among the exhibits. (The exhibit is a heavily bolted stick.) I also picked up from between the huts a length of half-inch galvanised iron piping.

I was present when an order was given by Mr Malcolm that the kitbags of 32 prisoners transferred from No. 3 compound to the small compound were searched. During the search some half dozen home made knives were found, which they should not have had in their possession . . . I am aware that the 32 prisoners were transferred to the small compound because they had expressed a willingness to die in the recognised Japanese way. In fact one of them asked me when they were going to be shot. When I replied that I did not know, he said, 'Give us the tools and we will do the job ourselves.'

*During this uprising, some 240 rebellious Japanese prisoners rushed their guards en masse. The guards shot 48 prisoners dead and one New Zealand guard was killed by a ricochet. Another 11 guards were injured by stones thrown by the prisoners. Lieutenant Robertson had spent three years as a missionary in Japan and acted as an Intelligence Officer.*

## BATTLE FOR THE MARETH LINE                  *Tunisia, 1943*

## General Freyberg

At three o'clock on 26 March, as I drove up the valley in my tank, all was quiet except for occasional shellfire. There was no unusual movement or sign of coming attack. Exactly half an hour later, the first squadrons of the RAF roared overhead and relays of Spitfires, Kitty-bombers, and tank-busters swept over the enemy positions giving the greatest measure of air support ever seen by our army. At four o'clock 200 field and medium guns opened their bombardment on a front of 5000 yards. In an instant the attack developed and 150 tanks and three battalions of infantry appeared as if from nowhere, advancing in the

■ 180

*General Freyberg.*

natural smokescreen provided by the dust storm. It was the most awe-inspiring spectacle of modern warfare. The roar of bombers and fighters ahead of our advance merged with our barrage of bursting shells. Following close behind this intense barrage as it advanced came waves of Sherman tanks, carriers and infantry, sappers on foot, preceded by three squadrons of Crusader tanks. Behind New Zealand Corps, coming down the forward slopes, just in the rear of our front line, were 150 tanks of the 1st Armoured Division, followed by their Motor Brigade in lorries, advancing in nine columns.

Hitherto all our big attacks had been by moonlight, and although the enemy was expecting us to attack we again achieved surprise by attacking in daylight.

Without check our armour swept through to the final objective, a depth of 6000 yards. Enemy tanks were destroyed or driven back, Anti-tank guns and artillery were overrun or recaptured. Meanwhile our infantry battalions, moving behind the armour, attacked the remaining enemy strong points, and fierce hand-to-hand fighting took place to clear the objectives and secure the high ground on both flanks. By dusk all enemy resistance had been overcome, except for the high ground at Point 209 and a strongpoint outside the left flank where the German garrisons held out. During the night the 24th (Auckland) Battalion attacked and cleared the left flank, taking a large number of prisoners.

By moonlight on the night of the 26th, Phase 3 was completed when the 1st Armoured Division was launched from our bridgehead. Next morning they had reached the outskirts of El Hamma.

All day of the 27th mopping up the enemy garrison continued. At Point 209 a bitter fight raged between the Maori Battalion and the Second Battalion of the 433rd Panzer Grenadier regiment, which finally ended by remnants of the German garrison, complete with commanding officer, surrendering.

The capture of the defile was decisive defeat for the enemy and a triumph for our co-ordinated attack by tanks and infantry with powerful air and artillery support. It is true to say that all three German divisions as well as the Italian divisions opposed to us were severely mauled. A great many enemy killed or wounded were left on the battlefield and between 5000 and 6000 prisoners were taken, many being Germans from the Afrika Korps. Over forty tanks and a great many guns, MT, and all kinds of equipment were destroyed or captured. But the most important result of the battle was that the Mareth Line became untenable, and heavy casualties, which further frontal assaults would have involved, were avoided.

As soon as all resistance had ceased in the defile, New Zealand Corps, led by the King's Dragoon Guards, New Zealand Divisional cavalry, and 8th Army brigade, fanned out north-east and east towards the coast road. Many prisoners were taken, including two battalions of Italian infantry with all their equipment. The 8th Armoured Brigade dispersed the last rearguard of the 154th Panzer Division, knocking out four more tanks and three 88-millimetre guns, and Gabes and El Hamma fell into our hands.

The battle was the hardest since Alamein and we have suffered inevitable casualties. I would like you to know that as usual in these wide desert moves our fully equipped surgical teams were with us, together with every possible facility for looking after our wounded, who were then flown out by air ambulance to our Base hospitals in Tripoli and Egypt.

Once again the officers and men of your Division displayed the fighting qualities that are now expected of them. Our staff and Divisional organisation and all our services worked smoothly and carried out most efficiently the additional responsibilities of a Corps. The exploits of units and individuals cannot be described in so short a report as this, but many of these will become known when immediate awards for gallantry on the battlefield are published.

*A despatch from Freyberg to the Prime Minister of New Zealand, Peter Fraser.*

## SHOT DOWN IN THE PACIFIC          *23 September 1943*

### Warrant Officer George Luoni

The Zeke which attacked me, fired a fair burst as he came up, hitting the oil tank and cowling in several places, with the result that oil spurted into the cockpit and into the canopy.

Losing height slowly, I broke away and headed for Treasury Islands having been told by the squadron intelligence officer, in briefing before the mission, that the natives there were very friendly.

The oil pressure went off the clock and the temperature dropped away very rapidly to 30 degrees, by this time the engine was running roughly and smoke started to belly into the cockpit so I rolled the plane over onto its back and bailed out at 4000 ft when about 2 miles north of Mono Island.

Geoff Highet, in a RNZAF P-40 had followed me all the way down, weaving as he went. After the attack, the Zeros broke off and did not follow.

I bailed out with my hand on the ripcord and pulled it fairly soon. The P-40 circled around following me until I hit the water. I released my parachute just before landing on the sea. I stayed in the water supported by my mae west until dusk. The water was warm. I never thought of sharks and saw none.

At dusk, I stripped off everything except my singlet and underpants, took my arms out of my mae west and tied it tightly around my chest. I then swam ashore taking regular spells and heading for the mouth of the Soanatala River. When I finally made the shore it was dark, so I folded up on the beach and went to sleep feeling exhausted.

I woke at sun-up, finding myself on a sandy strip of beach at the river mouth and for breakfast ate a coconut that was lying on the beach. Then I decided to head west as I could see what appeared to be dense jungle off the coast in that direction.

I climbed the ridge along the shoreline and headed west through broken jungle, and taking frequent spells. My aim was to contact the natives as the intelligence officer had warned us that there were Japanese on the south coast of the island and I had an idea I might contact natives on the North coast.

I had no food that day but drank plenty of fresh water from the streams running off hills. I sighted nobody that day and at night slept in the bush on the hillside, making a bed from what looked like huge lily-leaves, using them also as a covering. The next day I kept going in a westerly direction, moving around the foot of the hills and a swamp that ran down towards the North coast. I had no food since the previous day and saw none of the plants or trees with edible fruits that are described in the pilot's kit or castaway baedeker.

At about 1400 hrs I saw three Japs, approximately half a mile away, they appeared to be on patrol, were dressed in khaki with what looked like a white bandolier and were carrying rifles. I don't think they saw me and I didn't wait to find out, taking to the hills through the jungle. It was there I found odd coconut trees, growing where the jungle was less dense, so I had a feed of coconut meat, washed down with coconut milk.

I slept well that night and remained in the central part of the Island, lost among the hills for some time. I was able to find plenty of coconuts to eat but they lacked nourishment and I was steadily getting weaker. Apart from this weakness, I was perfectly fit and did not suffer from dysentery, the coconuts I ate were matured. My constant aim was to reach the coast and I wandered long distances each day. I made the coast, somewhere near Soanatalu, my original starting point.

I then made my way along the coast in an easterly direction. All this time I had not seen a native, it was not until I reached a position near Lua Point, on the North east coast that I met natives. This was on the Saturday night, two days before the New Zealanders landed on Mono Island . . .

I was found wandering about a small village by a party of eight natives, four men and four women. The village consisted of two small huts. This was 32 days after I had bailed out of my aircraft, I was very

*Kittyhawk plane.*

weak and could hardly walk. The natives carried me to their village and gave me a large boiled egg and cooked root food, like potato but very stringy and indigestible. They were perfectly friendly and spoke broken English, having been taught by Australian Methodist missionaries, who had a church on the south coast of the island.

The next day they hid me in the jungle from the Japanese, whom they described as 'demon men'. They built a lean-to shelter of stakes and branches and brought me hot water and lemons. The juice they squeezed into the water and this I drank.

I returned to the village that night and slept there as before. The next day I was already feeling better. That night I was strapped across an outrigger canoe by two natives and taken to a place I think is Taoloko Point, on the eastern tip of the island. With the natives I spent the night in a cave.

A Yank destroyer force bombarded Jap positions on the southern coast the following morning, 27th October, and it sounded good. Afterwards, accompanied by four natives, I headed overland back towards the village from which I had been brought, and at about 1300 hrs I arrived among New Zealand troops. I was very weak and been carried most of the way by the natives.

*While flying fighter cover for American bombers attacking 'Kahili Air Strip' on Bougainville, George Luoni's kittyhawk plane was attacked by Zero ('Zeke') fighters. After his island adventure he served one more tour of duty.*

## 'MOVE OR NOD YOUR HEAD IF YOU CAN HEAR US'

*Italy, 3 January 1944*

### Nursing Sister Gay Trevithick

We had packed up the hospital and moved to Italy on January 3, 1944. It was here, at Bari, I experienced the most memorable event in the war, soon after we arrived and before much of our medical equipment had been unloaded from the supply ship. I first heard loud explosions coming from the dock area, just walking distance from 3GH hospital, set up in buildings in a partly finished sports stadium, which the Italians called the 'Polytechnic'.

The ack-ack had been going at full tilt for over an hour and there were lots of explosions outside. We were on the seat watching the brightly lit-up display—very beautiful, I thought at the time (though I now regret feeling this)—when we were thrown onto the floor and all the windows came in. I believe an ammunition ship and a petrol tanker had received direct hits.

Another blinding flash followed an hour later. There were many explosions at Bari over the night, and the whole sky was lit up by both explosions and Very lights. The harbour was crammed full of ships,

*Gay Trevithick.*

literally sitting targets for the Luftwaffe's bombers. The first ship seemed to be hit by a German bomber, with a lucky shot down the funnel.

Casualties came in quickly. Every single person was covered in oil and many could hardly move at all. They were, in fact, of all nationalities—New Zealanders, Brits, Americans, Indians—although it was impossible to tell who they were, even to discern skin colour at first. Some could move, some couldn't and were either dead or paralysed. We would just say, 'Move a finger or nod your head if you can hear us.' Some did. Many didn't.

We had a real supply problem here, as one of the ships which was blown up was carrying most of our supplies, including blankets. To make it all worse, we had just received a whole trainload of casualties from Cassino, and had been quite busy with them. After warming the Bari boys up, the next step was to get fluid into them, but this had to be done with drips, as most of them had faces and mouths so swollen it was difficult for them to drink. There were hundreds of men in bunks in the corridors, with life jackets and oily clothes strewn all over the place. There were many hundreds who it was too late to treat, and who died.

Without our own supplies of blankets, etc, we kept the patients warm by putting clothes on top of them. Many died soon after they were brought in. People were still dying up until a week or so after the bombing.

We stayed on duty all night. The oil itself was difficult to get off—soap and water were useless and we had to use kerosene instead.

Eventually the whole building became full of casualties to the stage where it was difficult to move without bumping into a stretcher. 'We're full, try the Indians,' I heard Colonel Gower telling ambulance drivers from the gate. I felt glad it was not me with the job of refusing entry to dying men.

We heard that the heat was so intense that it was not possible for boats to go out into the harbour to rescue drowning men.

That so many died so quickly was a mystery to our doctors. It wasn't until well after the war that we discovered that it was mustard gas— apparently kept in storage on a freighter—which was responsible for these deaths. The minority who survived being poisoned seemed to be those who had managed to keep their heads out of the oily mix of liquid poison and oil—people said that this layer was about 12 inches thick on top of the water. As many men had been blown off ships, or had to jump, it must have been difficult to avoid the oily poison.

*Gay Trevithick, a sister with the New Zealand Nursing Corps, recalls the scenes which greeted her in the port of Bari, southern Italy. She thought the motherly presence of women nurses had a powerful, therapeutic effect on wounded men.*

## GENERAL KIPPENBERGER LOSES HIS FEET AT CASSINO

*Italy, 2 March 1944*

## Frank Massey

With 1400 hrs in mind I made my way back to Kipp and remarked that there were a number of wooden boxes dug up and left on the rocks. Kipp verified that the hill had been heavily mined and that casualties had occurred—the mines were covered over between the rocks—my intuition made me tread from rock to rock—only about two steps and I was sailing through the air—the explosion was enormous—blown several yards down hill. I knew it was either a direct hit on 'the man with the red band on his hat' or that he had trodden on a mine!! He was lying awkwardly and knew he had trodden on a mine and asked if his feet were still intact—my left side was a mess. This extraordinary man asked me to open my left eye and when he saw that it was in place I rolled my jacket for a pillow under his head and he said to make sure morphia was brought up with the stretcher bearers—he also told me not to go directly down the hill but to go along the ridge till I found a taped lane down to the artillery lines which were clear of mines . . . One booted foot was not there and the other a mess but intact, and I noticed one of his fingers seemed to be around the wrong way. He talked to me about his feet which I assured him were there—there was blood but the blast must have sealed the wounds so I waited with Kipp for help to come.

*Frank Massey (grandson of Prime Minister Massey) was General Kippenberger's aide-de-camp. Kippenberger had been given the all but impossible task of storming Mount Cassino, Germany's 'strongest fortress in Europe, with a single corps of New Zealand troops, unsupported by diversionary operations'. Following Kippenberger's wounding, a cloud of depression settled on the New Zealand Division.*

## KIWI KEITH'S HIGH-FLYING KITES

*about 1947*

Roger Holyoake

*Keith Holyoake.*

When we were schoolboys together on the farm at Pahiatua, my father built kites for us. Big strong well-made kites which we flew round the farm. He also found us large rolls of bindertwine, miles long, to fly these things. They would go hundreds of yards into the air. We used to put them up in the morning, tether the things to a fence post and they would still be way up there almost out of sight when we came home from school. The kites would sometimes stay up there for days. Then one day the local cop came round and not very respectfully suggested that we take them down as they were a hazard to power lines and low-flying planes.

*Roger was Prime Minister Keith J. Holyoake's oldest son.*

## HOTEL SERVICE

*14 July 1947*

Alistair McIntosh

My dear Berendsen,
You say in your note that you don't know why we are not pressing the tourist side in North America. It would be absolutely

impractical. You cannot get into a hotel in New Zealand and, if you do, you cannot get any service, because there are practically no servants, and those there are, won't serve. If you are privileged to enter the dining room you do so for a fleeting moment only at the earliest possible hour and you can't be served at the latest, after 7 o'clock at night. Any tourist coming to New Zealand at the present time, or for the next two years, is not likely to return, or, probably he would spend the rest of his life telling his countrymen and any others who would listen what an appalling place New Zealand is.

I should add that we are very short of electricity. The 'Limited' practically never runs because we have not any coal—the miners won't produce it and even in the remote contingency of them doing so the West Coast bars (harbour) have for some extraordinary reason become too shallow to permit the passage of ships.

You can't eat in hotels without coupons and, as far as I can see, even if you have got them—and the Tourist people never think of giving them to tourists for weeks after they arrive—then the hotels have mostly got ill-cooked scrag ends of meat with which to honour them.

Alistair McIntosh

*Alistair McIntosh headed our Department of Foreign Affairs from Wellington. Carl Berendsen was our man in Washington.*

## BALLANTYNE'S FIRE

*Christchurch, 18 November 1947*

## Margueretta Nicholls

*Miss Nicholls.* I was sitting down at my machine and the girls near the window jumped up and said, 'Ballantynes is on fire!' I said, 'Don't be silly.' Because I was used to the girls jumping up and screaming out at anything that went past the door. Then they jumped up again and put their bags under their arms and said, 'Ballantynes is on fire: we are going home.' I looked through the window and there were quite a number of people at the corner, and then smoke was coming straight up

Colombo Street. I said, 'I don't think it's Ballantynes. The people don't seem to be looking at our building.'

The girls all put their coats on. I did not think it was serious. I did not think the girls did either. I was trying to talk them out of it. I did not think there was anything definitely wrong, even then. We were dazed when Mr Hamel who is in charge of the room, and who had not been into the room for some considerable time, came in. I said to him, 'Is there something wrong? Is Ballantynes on fire?' He said, 'No. Sit the girls down.' I asked the girls to sit down and they sat down and jumped up again and said, 'The people are waving and calling to us.'

*Mr Watson.* When he told them to sit down, he meant at their work?

*Miss Nicholls.* Yes. He asked me to sit them down. They sat down and immediately jumped up again and said, 'The people are waving and singing out for us to go.' Then the girls all began to cough and said they were choking. I asked the girls to close the windows because the smoke was coming in from the street, and asked them not to panic. 'If there is anything wrong we will all be killed trying to get out the way you are carrying on.' There were three girls in the habit of leaving at four—married women on part time—and they picked up their bags and said, 'We go at four. It is good enough for us. We're off.'

*Mr Watson.* Did Mr Hamel come on the scene again?

*Miss Nicholls.* He was there, and he said he would go and see what was wrong. He went away and by that time all the girls were near the door, with the door open. He came in and said there had been a bit of a fire, but said, 'Tell them not to panic. I know you will not. Everything is all right. It is under control.' And then a girl came down from the ladies' toilet room—a girl from the tailoring room. The stairs came down and faced our door, and we were all at the door, Mr Hamel included, and she said, 'The toilet room is absolutely suffocating, we could not see.' I went to the fire escape and looked down, and heard a man sing out, 'Help me with this woman.' So I said, 'Get out.' But Mr Hamel was very reluctant to let us go. However, I said I thought we had better go. The girls got their hats and coats from outside the door and went. Then Mr Hamel went away again—before the girls went—before the girls went out—and said, 'I will see.' I do not know where he could have gone, the building was on fire outside the door. He came back and put his head to the door and said, 'For God's sake run for your lives.'

*Mr Watson.* At the time he said that who was left in the room with you?

*Miss Nicholls.* The other girls and Mr Duthie—before the three that went; they were not at the door.

*Mr Watson.* Did he wait to see what you did?

*Miss Nicholls.* He did not come into the door where we were standing near the door. He ran through the tailoring room and that was the last I saw of him till I got into the street.

*Mr Watson.* They stayed and put their coats on. What did you do?

*Miss Nicholls.* The coats were just outside the door. They put them on and off they went. I walked back to the machine where I was working. The lights had failed by then. I thought I would finish pressing some collars I had already made. I took up the iron and the presser.

*Mr Watson.* He stayed with you?

*Miss Nicholls.* Yes. I said to him, 'I don't know what all this excitement is about.' I pressed the collars and took them back to the box.

*Mr Watson.* All this after the girls had left?

*Miss Nicholls.* Yes. By that time the room had a lot of smoke, but I did not take any notice of that. I thought it came from the windows while they were open. The presser said to me, 'Every one has gone; we will go.' I took my coat off the peg and hung the coathanger on the peg, and then thought I would open the door and see before I put my coat on. When I opened the door the heat threw me back. The smoke was about two feet from me, billowing round, grey and black in colour. The heat was terrific, but I saw no flame. I got a fright. I do not know whether I screamed or not, but threw the door closed and ran back into my own room. I did not see anyone. I went into the room. I had some cat's meat on the machine for the cat. I picked up this meat and saw my belongings and thought I would get those in the morning. I grabbed the cat's meat and ran out the door, and some one grabbed my shoulder and said, 'This way.' We managed to get through into the street. I was very upset, and nearly fainted. I know some one was holding me up . . . And when I got into the street I recognised him as the presser . . . Charles Duthie.

*Margueretta Nicholls was forewomen of the shirt department on the second floor of the building.*

## Nancy Nash

*Mr Watson.* Half the girls were through the door and half were not when the lights failed. What happened there then?

*Mrs Nash.* After that nobody seemed to know what to do or where to go.

*Mr Watson.* Did any one give any instructions?

*Mrs Nash.* Not that I heard.

*Mr Watson.* What did you personally do?

*Mrs Nash.* I stayed where I was and saw some one trying to jump out the accountancy window. Someone from the credit called out: 'Do not jump yet; there will be someone here.'

*Mr Watson.* Do you know whom you saw trying to jump?

*Mrs Nash.* Miss Blair.

*Mr Watson.* What did she do?

*Mrs Nash.* She came back.

*Mr Watson.* What did you do?

*Mrs Nash.* It was getting hotter and hotter. Miss Kennedy sang out my name and I answered. We kept hold of each other and said we would have to get out. We mentioned the fire escape again and went to go there but were stopped [by the smoke].

*Mr Watson.* Did you open the door?

*Mrs Nash.* No. We did not get as far as that. We said we would go to the fire escape before we opened the door to the credit office.

*Mr Watson.* When you did open the door to the credit room, what did you find?

*Mrs Nash.* All the leadlights above the safe and the roof were one mass of flame and it was falling. You could see the timber above the leadlights falling on to the leadlights and coming through.

*Mr Watson.* Did you then close the door?

*Mrs Nash.* No we were in the credit office. We turned and made for the window of the credit room. We opened the window and sang out for help. As we opened the window there was one mass of flame from the furnishing department underneath the other side of the building. From the appearance of the people on the road it seemed some were telling us to jump and some not to jump. I saw a ladder on my left being put up on the verandah and some one was on it and it caught fire in the middle of the ladder and they had to get it down. We looked at the crowd and the smoke went white. We jumped in between the billows of smoke. Miss Kennedy jumped first.

*Mr Watson.* You followed?

*Mrs Nash.* Yes.

*Mr Watson.* You landed on the verandah and do you remember what happened?

*Mrs Nash.* Yes I remember falling and some one grabbing me by the shoulder and they tipped me into a net or tarpaulin held from the street.

*Mr Watson.* You were unfortunately injured and taken to hospital.

*Mrs Nash.* Yes.

*Mrs Nash was lucky—41 staff and customers died in this fire, the worst in New Zealand's history. The Commission found that shop fire precautions were almost non-existent, and the work of the Christchurch fire brigade seriously defective in organisation, leadership and command. As a result, new national fire regulations were gazetted and the fire brigade restructured.*

## WATERFRONT DISPUTE                              *Christchurch, 1951*

## Colin Clark

The five months of the waterfront dispute were a bitter but very hectic time for me. I and a handful of other students tried our best to get the wharfies' case through to those around us at the university, by distributing leaflets, by holding meetings, by talking to anyone who would listen. The Emergency Regulations, of course, meant that all such activities were illegal and we knew that the Police were raiding private homes (they did not even need a warrant). I found it hard to cope with the venom and hostility directed towards us by many students, who were mostly middle class, and I was appalled that many of them supported the punitive actions taken by the Holland government. Many a time I was surrounded in the quad after a lecture patiently trying to argue the watersiders' position in the face of incessant opposition. I liked to think afterwards that some of the quieter ones might have been interested at least to hear the other side of the argument. The issue of communism was often to the forefront in such discussions. Catholic Action students in particular were paranoid about it. I was usually assailed by them after a Latin lecture. Much of the government's far-fetched propaganda against the Watersider Union plugged the anti-communist theme, i.e., that the militant unionists were fomenting class war and were essentially traitors to New Zealand. It was pretty nasty stuff and there was never any rebuttal in the newspapers because of the Regulations.

I also tried hard to collect money for the locked-out workers and their families. That was illegal too. Many wharfies' families were in desperate straits. I approached a number of the university staff, but only two or three were willing to contribute. It was a very conservative environment.

In May, halfway through the drawn-out dispute, I left university and went down to Central Otago to work on the giant Roxburgh hydro project, living in one of the two large single men's camps. What a contrast! While there were plenty of my fellow workers who did not support the wharfies and plenty of others who were totally apathetic about anything political, there were lots who were solidly on the Union's side. I no longer felt like a pariah.

I was pleased to find that the local Workers Union branch regularly collected funds for the watersiders. The system fascinated me. Roxburgh hydro was a huge site, with the workforce totally scattered. The Public Works Department pay car would circulate on pay day every fortnight. There were always four people in the car. In front were the driver and a local police constable. In the back were the two pay clerks who found your pay envelope (everyone was paid cash) and got your signature. The policeman was rumoured to have a gun. There was obviously a lot of money in that car. During the waterfront dispute the pay car was followed by the Union car, with two or more officials there collecting donations. It was voluntary, but many of us went from the pay car to the Union car to make our contribution. The police constable must have guessed what was going on, but he did not interfere.

I was very proud to be part of such a group and was a member of the Union Branch executive for a brief period before moving to the Homer tunnel project in November. The waterfront dispute was well over by then and the National Government had convincingly won a snap election on the strength of its stand against militant unionism.

*Colin Clark came from a large working-class family. In 1951, he was a 20-year-old student of classics at Canterbury University and secretary of the University Socialist Club. Subsequently he was in charge at the Raoul and Campbell Island meteorological stations and leader at Scott Base, Antarctica. Later he became secretary of the Public Service Association and the Combined Trade Unions.*

## UNDREAMT-OF-SUCCESS  *Wellington, 9 July 1951*

### Sidney Holland

My first words are, I am glad to meet you. It did not take me long to accept the invitation, It is heartening to hear what you said Mr Poole, and all your friends, and for us to hear you say 'Things could not be better'—well, I am almost shaking myself every day, whether my ears are letting me down. Am I in a dream or what? I did not think I would ever see the day when I would be cheered by a Watersiders' meeting. When I heard them moving votes of confidence with the government, I wondered if I was in the same world. When I hear the union say they are happy, they are earning good money, and they want to work well, and when I hear the employers saying they have never known anything like it, it does me good . . .

I was out with Captain Robinson on Saturday. He said, 'I want to thank you for what you've done', and then he came out again and said he did not think that was adequate. 'I want to tell you,' he said, 'what has happened. My ship arrived ten days ago and I'm off in a week or ten days. This is back to pre-War.' I said, 'Have you told the shipping companies back in England?' and he said, 'Yes, I have.'

You are in a tough business gentlemen. You have had to deal with tough men, and how you have retained any sense of balance, I do not know . . .

We have been through a dreadful time, nobody knows what we have been through—Mr Sullivan especially . . . We are not in any sense jubilant or boasting, but we have achieved a success you never dreamed of and, frankly, we did not either. We made up our minds that no matter what it cost, we would see it through, and when you set your shoulder to the wheel you don't like to take it away: and when your country calls you, you don't like to fail and we knew the showdown had to come some time. We are a happy community today. Watersiders and shipping companies are thinking well of each other. You haven't done that for many years, have you?

*The most serious strike in New Zealand's history started when the wharfies' union refused to accept a 15% general wage increase. Nearly 5 million man-hours were lost. Sidney Holland, the Prime Minister, resigned his government and was re-elected on his policy of breaking the Waterside Workers' Union. The 'old' union was deregistered, the army employed on the wharves and a new, tamer union set up. Holland is here gleefully reporting on the success of his policy to a deputation of port and shipping managers. Mr Poole was chairman of the Port Employers Association and Mr Sullivan was Minister of Labour.*

## THE HULK DOES STILLWATER                                    *1951*

### George Fraser

I had caught a glimpse of an advertisement in the local newspaper about a country dance in the mountain-graced Stillwater. A special bus had even been arranged to take revellers to the dance hall and adjoining public house.

At an appointed spot I joined a group of Greymouth lads and lasses and later boarded the 28-seater as it shuddered to a stop on its 1937 chassis in Main Street. It was already packed with a sweating mob, some clinging to handstraps and a heady aroma of cheap perfume mixed with cloying remnants of old french fries and burnt grease from an ancient and over-strained engine permeated the air.

On the outskirts of town the bus made another stop, picking up a trio of boozed football players in black woollen singlets and grubby shorts, glazed of eye and fresh from the team's clubhouse.

They were big guys, one so tall and wide that his massive hulk filled all the front port-side of the bus even with his feet still planted on the entrance step . . . But even in his alcoholic haze, perhaps the Hulk had a sense of humour. As we bumped along country roads he grabbed one of the handrails and in a couple of grunts had torn it from the roof. The chromium rod holding leather handstraps clattered to the floor and standing passengers collapsed like a row of 10 pins.

'For Chrissake, what are you doing mate?' the driver yelled.

The Hulk did a slow-motion turn of his head, stared unseeing at the bus captain and pivoted his gaze again to the bevy of startled manicured maidens.

'Guess it's his weight that done it,' the driver grunted through his PA system as he tooled his ancient vehicle towards the cluster of lights—the Stillwater hotel and dance hall.

The starburst of lights must have suddenly activated a tiny portion of the Hulk's brain and triggered an animal response. Fighting as though caught in a speeding cage, he lunged at the door with massive paws and spilled out on to the roadway as the bus was rounding for its final approach to the hotel entrance. Faces peered with relief as the mountain of flesh was reshaped into humanoid form, but instead of brushing himself off and heading for the boozer, the Hulk took giant stiff-legged strides to the darkened greenery of the roadside.

The creature, however, was unaware the greenery belonged to acres of barbed and skin-flaying blackberry bushes which hid swamp holes by the dozen. He slowly disappeared into the darkness only to crash back into sight minutes later like some Frankenstein monster emerging from a sulphur pit.

His flailing arms, as he struggled from the mire, bore whiplashes from the thonged bushes and blood mixed with slime as the creature from that foul lagoon regained his stance on solid ground. Legs apart, he stood shuddering in front of that brooding marshland backdrop before the slow-motion head turned towards the public bar. With the brain being reactivated on seeing the lights, the Hulk departed in that direction in painful pendulum motion while the bus passengers disembarked and hurriedly headed for the adjacent dance hall.

The three-piece country-and-western band discordantly hammered away for its allocated four-hour stance in that carousel of casual courtship; the daring grabbing gals for each dance while the more gutless guys formed a gallery near the door for easy escape.

The clumsy choreography was nearing its shuffling finish when I heard a commotion coming from the hotel. Voices were raised in fear and concern. There was the Hulk, his arms, Samson-style embraced around one of the wooden pillars which supported the hotel's expansive second-floor verandah. Like a malfunctioning robot, he started rocking the structure. Clouds of dust and dirt, accompanied by ominous creakings, billowed down from the 70-year-old floorboards to the amazed spectators below and, just as the ancient structure was about to give way, the Hulk suddenly stopped playing with his new-found toy.

He had espied the bus, already loaded with the dancehall patrons—including myself—which was about to make the return journey to town.

Fear and apprehension spread over the faces of its occupants.

The motor started and with a clash of gears the driver manoeuvred for a U-turn up a slope with the Hulk in hot pursuit, only to crash thuddingly into its rear when the vehicle suddenly reversed. A couple of the passengers then alighted to inspect a more bloodied and bruised Frankenstein and helped him into a rear seat.

Halfway to Greymouth, life again was breathed into the monster. He awoke with a growl and with his massive hands began demolishing the inside of the bus. The rampage continued as the driver wrestled with the gears, steering wheel and climbing acceleration to reach town before there was bloody murder on his hands.

Crossing the Greymouth bridge, with its infamous glacial fog, he turned into the main street at full speed.

'Hold on, folks, we're heading straight for the police station. They'll put him safely in the lock-up.'

Suddenly the violent rampage stopped. A look of shocked amazement spread over the Hulk's face and with ripping desperation he attacked the passenger door and catapulted on to the footpath. Amazingly, he took the leap as though riding a bicycle and kept up his rapid perambulation still looking at the row of startled faces lining the bus windows.

It was that fixed stare at the hurtling vehicle that finally destroyed the monster. At full running speed he had not noticed the oncoming phone booth. He ploughed straight through the timber and glass structure in a full-throttle demolition act. With his legs still pumping up and down, the Hulk disappeared in a spray of splinters and glass shards into the gloom of an alleyway.

About 30 minutes later, when remnants of the dance hall gang were quietly sipping coffee in a wharfside dining hall, the front door suddenly opened to frame the image of—the Hulk!

The wounded monster, now obviously sobered by his encounter with the phone box, sullenly slid into a stall with his face and hands dripping blood on the clean serviettes.

A look of penance came over his face as he sought companionship at our table. Grudgingly, and with a self-conscious embarrassed smile, he joined our group.

'And what were all those shenanigans about, Sport?' came the question.

'Well, it was a celebration that sort of got out of hand,' he said.

'What were you celebrating?'

The Hulk smiled dreamingly at his audience. 'I've just been accepted into the police force. Start my training next week.'

*George Fraser, a radio announcer and agent for the New Zealand Security Intelligence Service, infiltrated the Greymouth branch of the Communist Party. To cover his tracks, Fraser had to fraternise with the locals—an activity he found rather distasteful. After nine years penetrating the Auckland, Lower Hutt, and Wellington branches of the party, the SIS abandoned Fraser in the United States. The fate of the Hulk is unknown.*

## KNOCKING OFF MOUNT EVEREST — *29 May 1953*

### Edmund Hillary

We set off from the tent at 6.30 in the morning. After going for some time we reached the bottom of a 400-foot slope which reached up to the south summit. And this slope was a tremendously steep one and I think was the actual piece of the whole climb that Tenzing and I disliked the most.

After cutting steps for about an hour we had made quite a distance along the ridge and then we came to the biggest problem . . . *technical* problem we had and that was a rock bluff that barred the way along the ridge. We'd seen this rock bluff, actually, from far below, and we knew it was going to be a major problem in getting along the ridge, and we knew that it could stop us. Certainly when I first saw this rock bluff, I must admit that I thought that this was as far as we were going because the actual rock itself was very steep and at that altitude I should think would be quite beyond our powers. However, on the right-hand side of it, it was plastered with a great ice cornice and this cornice had come away a little from the rock with the result that there was a crack between the rock and the ice.

Well, this crack was about forty feet high and I managed to wedge myself into the crack and by jamming back on the ice with my crampons or icespikes on my boots, and scrambling on the rock in front I was able to wriggle and push my way up the crack and on to the top and then I, after recovering my breath, I took the rope and with many a heave, and old Tenzing wriggling and scrambling, got him up the top too. Well I really felt then that the last, the worst of our problems were over and it was mainly a matter of just hard work and time before we got to the summit.

And so it proved. We cut steps along the top round bump after bump, keeping looking for the top—it was rather hard to see where it was—and finally, after quite a long bout of step-cutting, we actually reached the summit itself. And it was certainly a thrill for both of us. We were conscious all the time that our oxygen was running short and we had no time to waste and we must get down again, so we, on top, we only spent a quarter of an hour. I took my oxygen off in order to take photographs and photographed Tenzing waving his ice-axe with four flags tied to it on the top.

*Hillary and Tenzing.*

I had a good look round at the view and spent some time actually, looking at our very large neighbour Makalu which we had hopes of attempting next year with the New Zealand expedition. And also I took photos down all the main ridges of the mountain just to have some proof that we'd been on top. After quarter of an hour we got our oxygen up again. I worked out how we were going, and decided we had enough to get down perhaps with no margin but at least to get down safely. We set off quickly back down the ridge and descended finally down to the South Col to be met by George [Lowe] yet again, and a great relief it was to get back to the South Col and back to our friends and relative comfort again.

## TANGIWAI DISASTER                    *24 December 1953*

### Cyril Ellis

I did not know what train, but I realised that with the river in that state it had no chance of crossing the rail bridge. I jumped the railway fence and ran up the embankment. I ran down the middle of the track brandishing my torch and shouting at the top of my voice in an endeavour to attract the attention of the engine driver or fireman. I ran away from the bridge to try and give the crew more room to pull the train up, but it was no use they just didn't see the torch. I jumped clear and yelled to the driver when the locomotive roared past me about 200 yards from

*Prime Minister Sidney Holland (right) surveys the scene of the disaster.*

the bridge, but he had no chance of hearing me above the roar of both river and engine. As the train passed I realised for the first time that it was the express. I didn't know the bridge was damaged; I had merely realised that with the flood they could not get across.

*Late on Christmas Eve, while driving his truck north, Cyril Ellis, a postal clerk from Taihape, found the road bridge over the Whangaehu Stream blocked with floodwaters which had poured down from Mount Ruapehu. Armed with his five-cell torch, Ellis got out to have a closer look, but saw the light of a train approaching the nearby railway bridge. After the train plunged into the river, Ellis knocked out the window of a flooded coach and rescued all but one of its occupants. He was awarded the George Cross for bravery. New Zealand's worst railway disaster resulted in 151 deaths.*

## THE QUEEN VISITS STRATFORD 1954

## Jill King

We had all been very excited when we heard the Queen was coming. The whole school had been abuzz. We wondered which one of her dresses she would wear. I hoped it would be the one she got married in. I liked it better than the Coronation dress. When she'd got married, we cut out the pictures in the paper and kept the photographic supplement. We knew the wedding dress intimately. We'd drawn copies of it for our cut-out dolls. It had a wonderful long, filmy veil with embroidery on it. It was every little girls' dream, feminine and romantic. I pictured her arriving in Broadway with it billowing gently in the breeze as she stepped from a glittering golden horse-drawn coach.

Then the bubble burst. Someone asked the teacher which dress it would be. The Queen would not be wearing either dress, nor even the crown we were told! I felt betrayed. In spite of this, Royal Visit fever over-took the town.

Dad, who was in the Jaycees, was heavily involved in arrangements. Seating and flags were put up in the main streets, a lot of shops had royal displays in their windows and, at school assemblies, instructions were issued and children drilled in the art of cheering and flag-waving.

The Queen was to arrive in a train at one end of town. She was to get out, walk down the main street and then get back on the train to go on to the next town. The railway station was painted. It was rumoured that only one side—the side the Queen would see—was done.

Mrs Dillon ran the milkbar by the Plaza Theatre. Anticipating a big increase in trade that day she asked Mum if I could help out. I sometimes earned pocket money rolling icecreams ready for half-time at the movies. The icecream was in big, frozen metal cans in the fridge. I used to stand on a stool to reach inside, careful not to touch the sides. If you touched the sides your skin could stick and hurt. The icecream was hard and the scoop had to be dipped often into a basin of warm water. Each scoopful was put on a cone and stored upside down in an empty can ready for the rush.

Mum was reluctant. Royal Visit fever was rampant and she didn't want me to miss out on the great event. As the wife of one of the organ-isers she had herself been promised a good seat, and even sister Jan, who was still in the primers, was practising flag-waving. However, my perversity and pique at being deprived of the wedding dress prevailed. Came the great day and I was in the milkbar rolling icecreams.

But all the business and bustle outside proved irresistible. I had never seen so many people in their best clothes, ladies with hats and gloves and men in suits. There were people everywhere and busloads of school-kids kept arriving.

Flags were distributed and the noise was deafening. It reached a crescendo. The Queen had arrived! Mrs Dillon shut the shop and I ran along the footpath behind the seats hoping to catch a glimpse. But there were too many people shouting and cheering. Then it faded and it was all over. People were leaving, telling each other how beautiful she looked, how close they had been, and how handsome Philip was.

That night I was depressed. I never saw the Queen. I felt I had missed out on something important.

That night my mother was depressed. There had been a mixup in the arrangements and Dad had asked her to give up her seat. She never saw the Queen.

My sister Jan was upset. All the little kids had been put behind another group of bigger kids and even though she waved her flag, she never saw the Queen.

My father saw the Queen. He walked down the main street, behind the mayoress who was behind the Queen. We know because there is a photograph and he is in it.

*Jill King, a journalist, recalls the big day.*

## MOIDERING MOTHER                    *Christchurch, 1954*

## Pauline Parker

*February.* Why could not mother die. Dozens of people are dying all the time, thousands, so why not Mother and Father too. Life is very hard.

*20 April.* Mother went out this afternoon so Deborah and I bathed for some time. However I felt thoroughly depressed afterwards and even quite seriously considered committing suicide. Life seemed so much not worth the living, the death such an easy way out. Anger against Mother boiled up inside me as it is she who is one of the main obstacles in my path. Suddenly a means of ridding myself of this obstacle occurred to me. If she were to die—

*29 April.* I did not tell Deborah of my plans for removing Mother. I have made no [illegible] yet as the last fate I wish to meet is one in Borstal. I am trying to think of some way. I do not [illegible] to go to too much trouble but I want it to appear either a natural or accidental death.

*19 June.* . . . our main idea for the day was to moider Mother. This notion is not a new one, but this time it is a definite plan which we intend to carry out. We have worked it out carefully and are both thrilled by the idea. Naturally we feel a trifle nervous, but the pleasure of anticipation is great. I shall not write the plan down here as I shall write it up when we carry it out (I hope).

*20 June.* I tidied the room and messed around a little. Afterwards we discussed our plans for moidering Mother and made them a little clearer. Peculiarly enough, I have no (qualms of) conscience (or is it peculiar, we are so mad).

*21 June.* Deborah rang and we decided to use a rock in a stocking rather than a sandbag. We discussed the moider fully. I feel very keyed up as though I were planning a surprise party. Mother has fallen in with everything beautifully and the happy event is to take place tomorrow afternoon. So next time I write in this diary Mother will be dead. How odd yet so pleasing.

*The Day of the Happy Event*

*22 June.* I am writing a little of this up in the morning before the death. I felt very excited and the night-before-Christmas-ish last night.

*Pauline Parker, age 16, and Juliet Hume ('Deborah'), 15, carried out their plan and murdered Pauline's mother, Honora, in the Port Hills, above Christchurch. They were sentenced to be 'detained during Her Majesty's pleasure'.*

---

## FIRST HOLY COMMUNION                    *New Plymouth, 1958*

## Therese O'Connell

All the preparation for First Holy Communion was amazing because you had to learn everything off by heart. I should tell you I actually won the catechism prize just about every year.

There was lots of thought about how you were going to take the body of Christ into you, and therefore you had to be really pure and ready. That's why you had the First Confession, to clean yourself of all those sins that you would have committed by the time of seven. I mean, imagine the amount of sins you could commit!

But the thing that worried me was there were these stories that people were so pure and so good that after they had their First Holy Communion they just died and went to Heaven. I was terrified that if I was so pure, which I knew I was, that by having my First Holy Communion, I might just die.

I think I was terrified of being a saint too! During part of Easter they would cover up all the statues in the church in cloth and there were no flowers. And then on Good Friday, Jesus on the Cross, you had to get up and kiss his feet. And I know I was always terrified that as I bent to kiss the feet they would become human and then I would know that I was a saint.

At seven when we did First Confession, you learnt the little litany, 'Bless me Father, for I have sinned . . . ' and then you'd go to the list of sins. And of course after a while the list of sins became pretty normal—things like 'I have not said my prayers properly'.

This was an obsession of mine. To say your prayers properly meant that you knelt beside your bed in the cold—it was always cold in our house because we could only afford one heater and that was down in the living room—and you placed your hands in the prayerful position, not clasped loosely, but fingers matching totally, and you thought every word of your prayer. If you hopped into bed and screwed up your hands, you could confess that. I'm sure it's not really a sin, but it was a good filler.

'Answering my mother and father back'—because you've got to be obedient. I think I must have said that every time because I don't think I could have lived without answering them back. 'Fighting with my brothers and sisters'—now that was also one that probably popped up every time. It may not have been an actual sin, but it sounded good. That was about it. I don't think I was heavily into any other sins; I had to *find* those ones. You had to be careful about not doing the same one every time or else the priest would know.

The most agonising bit about Confession was you hoped you wouldn't be recognised. You would be telling these dreadful things about not saying your prayers properly and swearing, and the priest would say, 'And how's your mother, Therese?' And you'd think, damn, how does he know it's me? 'Fine Father.'

But the big thing about going to Confession is that you came out of it feeling aaah—you could almost hear yourself sigh. It was like a good massage would be nowadays.

*Therese O'Connell recollects her experience of St Joseph's Church, New Plymouth. In later life Therese involved herself with the women's liberation movement, the Progressive Youth Movement, Communist groups, the Federation of Labour, and sang with an Irish band.*

## THE WORLD MILE RECORD  *Wanganui, 27 January 1962*

## Peter Snell

By 9.15 p.m. it was apparent that the programme was hopelessly behind schedule so we asked the meeting manager if he would break into the order of events to allow us to get under way on time. After consultation, he agreed.

The track wasn't quite the full 440 yards so we started half way down the back straight with four laps to run when we passed the finish the first time. When the gun shattered the tense silence, heightened by the ominous clouds hanging motionless overhead, I didn't leap away with my usual keenness. Normally I would have run out and jockeyed for a suitable position fairly near the front from which I could watch developments. But this time, taking the view that there were plenty of others to help me, I decided to sit in well back.

The expected didn't happen. There was some shuffling around and to avoid running too wide round the first curve, I was forced to drift back to the rear of the field. Tension probably caused this mix-up and it also affected my pace judgement because as we passed the quarter mark I heard 61 seconds called. This was still reasonably within the four-minute schedule so I wasn't unduly disturbed. The field was now in fairly close Indian file and I was content to stay where I was, 12 yards back from the leader Barry Cossar.

Midway through the second lap, I sensed the thinning of the field and surged forward to the middle and then again into a gap between Murray and Bruce. This put me third. Murray, my hope for the third lap, dropped two yards on Cossar. I had to leave him and go past to get a close trail on Cossar.

He was doing a tremendous job and two minutes were called as we passed the half-mile. I moved up to his shoulder and glanced back to see who was coming through for the third lap. All I saw was a large gap.

Impatience got the better of me then. I moved into the lead myself, determined that I would make the three-quarter mark in three minutes. It wasn't going the way it was planned but all was not necessarily lost. I concentrated purely on the time and on keeping my running as relaxed as possible and I was still moving comfortably as I came up to the three-quarter timekeeper and heard him calling ' . . . 59 . . . 60 . . . '

Then a surprise. Tulloh drew level as we approached the bell, the bell clanged and Bruce was out in front, sprinting like a rocket and obviously intent on stealing the race. Even though it came from the runner I'd discounted, this was the stimulus I needed.

Rather than fight him round the bend, I stepped up pace only enough to poise myself on his shoulder. As we swung into the back straight with 300 yards to run, I knew I had him covered. I wasn't worrying about him. I was racing time, not Tulloh.

At that point I abandoned the studied relaxation of my running and let go with my finishing drive. This is the moment when you stop consciously controlling what you are doing and pour everything into driving out the utmost speed.

I found myself running in complete freedom from restraint. I was holding nothing back and I don't think I've ever felt such a glorious feeling of strength and speed without strain as I did during the final exhilarating 300 yards. I knew I must be well within the four minutes as I raced round the last curve. I straightened, heard for the first time the rising roar of the crowd and kept on driving. Still there was no conscious effort and I flew through the tape in full free flight.

I ran straight into chaos. That moment was virtually the end of the meeting. There were people everywhere, an endless din and confusion. Someone came out of the crowd and showed me a stopwatch. It was inside four minutes but I didn't bother to read it properly. Over it all the crowd announcer kept calling out that he, too, had a stopwatch but that all he could say was that it was definitely well under four minutes.

It seemed ages before the official time was announced at 3:54.4 and, because the printed programme was in error, this was announced as equalling Herb's world time. By now, I'd given up waiting and had run a victory lap. The crowd never stopped yelling and I felt in the same chaotic state of mind I had experienced after the final in Rome.

Finally, it was established with the officials and the crowd that my time was a tenth inside Herb's record and we had the tumult all over again.

## MEETING THE RIGHT PEOPLE IN HERETAUNGA

*early 1960s*

## Robyn Du Chateau

Convent life was so strict. I came from this highly unhygienic family with dogs and cats in the bed and everyone using each other's toothbrushes. It was a warm easy environment where people said what they thought quite spontaneously, although now I realise lots was censored—direct criticism, any mention of sex, any sadness. We were not allowed to cry or be sick; when I was sick I was told I was making it up—which caused a crisis the day my appendix burst and no one believed I was in real pain.

Then I went to the convent where no one said anything. We had to get up at 6.25 a.m. and weren't allowed to talk until breakfast. When we walked around we weren't allowed to talk; they used clickers. You weren't allowed a special friend. If you spent too much time with a girl you'd be separated. Here we all were in this monastic atmosphere—hormonic and longing.

My family were upwardly mobile. They lived in Heretaunga and then moved to the Akatarawas where we rode ponies. I got a passport into the Woodford House-type ball scene and was inundated with invitations to woolshed dances, which were fantastic fun. This was the early sixties—hooped petticoats, easies, seamed stockings.

I think the scene was all about country mothers looking to marry off their daughters, or perhaps just to give them a jolly good social life and the right connections to make future marriages. 'The right connections' was huge. Part of going home on holiday for me was being taken down to the Heretaunga Golf Club and being forced to learn golf because I'd meet 'the right people' in the golf club. But the more they pressured me, the more I couldn't do it. I couldn't play golf, but I couldn't actually relate to those people. I'd been sent to this monastic school which was into pain and suffering, and being good and pure and going to confession, where real love was giving up everything I had—and then there was this pressure from my parents to get out there and gad about socially.

There were strict rules of conduct, but no one would tell you exactly what they were. At my first dance—it was my sister's dance, held in our woolshed—I went outside with a boy, sat in the car with him. Dad came out with a spotlight and found me and hauled me out. The boy was sent home and I was put in my room for three days. I kept saying to Dad, What have I done? He'd say, You know what you've done, disgracing the family. I asked Mum, What's the story? Don't talk to me, you're a filthy dirty girl. My sister: You know what you've done. No one would tell me what they thought was so terribly shocking.

---

## VIETNAM TEACH-IN                     *Wellington, 1965*

## Prof. Keith Sinclair

Victoria University students put on New Zealand's first 'teach-in', ably organised by Helen Sutch, daughter of the historian Bill Sutch. The teach-ins in New Zealand were not simply anti-government rallies. Some of the speakers outlined historical, geographical and other background information. Cabinet ministers and Opposition Labour MPs took part. I have never attended such exciting meetings. Often the atmosphere was electric.

I was asked to speak and, before I left for Wellington, received a long and surprising telephone call from Tom Shand, the Minister of Labour. I wondered whether he was trying to put me off; certainly he was sounding me out. But I think he was sincere in explaining to a reporter that he simply wanted to find out whether a good number of students would be present and that it was simply not another wild scheme, and also to satisfy himself that the government was not going to be an Aunt Sally.

About a thousand people, not by any means all students, sat for fifteen hours listening to the debate. There was a great deal of heckling of pro-government speakers. Sir Leslie Munro, a National MP, said that such a meeting would not be allowed in Hanoi; my interjection, 'Or Saigon', was widely reported in the press.

One journalist, Ian Templeton, reported that 'the critics clearly won the day' but the presence of Tom Shand, Minister of Labour, and D.S. Thompson, the Minister of Defence, gave the meeting a dignity and seriousness that it would not otherwise have had. Indeed, I doubt whether such a serious debate on foreign policy had ever occurred in New Zealand. When Walter Nash, a former Prime Minister and our senior statesman, spoke, he received tumultuous applause. A former MP,

Ormond Wilson, said to me that he had never heard Walter speak so clearly about anything.

When I spoke I began with our war graves. I had stood in the cathedral at Amiens and read a notice commemorating the thousands of Australians and New Zealanders who had died in defending the town during the First World War. 'My feelings when I read that notice were very emotional and not those of satisfied patriotism. Amiens is a scruffy-looking town and I wondered why those men had been there.' In Lebanon, not long before, driving from Beirut to Byblos I had come across a cemetery: 'War graves: Australia and New Zealand.'

When would this end?

Most of my speech consisted of criticisms of the government's arguments for joining in the war. Sir Walter had made a couple of errors about SEATO. Shand and Thompson had not attacked him, but waited till I had finished and then questioned me about SEATO. Anticipating questions, I had put the text of the treaty in my pocket and now brandished it, saying that I always carried it about with me in case, like South Vietnam, I should need aid.

The academics were certainly not inferior to the politicians as speakers. Bill Oliver from Massey and Keith Buchanan from Victoria were excellent. A man later wrote to Nash saying that he had enjoyed the 'spate of wonderful oratory from the "intelligenzia" of the university'. Only a few years earlier it is doubtful we had possessed an intelligentsia, but we had the beginnings of one now. This was the first occasion on which academics had taken a lead in public dispute and, indeed, proven a force with a little political clout. Of course, before the Second World War there were not enough academics to possess any force.

*Keith Sinclair was Professor of History at Auckland University.*

## VISITING RIO AND BERLIN                                       *1967*

## Robert Muldoon

The IMF meeting was held in the newly-completed Museum of Modern Art. They were laying the lawns outside when we arrived, but inside the building was already falling apart. When I washed my hands at a hand-

*Robert Muldoon.*

basin in the bathroom, I put too much pressure on the tap and the basin fell off the wall.

At the official dinner, I was seated next to a delegate from the Malagasy Republic—Madagascar. As we sat down, I realised that my plate was the only one that did not have a bread roll in front of it. I beckoned to the waiter, pointed to the bread roll alongside the plate of my neighbour, and to the fact that I did not have one. He went out to the kitchen. He came back looking worried. It was obvious that there were no more bread rolls. When I still expressed concern he picked up a bread roll from my neighbour's plate and put it in front of mine.

As the soup was being served, I decided that I needed the bread roll, picked it up and just as I was about to eat it, realised that my neighbour from the Malagasy Republic had already taken a bite out of it. Making the best of a bad job I ate the rest.

I then tried to make amends by conversation. His second language after his native dialect, was French. My French was not bad, indeed about as good as his. Desperately seeking a subject on which we could converse, I put it to him that where he came from was the home of the remarkable extinct bird, the dodo. It took us fifteen minutes in our limited French to identify a bird which he knew by a quite different name, but which we agreed was the dodo.

That brought us together and for the rest of the meal we conversed on various subjects that were within the range of our respective vocabularies. It was only when I got home that night that I realised that the dodo did not in fact come from Madagascar; it came from Mauritius.

Each delegation at the meeting was given a brand new Willys

motorcar locally made at the factory that had recently been set up. By the end of the week of our meeting, the motorcars were falling apart and pieces were dropping off them. We had a driver called Placido, assigned to us. After the first day, we rechristened him Rapido.

I had heard that in anticipation of the visit of several thousand delegates, bankers and others, the Government had had a round-up of all the streetwalkers and taken then out of the city so that its reputation would remain unsullied. They missed one, however.

Willys cars of over a hundred delegates were lined up outside the Copacabana Palace Hotel, waiting to take us to the dinner that was on that night. I came out of the hotel and rather than send out a call for Rapido . . . I walked along the line of cars to where I knew he would be. In front of me walked an attractive young woman who had murmured as I went past her some words in the local tongue which ended up, 'Casa mia', and which, clearly, were an invitation to accompany her to her place. As she sauntered in front of me, and I went equally gently behind her, the drivers, each standing by their motorcars, began to murmur in chorus: 'Bravo, bravo, bravo.' To their disgust when I reached Rapido's car I leapt in, told him where we were going and off we went . . .

We visited West Berlin about the time of the Polish crisis. We had lunch with all the mayors in the Reichstag Building, right alongside the Berlin Wall near the Brandenburg Gate . . . I was sitting next to one of the mayors when he expressed concern about the Polish crisis and said that: 'After all, we are only fifty minutes from the Polish border.' Innocently I inquired: 'You mean, by air?' 'No,' he grimly responded, 'by tank.'

On the other side of me was the wife of one of the mayors and when I idly commented on the fact that there were kiwifruit in the bowl on the table she asked me: 'Do you grow kiwifruit in New Zealand?'

---

## SAVED FROM THE SINKING *WAHINE*                *Wellington, 1968*

## Ada Woolf

We were about the last passengers off & lifeboats etc were far away— looked about and saw people floating in their life jackets all over the sea—the Captain on the deck below, bellowed again—'Get them off— she's going—make them go!'—The man tried to loosen the woman's grip on the rails to make her jump but she just screamed and refused—He turned to me and said 'Will you jump!' 'Of course!' I said, 'but give me that handbag there—it is mine and she slipped it off my arm as she skidded past me? He looked at me amazed & said 'But no one is taking their handbags!'—Indeed I'd seen handbags lying all over the decks—I said 'My specs are in there & I cannot see without them—I hate being blind—give it to me—there's a good fellow—then I'll jump.' He handed it to me and helped me up on the rails. I clasped both hands over my bag on top of my chest and jumped. The water felt amazingly soft and I felt good after all the struggling on deck. I turned on my back and lay there—kicking my feet to drive me away from the sinking ship. My lifejacket had come undone around the waist so I firmly set my bag on top of it to keep it flat down and crossed my arms tightly over the bag & all—& there I floated. My leg was aching and my head throbbed from my bumps and bangs. From the time I'd pulled out from under those chairs I had been praying to God to still the tempest so we might all get off safely—I prayed to him to save us (not me but us) and I always ended 'not my will but thy will oh Lord.' As I floated around I realised the rain had stopped and although I was going high up and down the breakers weren't breaking over me. After a while a rubber raft came by but was too laden to take me—perhaps it was as well because it was reported afterwards that some of them overturned and another one spilt. So I floated on—lapsed into unconsciousness from my cracked head—but suddenly there were two lifesaving boys from the Worser Bay Lifesaving Club bending over me and shouting, 'Come on Mum—Come on Mum.' They were in a little boat with an inboard engine that they started with a rope like a motor mower. I said, 'You boys can't get me into that wee boat—I'm a big woman—and my clothes are wet and heavy—Leave me—I'm alright—Get some one younger—!' But they persisted saying 'Come on Mum. There's plenty for you to live for yet—Come on Mum —' And they grabbed me—one by each arm and hauled me with a wallop into the bottom of that boat—I said 'Don't lose my handbag— I've hung on to it because my glasses are in it—and I can't see properly without them.' They laughed and said 'Alright Mum'—and one put me up near the front with my bag on my knees. I pointed into the water and said 'Oh look—there's a baby floating.' One of the boys grabbed it and laid it at my feet—It was dead. Poor wee soul. Then I began retching and retching—all the salt water I'd swallowed I suppose. I said 'Sorry boys to be messing up your boat.' They laughed—and hauled 3 or 4 more people in—I was busy being sick—I heard them arguing over an old man clinging to a raft. One wanted to get him aboard and the other said they had a full load and if they took any more they would drown everyone—so they left him. I saw him—just another face that will always stay in my mind. I lapsed into unconsciousness. Those boys did not go to the depot where all the lifeboats etc. were gathered together by police—they shipped their boat on some little beach and I felt myself being lifted by many hands—I came 'to' with the Siren screams so knew I was in an ambulance.

*Sixty-three-year-old Ada Woolf had been a matron of a large old people's home. Her family say that she was trained to handle emergencies and crowds. 'The man' mentioned here is Mrs Woolf's husband.*

## Anti-Vietnam Demos in Auckland                    *1968*

## Tim Shadbolt

The emphasis was on small but persistent action. Guerilla protest. Pickets, leaflets, posters, parades. We were hounded and persecuted by police and public alike. Three times during the year I was assaulted. One guy spat in my face, another time about six clean-shaven rugby types surrounded me and started taunting. Then one of them opened a bottle of beer,

'If you move one single muscle, I'll kill you, you bloody commie cunt.'

He started pouring beer over my head. I defied him totally and moved every single muscle in my body, man, you should have seen me run.

We used to have marches down Queen Street. Our biggest rallies drew as many as 35 people. On one occasion we had six. Rod was walking along at the rear with one of his anarchist mates when two smooth young men started pulling his hair.

'Ya longhaired, peacenik hippie' and they'd pulled his hair again. Now brother Rod, though his hair was well past his shoulders, isn't the sort of guy you could describe as a peacenik hippie. He was a boxer in Sydney, he'd played six years of rugby and he fought in the mod-rockers wars of the sixties. Rod grabbed this guy by the tie and dragged him out

*Tim Shadbolt.*

into the middle of Queen Street. All the cars halted and a crowd formed as he dragged the guy round in circles at the same time telling everyone what a bastard he was. A few seconds later the police arrived, saw this ridiculous scene and thought they were a couple of drunks. I don't think the guy ever picked on a 'peacenik hippie' again.

We also picketed American warships and caused so much embarrassment that they finally had to moor them at the Devonport Naval Base. We didn't do any damage or cause any violence but the police moved in and made arrests. An Auckland housewife was arrested for singing anti-war songs on an American warship and charged with offensive behaviour.

We were small, we were social outcasts, but we kept going. Gradually things began to change. It was the efforts of the Vietcong as much as our own that brought about this change in New Zealand. Nobody likes supporting a war their side is losing.

The first sit-in was a real shock for New Zealand. The police just couldn't work it out: we were really nice young students all wearing suits. Even a lecturer came with us—Walter Pollard, a French lecturer who had been a tower of strength in the Auckland movement for many years. He's one of only a few lecturers in New Zealand who has been prepared to commit himself actively to civil disobedience. While we all sat in the US Consul's office, as nervous as hell, waiting for the police to arrive, Walter read from Bertrand Russell's book on war crimes. A few of us actually took over the consul's office and it was amazing what a nervous, weak-looking man the consul was. He was so scared that he couldn't even speak. He just sat there shaking, beads of sweat rolling down his face. He was just a trade consul and it was amazing to think that this terrified little man represented the greatest imperialist power in the world.

'Hello,' said Bill Bone, trying to help him relax. 'Don't worry about us. We're occupying your consulate like you're occupying South Vietnam.'

This seemed to make him even more scared but then his bodyguard arrived, a big man with a patch over one eye, and the consul was a lot happier with him around. I had a funny feeling that the bodyguard was armed but there is always a funny atmosphere around a man who is carrying a gun.

There was no yelling, no emotions, no chants. Just peaceful protesters. The police were really funny. They didn't want to arrest us. They carried one girl out of the building and actually pushed her into the crowd. Then they carried Maureen out and told her to get lost. The Whatleys had just been married and the sit-in was almost their honeymoon. The police carried them out of the building and refused to arrest them or put them in a police car. So they had to catch the lift back up and re-occupy the consulate—just the two of them, and get arrested. No one struggled but we all went limp. A large crowd gathered and they were amazed to see thirty limp bodies being carried out of the AMP building in Queen Street.

For every one of us it was our first arrest and for New Zealand it was the first mass arrest. It received massive national publicity and created a lot of controversy.

Back in the police station, it was really interesting getting our photographs, our fingerprints taken—and getting our belts taken off just in case we hung ourselves. There wasn't time to lock us all up in cells so they locked us in the dining hall. We rolled up a pair of socks and were soon playing soccer, watched by the stern eyes of two closed circuit TV lenses.

The police wanted to keep us all night but after a lot of yelling by lawyers and JPs we were soon all out on bail.

*Shadbolt was later elected mayor of Waitemata, then Invercargill.*

## Qui Nhon Hospital Viet Nam  *31 March 1969*

### Dr Peter Eccles Smith

I have just been getting my monthly report done, and there were 519 operations this month, of which we New Zealanders did 422, of which 240 were war casualties, so that you can see we are not just sitting around boozing. Apart from a few official welcomes and farewells we have hardly been out at night, which suits me as the days are very tiring.

The rainy season seems to have stopped, and the Americans are beginning to repair the roads. This makes the journey to and from the hospital much better already.

I had a letter from Dr D.P. Kennedy, the NZ Director-General of Health, telling me he hopes to visit us in June. He also mentioned that we have replacements for the anaesthetist, physician and third surgeon when their terms finish. I will hear all this officially soon, but Dr Kennedy takes a very real interest in the team's work.

There is talk of sending a three-man Red Cross team here. I think they may have difficulty if they plan to come to Qui Nhon because the present policy is not to have any more foreigners here, in fact some may be moved out. This does not involve us. I think the main reason is the complete disruption of the local economy by the more highly paid foreigners, especially the Americans, and there have been instances of local people, some of them professional people like teachers, being turned out of rented homes so that the landlords could lease the property to Americans at a much higher rent. This hardly helps race relations. I think many Americans are quite unaware that these evictions are taking place.

Qui Nhon seems such a tempting target for some Viet Cong activity with its busy harbour, bulging military stores, oil, petrol, and ammunition dumps, but it is also referred to, jokingly, as a leave resort for the Viet Cong, and they may easily find it more useful to them if left quiet.

We treat many Viet Cong wounded or suspects, and there is no obvious ill-feeling towards us, and no evidence of friction between them and the other patients. They are in the same wards, and are only identified by the handcuff or chain which tethers them to the bed. It must be very strange for them. They are injured by Americans, then brought to the Vietnamese civil hospital, where 'New Zealand' Americans treat them. I don't think most of the less educated people know that there is any difference between us and the Americans. I think some of them look on us rather as they look on American Negroes, that is, as Americans who are different from the other, more common white Americans . . . I have met many Americans by now, mainly USAID men, most of whom are very sincere and dedicated. Some are as concerned as I am with the slaughter of innocent civilians, and as concerned with the future. Active military operations continue north of here, with the endless casualties and refugees. It is estimated that the An Lau valley action will create 40 000 refugees. Had a three-year-old die on me today. She came in with her guts torn apart by a grenade. Her mother, just a girl really, was with the child all the time, helping us to try and save her, and it was not until the child had died that we realised that the mother too had several wounds herself. The terrible sight of the dying child in the arms of the injured mother was most upsetting. It is horrible to think that our own troops will be inflicting the same sorts of wounds on the same sort of people. It is a blessing that they are not in this province. It would be awful to get this sort of thing inflicted by our own people.

*Dr Smith, for many years the Medical Superintendent of Dannevirke hospital, served voluntarily for 12 months as leader of the New Zealand civil surgical team in South Vietnam. The team won an international reputation for the success of its humanitarian efforts. Dr Smith reports here to his family back home.*

---

## STATEMENT TO POLICE          *Pukekawa, 25 October 1970*

## Arthur Allan Thomas

I am a married man 32 years of age. I reside with my wife Vivien Thomas on my father's farm at Mercer Ferry Road, Pukekawa. The phone number is Pukekawa 838. I lease the farm from my father Allen Thomas who is living at Pt Wells, Matakana.

I am being spoken to by Detective Inspector Hutton about the deaths of Jeanette and Harvey Crewe in June of this year. I have been warned that I am not obliged to say anything more about this matter or to answer any further questions unless I wish to do so and that anything that I may say will be taken down and may be used in evidence.

I was brought up on the farm that I am now leasing from my father.

In 1966 my father agreed to lease the farm to me for $2000 a year. I have been on the farm ever since. My marriage is quite a happy one. We do not have children but that is my fault.

I remember going to Pukekawa Primary School with Jeanette Crew. We were both in the same class right through primary school. On second thoughts I was a class ahead of her until she caught up when I failed a year in standard one. I had quite a schoolboy crush on Jeanette at school. When I finished primary school I went and started work on the farm with my father. Jeanette carried on her education by going to St Cuthbert's. After this she became a schoolteacher at Maramarua. At this time I was working in the Forestry at Maramarua. I met Heather Demler one night at a dance at Pukekawa and she mentioned that Jeanette was a schoolteacher at Maramarua. She told me that I should look Jeanette up. I actually visited her a couple of times but I never took her out. Not very long later I heard Jeanette had gone overseas to England. I went round and saw Len Demler and asked him for Jeanette's address so I could write to her. I think I wrote to her twice while she was away. She was away for about two years. She replied to my letters. I now hand one of the letters from her to the police. Later when Jeanette returned I took her round a Christmas present. The brush and comb set I have just looked at is the one I gave her. The card has my handwriting on it. I did not take Jeanette out.

She did mention at the time I gave her the present that she had a boyfriend.

I have been asked about my movements on the night of the ratepayers' meeting of 17 June 1970. I remember soon after Jeanette and Harvey were missing Vivien and I discussed what we were doing that night. I recall remembering that we were home attending a sick cow. Peter Thomas was home also. The cow had been sick for some time and I think Peter helped me the previous night but I'm not sure. The cow was in a sling in the tractor shed and was sick for some time. I finally had to shoot this cow with my .22 rifle. I also remember that day as I think Vivien and I went to our dentist in Pukekohe. We arrived back home about 4 p.m. We attended to the cow between 5 p.m. and 6 p.m. I think I intended going to the ratepayers' meeting but by the time we had tea it was too late to go.

I have been shown the axle that was found with Harvey Crewe's body together with the two stub axles found by the police on my farm tip. After looking closely at these and also some photographs I agree that the axle and stub axles belong together. I cannot recall any of these articles being on my farm. I cannot explain how the axle got with Harvey Crewe's body. After looking at the axles I think they must belong to the old trailer.

I faintly recall the old trailer and the fact that there was some blue on it. I do not know what happened to that old trailer. Seems like the axle must have been on my farm but I cannot help any further.

I have been asked about my .22 rifle and where it was on the night of 17 June 1970. I am almost certain that this rifle could not have been taken out of my house without me knowing. I certainly did not lend it to anyone round that time. I remember using this rifle to shoot the sick cow I have mentioned, about two weeks after Jeanette and Harvey went missing. The dead cow is now on the tip on the farm where the stub axles were found. I also used the same rifle about a month ago to shoot a blind dog. I also put the carcass of the dog down at the farm dump. I also used to use this rifle to shoot rabbits with. Vivien does not shoot and Peter Thomas has never used this rifle to my knowledge. I have been told that samples of wire found on my farm are similar to wire found on Harvey Crewe's body. I can only say that someone must have come on to my farm and taken the wire and axle. I have been told that the .22 bullets in Harvey and Jeanette's body had the figure 8 stamped on them and that similar ammunition with this number has been found on my farm. I cannot explain this. I was aware however that ammunition does have numbers stamped on the bullet.

I have viewed the brush and comb set I gave to Jeanette. I think the present cost me four or five pounds. This was in 1962. I know Len Demler quite well but he has never been to visit me at my farm.

I have been told that a detective overheard me say to Vivien when I was planting seeds on Friday something to the effect that if the police thought I was guilty then I must be guilty. I cannot remember saying anything like this to Vivien.

I have been told about a pair of overalls found in the boot of my car having blood on them. I do not remember any blood getting on these. I use these overalls to fix a puncture or other repairs to the car when I am in good clothes.

The rubbish tip on my farm is used by me when necessary. I use it regularly and take all sorts of things to it. I remember a few weeks ago taking some stuff out of the horse stable to the farm dump. I also remember some time ago cleaning stuff out of the stable to put the Dodge truck inside. This was about two years ago. I remember seeing one of the wheel rims found by the police on my farm dump but I have not seen the axles there.

I did not help the police and local farmers with the search for Jeanette and Harvey Crewe but by the time I had finished my daily chores by 1 p.m. I thought it would be too late to go. I thought that unless you could get to the Crewe farm by 9 a.m. you would not be able to assist. I was busy at that time of the year as my cows start calving on 10 June. I do not know how many cows I had in when the search started. I suppose I could of helped for a few hours but I was fairly busy.

I know I have been a suspect all along in this case. I suppose I did use to chase Jeanette along a bit and used to write to her.

I have read this through and it is true and correct. I have nothing to add.

A.A. Thomas

*These innocent statements became incriminating evidence in the hands of the Crown Prosecutor who argued that Thomas killed Jeanette Crewe out of sexual jealousy. Thomas was found guilty of the Crewe murders at two trials and sentenced to life in prison. He served nine years of his sentence before a Commission of Enquiry found evidence had been planted on him, and he was freed.*

# CHRISTMAS DAY IN PAREMOREMO 1970

## Carl Frederick Rosel

The only way I can describe D Block is that it is a small set of cells within one large cell, each having no window to the outside world. Across a passage from some source you can catch a small glimpse of the sky but apart from that an inmate never goes outside or even feels the rays of the sun upon him. Being in a cell in D Block is like being incarcerated in a steel oven of a large stove without the heat being turned on. There is just no possibility of escape and the whole place is bleak and hopeless.

In D Block one day followed the other with an invariable routine of absolute nothing. Each day I spent in my cell, walking up and down the two or three square yards of cell floor, sometimes talking to myself and sometimes just sitting with my head in my hands. My first spell in D Block was in the upper tier of cells and I spent about two months without any privileges at all, confined to my cell the total time except on rare occasions when I would be taken by three warders to a yard to exercise for an hour or so. These occasions were not regular and sometimes over a week would go by during which I would have spent the whole time in solitary confinement.

After these three months I was taken to the lower tier of D Block and placed in a cell there. Conditions were a bit easier . . . I was put in a handkerchief-size workshop with another inmate and worked there during the day sewing handkerchiefs and sometimes putting collars on shirts. Sometimes in the lower tier we would have the odd privilege such as seeing a movie and being able to go to the prison gymnasium for a maximum of an hour a week. If we went to the gymnasium we would never mix with other inmates. Solely lower landing D Block prisoners would be there. When there was an opportunity to go to the gymnasium I would always take it but it was not until later that I began to understand why some inmates in D Block did not do so. They had become so subjected and so overborne by their surroundings that they had lost any zest for life and even the temptation of going to a gymnasium and kicking a ball around held no joy for them.

After I had been in D Block for a while I became involved in the friction that always seems to exist between the warders and inmates. These little incidents were not important taken in isolation but over a period they mounted up and the atmosphere was one of discontent and bickering.

Christmas Day December 1970 found me in the 'pound', that is the disciplinary block. I ate my Christmas dinner off the floor as no tables or chairs were provided. I had been charged with failing to obey an order and assault. The assault consisted of my having tapped a warder on the shoulder and telling him he should have more bars on his shoulder and as a result of this I was sentenced to 14 days in the punishment block and also lost 14 days' remission off my sentence. In the punishment block the order of the day was nothing to do. At times I was allowed out into a small yard and the rest of the time I was locked in my cell. My main reading material consisted of old *Readers' Digests* and one of these was allotted at a time. On my release from the pound I returned to lower D Block and carried on there for about two months. At the end of this period I placed a broom in my door to stop it closing while I ducked out to get something and as a result of this I was placed on charge again and was sentenced to a further loss of seven days' remission and the loss of seven days' earnings and was told I was being taken back to upper D Block with no privileges. This started my long spell in upper D Block which commenced in February 1971 and lasted until the middle of 1972. I spent in total just under two years in D Block.

. . . the general routine was to sit in your cell and go mad. Prisoners were often transferred from D Block to Oakley Mental Institution but the symptoms of their insanity would have to be very, very obvious before this was done.

[On one] occasion another inmate had his arms out through the grill and he was also screaming out and he had a razor blade in one hand and was using it to try and saw his fingers off his other hand. His fingers were cut open to the bone and blood was pouring everywhere. On these occasions the other prisoners would press alarm buttons, scream and yell calling for medical assistance which never seemed to come.

One day another inmate complained that there were ghosts in his cell and he wanted a doctor. He was told in no uncertain terms that no one would be obtained for him. Following that I heard a noise like paper tearing and the inmate had ripped himself open from the shoulder to his lower stomach with a razor blade.

Living in D Block was like living in a madhouse. Almost every day a prisoner would either break down and become hysterical or some bizarre incident would occur such as a prisoner slashing himself.

Sometimes I would say to myself, 'This can't be real. These people around me can't be human beings. This must just be a bad nightmare and soon I must wake up and all this will no longer exist.' As the months went by this nightmare continued and I found myself deteriorating and feared that eventually I, too, would become completely insane and be transferred to a mental institution as an incurable patient.

*Rosel was released in June 1973. His account formed part of the Howard League's report on Paremoremo prison, written by Fred Jordan and Peter Williams.*

## NORMAN KIRK'S DAYS AND NIGHTS

*Wellington, 1974*

## Margaret Hayward

*Friday 2 August*

Brigadier Gilbert has been to see Mr K about 'something serious in New Zealand'. After he left, Mr K looked as stern as I have ever seen him. Brigadier Gilbert had told him about a sinister figure who had been concerning the Security Intelligence Service for years. A 'Mr Big'—who was Dr William Ball Sutch.

I couldn't believe it. But it seems from his own absolute certainty that they have told Mr K enough to convince him completely. He told me that for more than 20 years the SIS had suspected Dr Sutch of being a spy. Even worse, Mr K seems to feel, is what Brigadier Gilbert had to say about the activities of Dr Sutch and another Zealander in refugee relief during the war, and the means by which they had acquired substantial assets. Although Dr Sutch lets people think he is a man who can't afford a car, he is in fact leading a double life and is very rich. Brigadier Gilbert has also told Mr K it is only Dr Sutch's 'incredible arrogance that occasionally lets his mask slip'.

I cannot understand why Mr K is telling me all this. Although I

*Norman Kirk.*

haven't had lunch with Dr Sutch for some time he is circumspectly warning me against doing so again.

Mr K used to be gentle with Dr Sutch. When I asked why he was so patient with him he had explained that he was an elderly man 'who can't have much money, no future but an old age pension, and has only his reputation to cling to'. He had excused Dr Sutch's arrogance by saying that he wore it like a threadbare cloak. Now he is furious.

I think it is an incredible accusation to bring against a famous economist, writer and social reformer. And it seems a very conveniently timed revelation. I didn't point that out, though, because the SIS has obviously produced enough evidence to banish any doubts Mr K may have had.

But why, if the Security Intelligence Service has known about Dr Sutch for years, has it waited until now to take action?

Is it because the people there know that Mr K is unhappy about the way they tapped phones while assuring him they were not? The way they rarely brief him, although as Minister in Charge he has to take final responsibility for their actions? The way they vetoed his suggestion that a person of good standing be appointed to oversee the Security Intelligence Service and protect the rights of the individual?

Perhaps they are anxious to keep Mr K from introducing safeguards, or having their activities monitored.

Perhaps this is their way of trying to convince Mr K that a strong, unimpeded Security Intelligence Service is essential to our security. That indeed New Zealand does have reds under many beds.

Yesterday Mr K walked the two hundred yards or so to Kelvin Chambers in The Terrace to see his surgeon, Mr McIlwaine. He came back limping, but happy. Mr McIlwaine was delighted with the way his legs had healed after the varicose vein operation.

He also inspected Mr K's ingrown toenail, split it down the middle and took the ingrown half off. It's good Mr K had it done professionally instead of hacking away at it with a pocket knife as he did whenever it gave him trouble in his days on Opposition. He's still adamant it's the result of milk fester from his dairy factory days.

Dr Diana Mason, president of the Society for the Protection of the Unborn Child, has told reporters she has given Mr K a great deal of documentation on the controversial Aotea Clinic in Auckland. She contends that four of the clinic's six criteria for carrying out abortions are not covered by law.

Questioned by the press, Mr K says the submissions, which include case histories of four women who had abortions and later needed hospital treatment, will be quickly and seriously considered, but there will be no enquiry.

Although he's as against abortion as ever, Mr K surprises me by being suspicious of SPUC's motives. He's put the submissions through official channels, asking the Health and Justice Departments to investigate the allegations and report back.

The U.S. House of Representatives Judiciary Committee wound up its special debate last night, recommending that President Nixon be impeached.

*Tuesday 27 August*

Although Mr K is getting plenty of peace in the house on his own, he says he lies there all night listening to every creak, every little sound. He still dislikes the Forres Street house, and I gather it has been scarey at times, struggling to breathe and listening to his own sloshy irregular heartbeat in the empty house. He is still not eating because 'my gut's too sore and tum's too tight'.

To make matters worse, a fellow from Hastings had phoned at regular intervals all night. After the third call Mr K asked the toll operator not to let him through but he was told they had to, it was regulations. He asked for a supervisor but there was none on duty. So the calls kept coming.

He took the phone off the hook but the post office put the screamer on when the next call came through. The caller kept saying, 'I know you're dying, you bastard. And about time.'

I'm not the only person Mr K has been ringing fairly constantly. He's been ringing Gray, too, and I gather he has been on the phone to a lot of people—probably as a hedge against loneliness and also so he doesn't have too much time to think. He has been keeping close contact with Cabinet Ministers and the Senior Whip Ron Barclay, and I suspect he has also been phoning various members of the Broadcasting Board.

Dr Hallright phones me at work. He says he hasn't been out to see Mr K but is concerned about his condition, and would like me to come and talk to him about getting the family to understand how ill Mr K is. I say I'll have to think about the implications, and will ring him later. When I do, he is out, so I tell his wife I don't feel I should discuss the Prime Minister's illness with the doctor unless both Mr and Mrs Kirk know, and give their permission. She says the doctor will ring me when he returns.

*Margaret Hayward, Prime Minister Norman Kirk's parliamentary private secretary, kept a full personal diary of events. Norman Kirk died in hospital on Saturday 31 August 1974.*

## SUNDAY NIGHT AT THE PETER PAN CABARET
*Auckland, August 1974*

Bob Jones

Muldoon spoke for about forty-five minutes. Throughout my earlier address and in the initial stages of his, the chanting of the protesters could be heard inside. Ten minutes into Rob's speech it became distinctly louder. After twenty-five minutes such was the noise that, despite his microphone, it was now difficult to hear Muldoon. I slipped off the stage and went outside.

A large battalion of policemen were blocking the front doors. Beyond them the mob, which had grown into sizeable numbers, were plainly working themselves into an ugly mood.

When Muldoon had finished and the formalities were over we repaired to an adjacent room for drinks and food which awaited the hundred and fifty specially selected guests from among the audience.

Muldoon was in rampant high spirits. Triumphantly garrulous, he was shouting and laughing. Everyone was his friend. Very soon he was roaring drunk.

Outside the noise was becoming deafening. I went out again and felt the same electric atmosphere of pending show-down violence one senses in the arena before a heavyweight championship fight when waiting for the fighters to approach the ring.

A police sergeant spotted me and came over. 'For God's sake, get Muldoon out through a back door quickly,' he urged. 'If he comes out here there'll be bloodshed. I want to announce he's gone, otherwise we're in trouble.'

I promised to do this and suggested he get reinforcements. He told me he already had every available man on deck.

Back inside I took Rob aside. He was grinning from ear to ear. I told him what the sergeant had said and added my own view that the mob were really ugly and if he attempted a front door exit, violence was inevitable. He broke away from me and yelled for attention.

'Listen to Jones,' he shouted. 'He wants me to sneak out the back door in my own city. That's something I'll never do.' The crowd roared their support.

Desperately I looked around the room. Pat Rippin, an uncanny Norman Kirk look-alike, up from Wellington, six foot three inches tall and seventeen stone, hovered nearby.

I grabbed him and acquainted him with the situation. Pat, typically, knew nearly everyone there. 'Select some big fellows and anyone you know who is a tough bastard and get them over here,' I urged him. A few minutes elapsed and Pat gathered a dozen fearless types. I informed them of the situation. 'What's important is not to break rank. Surround Muldoon and don't forfeit your position,' I advised, then I went outside again to report to the sergeant.

When I told him Muldoon was insisting on coming through the front door he went white. I told him about my special support force. He looked about anxiously and shouted to a huge policeman in the phalanx of police and told him to select half a dozen especially big policemen out of the ranks to form an outer layer of guards. By this stage the mob were spread right across Queen Street.

Back inside and another appeal to Muldoon for a rear escape, and another public mocking of me.

I gathered my force and set out with Rob in the middle. The funny thing was that in all this carry-on it never occurred to any of us to actually enquire about Rob's car arrangements, which in the event were non-existent.

When we arrived at the double-door exit all we could see were policemen hefting, arms linked against the heaving crowd. We passed through with all the military strategy of a eunuch, heading to a non-existent escape vehicle. The police broke ranks to force a path; the crowd pushed forward and, aware that at long last after a wait of some hours, Rob had emerged, went absolutely hysterical. Chants of 'Heil Hitler' rent the air.

I had presented Rob with a boxed set of Verdi opera records as a guest-speaker gift and he was gripping these under his arm. We stumbled forward, awash in policemen shoved against us, my small force of

*Robert Muldoon . . . 'a politician to be both feared and loathed . . .'*

protectors now rendered almost impotent by the sheer weight of numbers against us. Onwards we joltingly continued and might just possibly have made it if there had been an 'it' to make, had a woman not thrown herself on a policeman and tried to wrestle his helmet off his head. Simultaneously the policeman was hit by a flour bomb. The silly bugger released his arm-link with his colleagues as he tried to arrest the protester. The dam was broken, through poured the crowd and it was all on.

One could hit or be hit. We lashed out, punches raining in all directions. People on both sides hit the deck; the night was rent with shouts as bodies and flour bombs flew in all directions. Muldoon, fiercely gripping his presentation records, threw punches with his other hand, and neat little hooks they were too. He was shouting. 'One at a time and you're welcome.' I saw him bowl a few over, although, typical of this type, a swag of women filed formal complaints the next day, insisting he had punched them. I was there alongside him and so were the police, and he did not. Ultimately their complaints were ignored, except needless to say by the news media. The police managed to arrest ten of the worst culprits.

Oddly enough, once the police ranks were broken and the mob was upon us, we actually made progress—or it would have been progress if we were going anywhere meaningful, which we were not. For no particular reason the goal became to cross Queen Street and the protesters' objective to prevent us doing so. Such is the nature of such nonsense. And so the battle raged, people were felled, the noise was horrendous, but after a few minutes we had 'progressed' to the middle of Queen Street and were beginning to prevail. Suddenly a pattern emerged: we began to win despite a flour bomb finding its target on Muldoon. The problem was we had no battle plan and had simply assumed there would be a car for Rob.

It was a fine clear night and at that point, about 10.30 p.m. as things slowly swung our way, a funny thing happened.

The Peter Pan Cabaret was near the top of Queen Street and looking about for Muldoon's government limousine, I spotted a large black saloon car turn slowly from Karangahape Road and head down Queen Street towards us. 'Here's Muldoon's car,' I shouted to the police and they turned their attention to the brawling bodies on the street's upper side so as to allow access.

Slowly the car approached and then, as it reached the seething mob, of necessity it stopped.

I grabbed Muldoon, tugged him towards the back door, pulled it open and shoved him in. A policeman climbed in after him, then another and another as Muldoon slid across the back seat to make room.

Then, horrors: the driver turned to look at his passengers, his face aghast. He looked like some black-suited Brethren-type churchgoer, quietly on his way home, or at least that was his intention. We all instantly realised the mistake. What then occurred was a classic Keystone Cops situation, bearing in mind all this happened very quickly.

Muldoon, realising it was not his car, but saying nothing, wrenched open the far side door and stumbled out; the cop next to him followed then the next one and another and a stream of at least eight policemen poured into the back seat and shuffled across and out the other door to surround Rob. I thought it all so hilarious I went through as well for the hell of it.

The wide-eyed driver gazed open-mouthed in disbelief. Meanwhile the mob had regained the ascendancy. Some followed the police procession across the back seat, while others climbed on to the car's long bonnet and began jumping up and down. There was a failed attempt to tip it over. I was all but hysterical with laughter, then to top it a policeman roared at the speechless driver: 'Listen, you bastard, I'll arrest you for trouble-making, get the hell out of here.' The last I saw of this car was it moving slowly off down Queen Street, still adorned with protesters.

Muldoon's car finally emerged and he was off in safety.

*The occasion marked the inaugural meeting of the newly formed Property Investors' Association, a meeting attended by about 500 landlords. Bob Jones observed that as much as anything, this single incident was to mould the rising 'Muldoon image as a stop-at-nothing politician to be both feared and loathed by political foes in the years ahead'.*

## Milan Brych Unmasked                Auckland, 1974

Kevin Ryan

I presented to the commissioner some impressive witnesses. There was the sub-matron of the Mater hospital in Auckland whose case had been written off as hopeless but she was back at work after a course of Brych's treatment. There was also a Father McKendry, who, when his pain had gone, was inspired to write a contest-winning song in praise of Brych. Both have since died of cancer.

The inquiry listened to evidence from the parents of children who, it was claimed, had been cured of cancer. The most touching testimony came from the little girl who performed a Scottish jig on stage. Until Brych treated her, she had been a hopeless invalid. Now she was bright and beautiful again.

Brych had treated hundreds of patients, yet nobody knew what treatment he was giving. The inquiry was supposed to clarify this, yet the longer it continued, the more confused I became about the treatment.

I began to have misgivings about Brych. During the inquiry, he pointed out to me a sinister-looking gentleman. 'That man has been sent here by the mafia to kill me if I disclose the secret formula,' he told me.

Brych did not realise that I knew the man. He was definitely not a Sicilian hitman. He was, in fact, a New Zealander of Lebanese descent. His only reason for being at the town hall was because he had throat cancer.

During the hearing, Brych also introduced me to an attractive blonde woman. He explained that she was his associate. When she was out of earshot, he added, 'She, Mr Ryan, is my colleague from the clinic in Helsinki.'

I was incredulous. I knew her as Mrs G——Before she had married, she had been a student nurse at the Mater hospital. Long before my own marriage, I had even escorted her to social functions.

The pair must have discussed it because Brych came back to me later and tried to explain. But it was too late. I was beginning to wonder what I was becoming involved in . . .

I noticed that Brych would tell outrageous stories while radiating a beatific smile, which would then be followed by sweeping denunciations and alarming accusations. He told me the Vatican wanted his cure because the Pope had cancer. He also claimed to have treated Emil Zatopek, the Czechoslovakian Olympic gold medallist.

On another occasion, he told me that two attorneys were arriving from West Germany to purchase his formula. He would bring them to my house and I was to draw up a contract. Could I advise him? Should he accept a single capital sum of $5 million or a sum of $2 million with a royalty of 5% of all sales?

I never met the attorneys.

Mirek Cvigr, the Czech who had helped Brych on his arrival in New Zealand, told me another Brych whopper. Cvigr was waiting with a Czech couple for Brych to arrive for a lunch date. As usual, Brych was late. When he finally arrived, Brych's excuse was that he had attended a luncheon given by the Auckland Medical Society in honour of Professor Christian Barnard, who was visiting the country. His conversation with the famous South African heart surgeon had proved to be of such mutual fascination that he had been unable to drag himself away.

But Professor Barnard had not attended the medical luncheon, his hosts informed Brych. According to the radio report they had heard while waiting for him, Dr Barnard had been delayed so long at Rotorua he had travelled directly to the airport.

Without the slightest embarrassment, Brych changed the subject . . .

. . . I decided it was time for a showdown with Brych. I phoned him and asked him to visit my house. When he arrived he chain-smoked so nervously that afterwards one of my young sons asked, 'Why does the cancer man smoke so much?'

I asked him to confirm the year he graduated from Masaryk University.

'1962 . . . no . . . 1964. Ha, Ha, Ha,' he laughed nervously. 'I thought it added up to 1962.'

'Are you sure about it now?'

'Yes, it was 1964.'

'In 1964, there was no such university in Brno. In 1948, the communist regime altered the name of Masaryk University to Purkyne University.'

I asked Brych about his 'extra medical degree' from Charles University in Prague as I knew this university had never had a medical faculty but offered courses in the humanities, history and the social sciences.

'You do not trust me?'

'Just answer the question.'

He could not so I added that in 1948 Charles University had had its name changed to Central University of Prague.

'I've got something else for you too,' I said as he sat there in silence. 'Your photograph was shown to the commandant of the police station in Brno and he recognised you immediately. He said he locked you up himself and that you had received a four-year prison sentence for attacking a woman. While you were in prison, you undertook a course to be a lab. technician . . . '

'That is all communist propaganda,' he shouted.

*Milan Brych, a Czech living in Auckland, claimed to have cured scores of cancer sufferers with his new secret treatment. Hospital doctors, sceptical about Brych's credentials and treatment, set up a public inquiry. Kevin Ryan, a distinguished lawyer, defended Brych, but later denounced him. In 1977 Brych was struck off the New Zealand medical register but took his method to the Cook Islands, where he is thought to have made over a million dollars, and then to California, where he was exposed again as a charlatan and sentenced to six years' gaol, the judge describing him as a 'callous, devious human being'.*

## MAORI LAND MARCH                                     *1975*

## Donna Awatere Huata

John Rangihau proposed a land march from the northern-most point of the country to Wellington.

When it eventually happened it began as a very lonely affair. No Maori wanted to host us or join us. We had no encouragement. Far from it—we had been warned against provoking a Pakeha backlash, that we would wake the sleeping giant of the state. But a handful of us started out nonetheless with Whina Cooper at the head.

By the time we got to Warkworth the mood was changing; marae started to receive us and support us. And then suddenly they came in their thousands and then their tens of thousands. When we got to the Auckland Harbour Bridge there were so many of us, walking in time, that the bridge began to sway, and I was scared we would bring the whole thing down. As we marched to Wellington no marae was big enough to hold us. We walked for weeks, and the day we walked into Wellington we had a larger crowd than I had ever seen. The country was behind us.

*The 'Maori Renaissance' gathered momentum during the 1970s, led by such people as John Rangihau, Donna Awatere and Whina Cooper.*

## WELLINGTON MAYORAL CAMPAIGN
## LAUNCHED                                            *1977*

## Carmen

My campaign was now launched. I felt like a new ship having a bottle of champagne cracked over my breast-work. I was so proud, yet inside a little humble too. It was all so new to me and I was afraid that I might say the wrong thing or even get plain stage fright for the first time in my life. But that never happened and everything went so serenely.

I felt that my platform really represented me and my desire for radical social reform. I stood for:

*Carmen.*

Hotel bars open to midnight or even 2 am
The drinking age lowered to eighteen
Prostitution made legal
Nudity on some beaches
Abortion decriminalised
Homosexual acts decriminalised
Sex education in schools for fourteen-year-olds

My supporting committee produced policies on local transport and city government finance. I realised from the onset that when I became mayor I would have to rely heavily on trusted advisors. But then all holders of public office are in that position.

The *Dominion* newspaper of Monday 3 October 1977 featured a large full-face portrait of me topped with the caption 'CITIZENS FOR CARMEN'. Underneath the photo was printed 'CARMEN FOR MAYOR'. Then followed a 'We Believe' supported by the signatures of a number of people and businesses.

I had to accept the 'We Believe' as part of my supporters' overall strategy to win votes. Part of that strategy was to take the stodginess out of local politics. So I quote:

'1. That Carmen, by her visionary intellect, her achievements in many diverse fields, her obvious capabilities and broad physical appeal, stands out above all the other candidates for this important public office.

'2. In this sexist age only Carmen can provide universal appeal and avoid a tragically divisive, sexist alienation entering into public life and the community.

'3. That Carmen has displayed in her announced Transport and Town Hall financing policies, a necessary comprehensive cognisance of sophisticated financial matters appropriate to the management of our city, this stemming from her wide commercial experience and being an ability clearly lacking in the other candidates.

'4. That a Carmen mayoralty is not merely feasible but will brighten all of our lives, compensating for the deplorable weather introduced during the present mayor's term.

'5. That Mayor Fowler must go, no one can seriously consider Sir Francis, and Mr Blunt is boring. We implore all voters to get in behind and make Wellington New Zealand's real queen city.'

Then followed: 'The undersigned fifty citizens, randomly selected from a pool of 250 offered, comprise a broad range of backgrounds including lawyers, scientists, financiers, publishers, editors, farmers, quantity surveyors, strippers, artists, TV personalities, etc. . . .

*Carmen (Trevor Rupe), a flamboyant stripper, exotique dancer, Maori Princess, drag queen and businesswoman* (Carmen's International Coffee Lounge), *stood for Mayor of Wellington and polled 6000 votes. Another thousand and she would have had a seat on the city council. 'Not bad for a beginner,' she thought.*

---

## Data Entry Error                    *Auckland, 1978*

Brian Hewitt

In about July/August 1978 I prepared on work sheets the data necessary to produce a computer flight plan for our Antarctic flights.

McMurdo was defined on the work sheet with co-ordinates latitude 77° 53.0'S, longitude 166° 48.0'E. These co-ordinates were for Williams Field as used in my original study. Whilst typing the information from the ALPHA work sheet into the VDU I inadvertently typed the longitude of McMurdo as 164° 48'E rather than 166° 48.0'E. It was standard practice to check the figures displayed on the VDU against the work sheet which I did but, in this case, I did not detect my error. Once this check was complete the data was entered into the relevant computer file to await entry into the test programmes . . . Since everything appeared to be in order, the data stored in the test programmes was then transferred into the 'live' computer flight planning system at Newton.

*Brian Hewitt was chief navigator for Air New Zealand. The changed flight path brought the aircraft directly in line with Mount Erebus. The erroneous recording of co-ordinates was part of a chain of events which led to the sightseeing airliner crashing into the mountain, killing all 257 people on board instantly.*

## MR ASIA RUMBLED                              *Auckland, 1978–79*
## Pat Booth

*16 August.* It had been a big day, one I had been looking forward to and working towards for months—8.30 p.m. and I was at home relaxing, the front page with the big headlines spread on the floor in front of my chair: 'A two-year investigation aimed at smashing New Zealand's biggest drug syndicate has come unstuck because two men have refused to testify against the ring's Mr Big. The syndicate leader, an Aucklander living in Asia, is wanted by Australian police who say he's that country's biggest importer of drugs—and he's being investigated by America's Drug Enforcement Agency. The *Star* knows his name and address and has a dossier on him.

'The men who refused to go into the witness box worked for the Aucklander's ring which is estimated to have imported $20 million worth of drugs into New Zealand since 1976. The ring is also responsible for several large heroin shipments to Australia—one of which involved nine drums of the drug . . .

'A *Star* investigation into the syndicate's dealings has revealed it to be the major link between drug manufacturers in Asia and local distribution networks. The Asian connection operates under the cover of an Asian-based company and an Auckland company with central city offices. The *Star* knows the address and details of these companies. The ringleader, whom we will call "Mr Asia", the most powerful force in New Zealand's growing drug market, continues to live in Asia, a free man.

'But, after months of investigation, the *Star* has a dossier of never-before published facts—profiles of Mr Asia, top drug dealers in the North and South Islands, details of their operations, how they use guns, and threats and money to stay at the top, how much money there is at stake and who gets it.'

That exposé—that's a media cliché but there is no other word for it—took only six hours to get a reaction.

The woman's voice on the other end of the phone was educated, anonymous and pressing. 'I am concerned about this Mr Asia drug syndicate story on the front page of the *Auckland Star* tonight. I think I know who you are talking about.'

For what the company thought were good legal reasons—a view I didn't share—we had not named who we were talking about. We simply said that a young Aucklander, a one-time Queen Street shop assistant, now in Singapore, was fronting an international drug syndicate operating in and out of New Zealand. We knew him to be Marty Johnstone, but gave him that legally safe label, 'Mr Asia'. The insistent voice went on. 'Well, I think you are talking about Martin Johnstone. If you are, I have to tell you, Mr Booth, you have made a serious error of professional and personal judgement. I'm telling you now, Martin will not be pleased.'

I had never believed, I said calmly, that the person we are writing about would be pleased.

And she replied, 'Well, I think you should know. Martin is not going to like it.'

*A year later, November, 1979.* British police retrieved a body from a disused quarry pit. The man, who had been shot, and had his hands chopped off, was identified as a New Zealander called Martin Johnstone, resident in Singapore. Later, his closest associate in the syndicate, the undoubted hit man of the group, Terry Clark, was convicted of murder. Johnstone was the sixth victim to be killed by Clarke or on his instructions in the 18 months we had been investigating the syndicate.

In Johnstone's luggage when it was found and searched was a plastic bag of newspaper clippings from the *Auckland Star*—the Mr Asia series.

*Campaigning investigative journalist and editor-in-chief of the* Auckland Star, *Pat Booth, reports on his unmasking of 'Mr Asia'. Booth later copped some flak for inventing and using this name—a group of Asian citizens in Auckland found the sobriquet offensive.*

## NEW YEAR'S EVE PARTY     *Palmerston North, 1980*

## Tom Scott

This New Year's Eve I sat around with friends worrying about the National Development Bill, the rice crop in Indo-China and mercury levels in fish. Ten years before to the day, things were very different. Encounters with the opposite sex had been brief awkward affairs, and women were as mysterious to me as the inside of a thermal power station.

Nevertheless optimism ran high and blood vessels that would later be rendered toxaemic with cheap sweet cider fairly bristled with testosterone. My old mate Dreadon and I, trailing Old Spice, hurtled towards Palmerston North—citadel of infinite promise and sensual delight, each privately hoping that tonight would be the night. As the Mini was Brian's he naturally had a better chance, but to make absolutely sure he wore a top hat and tails, a black velvet bow-tie and spats. The kid was a knockout.

Me, I favoured my trusty green corduroys, ripple-sole brothelcreepers, and olive-green Borthwick's freezer jersey. I relied heavily on my native wit and chicks digging the inner man rather than being distracted by mere physical appeal.

We checked out several parties and finally settled on one in Main Street where there were more ladies than jokers, which at least gave you a range of rejections. Things were progressing nicely until a herd of shearers and fencing contractors from up Apiti way burst in, hell-bent on smashing in university students' skulls. Dreadon and I skillfully decamped, only to find our path to the car blocked by even bigger guys who for some reason thought that Dreadon's attire was offensive. They dutifully and colourfully told him so.

To his credit Dreadon remained silent and impassive. I bounded up and explained that he was a deaf mute. The head man suddenly softened. Stricken with guilt, his eyes moist, he put his face close to Dreadon's and said very slowly, enunciating clearly, 'Sorry mate. We didn't know. Do you understand me? Sorry mate, no hard feelings.'

Dreadon stared back unblinking, then walked wordlessly to his Mini. I followed suit, but without his considerable dignity, and spoilt it by bursting into raucous laughter at the last minute. Within seconds I was surrounded with no chance of escape.

They pushed me, prodded me, stamped on my brown suede shoes, threatened to smash my glasses and move my nose to another part of my face, and generally indicated that I was a smart-arse who needed to be taught several lessons all at once. Dreadon hissed at me from the Mini to get in but I couldn't, at least not without running the risk of leaving certain choice parts of me behind.

'I hope you chaps appreciate that I am a haemophiliac,' I said as calmly as I could.

'So what!' said one of their number. 'We know all you varsity creeps are a bit that way!'

'A haemophiliac,' I reasoned, 'is a person deficient in one or more crucial clotting factors. The slightest blow causes a wound which bleeds continually.'

'Don't argue with him, Snow,' screamed a voice in the dark. 'Punch his bloody face in.'

'One punch,' I continued, cold sweat streaming down my armpits, 'would result in you being up on a manslaughter, possibly a murder charge!'

They drew back momentarily and I scrambled into the car as they surged forward again. Dreadon accelerated away as they rained blows on the windows and roof. It was quite the best New Year's Eve party I have been to, and nothing these past 10 years has come near it.

---

## FLYING TO WELLINGTON                                    *1981*

## John Banks

I arrived in Auckland feeling very good about myself and looking forward to changing the world in my first pair of brogue shoes. There was little I could be taught about politics because I knew it all. I proposed to leave my mark from day one, although there was a slight delay in the strategy when I arrived at Auckland International Airport, and wasn't recognised by anyone. The woman at the counter advised that Members of Parliament could choose their seats and, while I was negotiating a suitable place in the airplane, I saw the daunting figure of Mr Muldoon hunched over his famous briefcase (which I now own after buying it at a charity auction). I said to the woman, 'I'll sit anywhere on the aeroplane as long as it's not next to Mr Muldoon.' 'Oh,' she said, 'that's not a problem.'

I got onto the plane and to my absolute horror Robert Muldoon was sitting in seat 3A and I was placed in seat 3B. 3C significantly was empty. But there I was—very nervous. Getting into the plane I said, 'Good morning Mr Muldoon.' He was reading the paper and took absolutely no notice. I stored my briefcase, sat down. The next ten minutes till the plane took off seemed like an eternity. I said, 'Good morning, Prime Minister,' again, knowing that it was pretty rude not to say good morning. We took off, he was still reading the newspaper, he had a happy pastime of grunting, snorting and chewing his fingernails at the same time as he would read the *Herald* cover to cover on a Monday morning going to Wellington. This day was no different.

About New Plymouth, when I had become deeply anxious about the situation, worried that he might think I was rude and maybe he didn't hear me, I pulled down the newspaper and said 'Good morning Mr Muldoon,' to which he snapped back, 'I heard you the first time.' I thought that if every Monday morning was like this, with me stuck beside this bloke, my political career was not going to go very far, very quickly. We landed and I fled the aeroplane.

*John Banks, newly elected Member of Parliament for Whangarei, flies to his new job.*

## PROTESTING THE SPRINGBOK TOUR                    *1981*

## Sonja Davies

By this time, the Wellington game of the tour was fast approaching. I was by now quite skilled at padding my chest and shoulders and on the day of the match, I set out wearing Mark's crash helmet from Rangipo as well, with a real sense of foreboding. I always left my car in the union carpark where it would be safe, and walked to where the squad was gathering. This time we were not told where we were going, only that we should watch the marshalls closely. I must say that with my limited lung power, I found climbing up the steep hill of the Town Belt rather taxing. We came out of the trees and saw below us McAllister Park, opposite

Athletic Park where the game was to be played. By now the police had coopted the army, who had set huge piles of barbed wire in place on the edge of the park to stop us getting over to Athletic Park. The marshalls had had a tipoff about this and had provided large grappling hooks for us to demolish the barbed wire; and a number of protesters clawed at the wire with these.

Graham's squad was in Rintoul Street where the plan was to block access by rugby enthusiasts to the game. They sat down in a solid mass so they couldn't be pushed aside and police waded in with batons. Some people were pushed through a plate glass window. Things were becoming very fraught. At that time the press reported that their polls told them that 52 per cent opposed the tour and 48 per cent were in favour. This was later amended to 60/40, which gives some idea of the situation.

By then the game was in progress. Onto McAllister Park came police in full riot gear—metal helmets, long thick navy overcoats, riot shields and long batons. The protesters were now assembled in several rows right across the park and the police positioned themselves in front of us, eyeball to eyeball so to speak, although they stared straight ahead. It had rained during the night and my shoes sank into the turf. I hoped I wasn't going to have to leave in a hurry. Next to me was a Chilean refugee friend, Victor, who had come to New Zealand to escape the excesses of the Pinochet regime. Remembering that in Chile, thousands had been murdered in and around stadiums, I said to him, 'Do you have a sense of déjà vu?' and he said that he did, but of course in Chile one would be taken round the back of the stadium and shot.

It was a tense encounter. Ken Douglas appeared. He said, 'Go home,

Sonja, you've made your point. You'll get hurt.' I looked along the line and saw Joanna Kelly, Graham and Jeanette's daughter, and I knew I couldn't leave. Not long before the match ended, the police decided that, in order to avoid a major after-match confrontation, they would move us out and off down the road. The Springboks had spent the night under the stadium at Athletic Park and feelings were running high. We finally hit the road and started back to town. On the way we passed a pub where rugby fans who hadn't been able to get into the park had been watching the match on television. They poured out of the pub and assailed us, threw beer cans, and a young Maori spat in my face. Someone saw a man he knew behind me and lashed out with a punch. Unfortunately he missed and punched me very hard, catching me below my padding.

*Sonja Davies, 58-year-old Vice President of the Federation of Labour, actively embraced many causes, including the protest against the 1981 tour of the Springbok rugby team which was seen as an acceptance by the New Zealand Government of the apartheid policy of South Africa. This sporting event divided families, workmates and friends up and down the country. The punch thrown outside the pub broke three of Sonja's ribs and cracked two others. Six years after the tour, Sonja Davies was elected Labour Member of Parliament for Pencarrow.*

## Confronting the Anti-Apartheid Protestors
*Auckland, 1981*

## Ross Meurant

Every muscle and fibre was taut and alive. The adrenalin was screaming through our bodies. Our will was almost overpowering. All the training, all the planning now came into focus. We had been involved in other confrontations on tour and each of those in their place had been demanding and vital at that point of time. But this final showdown was the battle that had to be fought. Those opposing us were the protestors that had chosen of their own free will to take the police head-on.

Amongst those opposing us we could identify every description of thug, criminal, anarchist and radical. We would not ruin our impressive track record for the tour by going on an orgy of retribution and violence. But we would, in a disciplined, professional and positive manner,

*' . . . we would, in a disciplined, professional and positive manner, maintain the rule of law . . . '*

maintain the rule of law and defeat those who sought to bring anarchy to the streets.

The effect of our advance was greater than we could have dreamed of. The protestors were paranoid about us at the best of times but the sight of us advancing on them with precision and determination caused pandemonium to break out within their lines. At first we were pelted with rocks, bottles, cans and several incendiary devices, two of which had to be extinguished. The Squad smashed its way through what had seemed an impenetrable wall of shields and was, for a few moments, forced to baton down on those in front of them to stop the momentum of the mob. But within minutes the superior fortitude of the few overcame the brute force of the many and the tide began to turn with the relentlessness of our advance, shattering the resolve of the mob and precipitating their retreat.

During the penultimate advance made along Onslow Road, Constable Lewis, of Squad 1, went down and stayed down with a broken ankle. As he lay in agony on the footpath the rest of the squad were committed to holding the ground until an ambulance could be called to take the constable away. He had fallen some 20 metres short of the intersection with Dominion Road, just below the rock fenceline which was the source of much of the protestors' arsenal, and it was an uncomfortable five or so minutes we spent waiting for the ambulance. After Constable Lewis had been taken off we regrouped some 100 metres from the intersection but were physically exhausted and badly bruised. Then, like a present from heaven, Squad 3 came trotting up the street behind us. They were a pleasing sight.

The final advance of the day up Onslow Road was made by Squad

3. When it arrived on the scene Phil, Mark and I conferred briefly on tactics. While we were discussing the issue some of the mob began tipping over a car (mufti police vehicle as it turned out) which had been parked in Onslow Road near the intersection with Dominion Road. When we realised that some were endeavouring to set fire to spilt petrol we were compelled to take immediate action, for an explosion of that nature would have injured many and only inflamed the passions of the mob.

Mark, Phil and I conferred briefly. We reckoned we could take what was left of them—about 700, and finish the thing off.

When Squad 1 began its final advance down Dominion Road behind the protestors they were not noticed until it was almost upon the mob, so intent was it in pelting Squad 3 and Black Squad with missiles and abuse. When the protestors did see Squad 1 there was sheer panic. The protestors just did not know what to do or where to go. They were like a herd of springboks, fleeing from hunting lions. Some jumped over fences, some crashed through hedges, some ran blindly and some just froze. And some still wanted to fight.

As we walked onto the protestors our objective was to break them up—to destroy their cohesion and effect. Those who ran and scattered we left, but those who stood their ground, bringing their arsenal to bear on us, got their just desserts. With PR 24's at the ready we walked right into the mob and batoned all who tried to continue the fight. Soon we joined up with Squad 3. The protestors around us now gave up. It was over, and they realised it. We had won and they knew it. Some of the mob who had fled behind nearby houses reappeared momentarily to assail us with missiles once again but were put to flight with one or two sorties in their direction by Squad personnel. Then one of their leaders came forward to negotiate a peace. And at that point Red Squad withdrew. Other police were arriving on the scene who could quite capably deal with any pockets of resistance which flared up, while out of nowhere appeared enough 'brass' to handle an international armistice. Our job was done and we quietly slipped away.

*Anticipating protest against South African apartheid policy, the New Zealand government allocated $2.7 million for police to ensure the unimpeded success of the 1981 Springbok rugby tour. Thirty-two-year-old Ross Meurant was second-in-command of the police riot team known as the Red Squad. He reports here on the final confrontation of the tour. Six years later Meurant was elected National Member of Parliament for Hobson.*

## TURNING POINT                    *Christchurch, 1985*

## Zita Edmunds

The first day I came here to the house, when I came in the front door—
well, I didn't know whether to cry or laugh, or what to do. I'd never felt
so alone or out of place in my life. I didn't know what was going to
happen to me. The matron came and we talked and had a drink, and
then the matron said, 'I think you'll be happy here.' I said, 'Have I been
accepted?' 'Oh yes,' she said and took me in to show me the bed—and
she introduced me to the two ladies that shared the room. That was my
first look at the place. It all seemed so—so different. I felt like an intruder,
and I thought, I'm not going to be able to do it. That night I was very
upset and I cried and wondered to myself how I could go on. You see, I
just felt that all the life I'd once had was gone.

I suppose in that first week I gave them quite a bit of trouble. When
they gave me my first meal I had to leave some of the food. I didn't
actually refuse the food, but there was too much of it. I couldn't eat it. I
was so tensed up I was sick. Sick to the point of vomiting. I tried to sit in
the sun room—a lot of them were in there talking, but all I could think
was, I can't stay here. I'm not going to be able to settle in. I went up to
the lounge, and there were all these chairs. I didn't know if any particular
chair was for me; I just sat down. And then the matron came in and
said to me 'Are you alright?' I said, 'I think so,' and then I started to
shake. So she said 'Would you like to go and lie down?' Well, I came and
lay down, and I thought to myself, I don't think I can settle in here—I
don't care if I die now.

Later that night I lay on the bed, and my lip was trembling and
carrying on, but I thought to myself, it's no use crying, there's no one
here to sympathize with you. Then all through the night I kept wanting
to get up to go to the toilet. Five times I went out. It seemed so stupid,
but that's what I was doing. In the morning I woke very early. One of
the women had a light on in the room, and I wondered if something
was the matter. I didn't know what was happening, and I thought what
will I do? Will I get up? Will I get dressed? In the end I just lay there, still
shaking and shivering . . . and when some breakfast was brought to me
I couldn't eat it. She said 'Oh go on, you've got to eat.' So I had some
Weetbix, and I was sick again. I just brought it up. I was so unhappy.

And later there was something else—I had to be showered. I had to get undressed in front of somebody I didn't know. It's hard to explain, but getting undressed—there's nothing more undignified than an old person's body, and getting undressed in front of somebody I didn't know, I felt embarrassed. Of course you don't think about it now, but then it was my first time, my first experience, and it felt horrible. At the hospital I said I would accept this place, but I thought then I could never do what I'd said. I would never accept this place. Then I was wishing I had died in the hospital. I really meant that.

I looked out the window and I thought, if only I could just walk out of here. Just go and get right away from it all. But I couldn't. Anyway when Myrna came I felt a little better seeing her. She was most understanding. She said, 'Oh Nana, it will take a while.' I said 'No, Myrna, I don't think I am going to be able to settle in.' But she said, 'Look what you did for yourself up at the hospital—you'll settle in.' And the thing is that as time went on, I did start to settle in. Of course you get moments when you think, this is no good, this is the end. But slowly I got more confidence, and I could talk more to the other ladies, perhaps about the television and things like that. Oh yes, I was starting to come round. Then one night as I got into bed I said, 'Look, Zita, it's no use going on like this, this has got to be your home, perhaps for the rest of your life, so accept it and make the best of it.' I thought again about what I had said to the doctor at the hospital, how I was going to make the most of it, and I thought well, that's what I will do. I will just go according to the rules, and I will make the most of it. That's what I've done, and I don't think I've looked back since. I'm not going to say I'm a hundred per cent happy: no, I wouldn't say I was satisfied, that's not the word for it but I am contented, if you know what I mean.

*At 85 years old, Zita Edmunds, who had spent a busy life in New Zealand and Britain, experienced occasional blackouts and falls. After a spell in hospital she was accepted into a 'rest home'.*

## THE OXFORD DEBATE                                             *1985*

# David Lange

I drove to Oxford with my old friend Joe Walding, our new High Commissioner, but not even his comforting presence made me feel less tense. Our arrival was disrupted by an anonymous caller who announced that he had placed a bomb in the Randolph Hotel where we were staying. The Thames Valley police arrived with a bomb dog. After a while the Randolph Hotel was pronounced free of any peril greater than woodworm. None of this helped. I fidgeted through the afternoon.

Evening arrived and I strapped myself into my dinner suit. The Union building was jammed with people. On the way to supper, a Japanese television crew showed extraordinary self-confidence and unconcern for others by walking backwards in front of the official party up a winding staircase. The old debating chamber had a church hall feel to it. The audience filled the body of the room and the galleries above it.

The debate, when it finally started late in the evening, took the form of a series of set-piece speeches. On each side, as well as the two principal speakers, were student debaters and a British member of Parliament, Labour on my side, Conservative on Falwell's. Both the latter were engaging speakers. The Tory, I must say, won my heart when he began his speech by saying hullo to his auntie in Onehunga, just up the road from where I lived. Speakers from each side followed one another in turn, the affirmative, my side, going first. Members of the audience were entitled at any time to interrupt and ask whoever was speaking to give way. The speaker might then, if he or she so chose, allow the interrupter to hold the floor. This happened frequently. All the while the audience simmered and surged, now rippling with applause, now murmuring their agreement, sometimes hissing, sometimes jeering.

Once we got going, I knew it would be all right. Oxford was a conservative university, and a victory for the affirmative side in the voting afterwards was by no means certain, but a large part of the audience obviously felt warmly towards New Zealand. They applauded vigorously before I'd said a word. The moment in the debate that stuck in most people's minds afterwards was entirely unscripted. I gave the floor to a young American, who was, I later learned, a Rhodes Scholar from the US Naval Academy. He certainly had a military bearing. He asked me, in

view of New Zealand's decision to ban nuclear ships, how I could justify our membership of ANZUS. I said I'd give him the answer if he'd hold his breath a moment. 'I can smell the uranium on your breath,' I added. I heard later that they didn't like that at the Pentagon.

Falwell suffered more than I did from interruptions. He gave way to a young man who rewarded him by calling him the 'Reverend Ian Paisley of the sunbelt'. Falwell asked who Paisley was. 'The Ayatollah Khomeini of Northern Ireland,' came the reply.

Falwell spoke at length about the threat to civilised values posed by Soviet Russia. The fundamental aim of Russian communism was world domination and the West was justified in deploying nuclear weapons to deter Soviet aggression. He took up the point of other speakers on his side who argued that New Zealand was only allowed the freedom to disagree with its friends and allies because we were sheltering under the wing of the American deterrent. Falwell put it less pleasantly. He said, 'It is the moral code of the West to take care of those who cannot take care of themselves, or who don't wish to.'

For my part, I spoke about the essential irrationality of the arms race, which led to the greater and greater proliferation of weapons, even as the people who built them understood that they were daily adding to the risk of our total destruction. I got the warmest response when I referred to American efforts to make an example of New Zealand. We were being told by the United States that we could not decide for ourselves, but had to let others decide that for us. That, I said, was exactly the totalitarianism we were fighting against. The audience roared.

When the votes were counted, late in the night, the affirmative side won, 298 votes to 250. It mattered much more to me that I stood up for New Zealand and our nuclear-free policy and didn't fall over.

# THE EDGECUMBE EARTHQUAKE                     *2 March 1987*

## Bronwyn Joyce

It was the weekly cattle sale at Te Teko saleyards. The sale was half-way through and most of the small animals had been carted away. The auctioneers, stock agents, helpers and buyers walked and stood with amazing ease and agility on the narrow platforms around the tops of the cattle enclosure.

The stock stood motionless, like statues, hardly breathing, as if they were waiting for the 'starter's' gun.

And, as if at a given signal, they all started twitching, pushing, shoving, milling—they were determined to break out of captivity. 'What the hell's the matter with them all?' the agent shouted as they pushed against the rails and the gate and rocked the hefty platform he was standing on. The stockmen's dogs took off in all directions with the hair on their backs standing on end. They wouldn't be around if the stock did go berserk and break loose. It was worse than that, all hell broke loose.

The ground at the saleyards lifted at least six feet high in the air, leaving great cavities and fissures that a man could get lost in. It stayed up and shook like shaking a doormat. People were falling around on to the ground trying in vain to clutch at whatever was within their reach. They crawled and rolled and tried to lie flat on the ground but it kept opening up all around them and closing again.

Some men were clinging to the stock pens—they were being shaken like a rag doll in a puppy's mouth, their feet were swinging in the air.

Some of the stock agents had been thrown into the midst of the cattle in the enclosures. The concrete slabs under the pens had just about stood on end, the gates burst open. The cattle bolted and clambered through the broken gates stampeding over anything or anyone in their path. Then the ground and concrete slabs dropped back almost to the same position again, leaving only gaping cracks as evidence.

## SHARE MARKET CRASH                    *Auckland, October 1987*

### Olly Newland

As the soft morning light filtered through the curtains, I turned on the radio and lay half awake for the news. Bip, Bip, Bip. It was 6 o'clock.

'Here is the news. There has been a world-wide collapse of share prices. Starting in New York, the Dow Jones plunged 508 points, cutting 22% off the index. Trading in Hong Kong has been suspended for a week to protect the investors. The FTSE in London . . . '

Now I gulped into full awareness. This was it! This was the big one! I tried to hear what the announcer was saying but I suddenly seemed partially deaf.

Keep calm. It may be temporary. No, this is it! I have to get to the office. Man the battle-stations . . . it's going to be a rough day.

Into the garage, and start the car. I slide out into the traffic. Everything seems normal. What do I expect? Bodies falling off buildings?

Queen Street seems strangely quiet. I slip into the office early. The only other person there is Neville Lyne. He looks up from his desk questioningly:

'Heard the news Olly?'

'Of course I bloody have!'

'We won't be affected . . . we invest in buildings, not shares,' Neville says.

'The aftermath, Neville,' I retort. 'The aftermath.'

At 9.30 a.m. I walked as nonchalantly as I could up to the Stock Exchange. I wanted to see what the market did when it opened. What did greet me would remain forever in my memory.

A packed throng of onlookers was crowding into the public viewing area, more than I had ever seen before. With noses pressed to the sheet glass viewing window, they stood on tip toes or on brief cases. Some cases had already split. Nobody seemed to care. Binoculars were held in shaky hands.

All eyes were strained down to the floor of the exchange where the milling pool of brokers stood by their booths. Lights began to flash in rapid succession on the incoming calls board.

The market opened like the roar of a cannon. The steady hum of the operators' voices rapidly rose higher and higher until their shouts became clearly audible to those of us behind the glass looking on.

There was a momentary hesitation. Then the markets nosed straight down. 'Sell Brierley at $3.60! Sell Brierly at $3.30.' Brierley plunged in the opening moments from $4.20 to $3.10.

The noise became louder, the brokers more frenetic.

The bottom was dropping right out. Giant conglomerate and blue-chip Fletcher Industries crashed 90 cents within five minutes of trading. Now it was selling at $5.20, down from $6.10, and the end wasn't in sight.

The gap between buy and sell bids yawned wider and wider. Normally only a cent or two separated bids. Not now. Not in this sort of panic.

'Sell Equiticorp $2.80!'

'Buy Equiticorp $2.50!' 150,000 shares traded.

Brokers were now thrashing about in an ever-decreasing swirl of confusion and shouted orders. 'Buy!' 'Sell!' The sell orders were running ten to one against. With every sell order the market capitalisation slumped lower and lower. There seemed no stopping it.

Looking to the left and right of me, I saw a sea of white faces, mouths clamped tight, brows furrowed. This was even worse than my worst nightmares.

The roar from the trading floor grew even louder. The chalkies were flying up and down the catwalk writing up new quotes and then almost immediately wiping them off again as fresh and lower sale prices were recorded. Smoke from innumerable cigarettes made the air blue right across the floor of the exchange.

On the boards the scribblings of the chalkies became almost illegible as more and more numbers were hastily written only to be changed an instant later. Brokers were jumping and shouting, phones and paper waving in anxious hands. It was bedlam.

Suddenly the tone changed. People were looking and moving to one side. Strong lights switched on, casting strange double and treble shadows. Heavens above! The TV cameras had arrived.

The cold knot in my stomach squeezed tighter. I had to leave immediately. It would never do to be seen wringing my hands on national TV.

*Olly Newland founded the property investment firm, Landmark Corporation, in 1982.*

# The *Rose-Noëlle* Makes Land    *30 September 1990*

## John Glennie

That night we slept fitfully, the atmosphere below tense, wondering what the morning would bring. Then there was the welcome sight of lush green bush, the white outline of breaking waves on Great Barrier's coastline and a northeasterly wind that was steadily pushing us towards the island. It was obvious that we were going to hit land that day and I scanned the horizon anxiously for fishermen or pleasure cruisers who might be in the area.

While the sea had been relatively calm offshore, the waves grew stronger and angrier as we approached land, and now they picked *Rose-Noëlle* up and pushed her towards those rocks. She hit with a sickening crunch; the waves lifted her firmly on to the reef and abandoned her, leaving the full weight of the upturned trimaran to grind itself over the remains of the mast and rigging.

I sat there shivering, weak and cold, while we waited for *Rose Noëlle* to drift closer to shore. Finally we hit rocks near the foot of the cliff and waited till the wreck could go no further. It was time to leave. We stumbled and clawed our way through the water until we reached dry land. We had made it.

The four of us staggered round the rocky headland, only to be confronted by another obstacle—15 metres of deep water which we had to swim through to reach the beach. Phil went first, and Rick, Jim and I followed. By the time my feet touched the ground I was exhausted and the others again had to lift me from the water. I lay on the beach as the water drained from my heavy clothes, waiting for my strength to return.

We walked and walked through the bush as the darkness closed in until we could no longer see where we were going and the whack of branches in our faces was the only indication that we were still upright. We stumbled over rocks and fern roots, sometimes on our hands and knees, until eventually we had to stop. We had no idea where we were going and very little strength to get there anyway. Were we going to die from exposure here in the bush after all we had been through? Where was the force, the being, the God who had watched over us so far?

*A huge wave overturned the trimaran* Rose-Noëlle *off Hawke's Bay. Given up for lost, her four crew floated helplessly for 119 days, sleeping in the upturned boat. The day following their beaching, the survivors stumbled across an empty holiday home with a telephone.*

## DIALLING 111, ARAMOANA  *13 November 1990*

## Darren Gibbs

Ops: Police emergency

DG: Yeah, hi. We have got a guy down here at Aramoana.

Ops: Yep.

DG: He's trying to shoot people.

Ops: Sorry?

DG: We have got a guy running around with a rifle shooting people. (At this time the operator put Gibbs on hold and alerted Sergeant Guthrie to the latest news.)

Ops: All right, now are you able to talk to me?

DG: Yes.

Ops: Right. What's your name?

DG: Ah, Gibbs, Darren.

Ops: Sorry, Gibbs?

DG: Yep.

Ops: Right Darren, what can you tell me that's happening?

DG: Well I'm not sure, it looks like there's . . .

Ops: Yep, can you just speak . . .

DG: Sorry. (The operator knew of other 111 calls and spoke to Sergeant Guthrie. 'We are taking triple ones at the moment. It looks like the real thing. Take it with caution.')

Ops: Are you there Darren?

DG: Yeah.

Ops: Right. Now you are at the back of the address are you?

DG: Ah, yeah, we are on the other side.

Ops: That's on fire? How far are you away from the address?'

DG: About 200 yards.

Ops: Now, can you see anybody at that address?

DG: No.

Ops: You can't. Okay, you saw the guy with the gun did you?

DG: I didn't see his face, I seen someone running up the back of the house.

Ops: He was running out the back of the house, with a gun?

DG: Yeah. My friends were going on about a guy with a gun and how they had been shot at.

Ops: All right. Your friend was shot at. So you don't know anybody who's been hit?

DG: Not that I can see. The ute sitting in front of the driveway, I can see something has hit the windscreen but it didn't break.

Ops: Yeah, okay, where's your friend at the moment?

DG: Ah, he's disappeared, he's out of here, he's gone.

Ops: Right, do you know the guy who has the rifle and has done the shooting?

DG: Yep, Gray.

Ops: A guy Gray?

DG: Yep. (The operator immediately told Sergeant Guthrie what Gibbs had said and now the sergeant knew exactly who he was looking for.)

Ops: Can you hear shots at the moment?

DG: No, they stopped a couple of minutes ago.

Ops: How many shots did you hear?

DG: I'm not sure, twenty?

Ops: They stopped how long ago? Before you rang up?

DG: Just as I rang you.

Ops: You don't know of anybody being hit though do you?

DG: No, I seen one hit the windscreen.

Ops: Yeah, no that's all right. We have got other people talking about that anyway and I just wondered what you had seen.

DG: No I didn't see anybody else, I got out of there real quick.

*Darren Gibbs was reporting on the early stages of a mass murder in the Otago seaside settlement of Aramoana. David Gray, a solitary young man fascinated by militaria, the Ninja mystique, Rambo-like survival, and with a cynical bitterness towards society, went berserk, shooting 13 neighbours ranging in age from 5 to 70 years and including a police sergeant. Twenty-two hours later, police shot a heavily-armed and still defiant Gray to death.*

## THE AMERICA'S CUP COMES TO NEW ZEALAND

*24 March 1995*

### Suzanne McFadden

Two hours into the 13-hour flight from Los Angeles to Auckland, almost all the Team New Zealand crew were spread across rows of seats fast asleep.

They had their regulation glass of champagne before boarding the chartered Air New Zealand flight, watched video footage of their historic America's Cup win, and then flaked out.

Most of them were still out when the Boeing 767—with the flight number NZ1032—flew over Rarotonga eight hours later.

Well before the crew took a bus from San Diego on Tuesday night and arrived at Los Angeles airport, they were tired. And they knew what was ahead of them at the other end of the flight—the most spectacular welcome home ever seen in New Zealand.

*The Auld Mug as depicted in 1893.*

A Maori dance group from Southern California, Te Manawa Maori, performed for the New Zealanders in the Los Angeles airport lounge, before the Auld Mug was wheeled on board and buckled into seat 10A.

Then another 150 passengers filed on board—crew members, Team New Zealand staff, families and media.

No champagne magnums were allowed on the plane because of the weight restrictions, but the airline crew made a special last-minute allowance for skipper Russell Coutts' golf clubs.

All the passengers were treated to business class service and special attention was given to Craig Monk, a grinder, who missed celebrating his 28th birthday on May 23—the day the crew lost in the change of time zones.

As the plane approached Auckland, it made a special flypast at 2500 ft—flying over the East Coast Bays, where the next America's Cup will be raced, over the Harbour Bridge and across West Auckland and then back to Howick.

*Suzanne McFadden, a* New Zealand Herald *reporter, flew home with the team. Later that day the team made their way through a storm of tickertape and 400,000 screaming, whistling, clapping fans cramming central Auckland streets.*

## FALLING INTO CAVE CREEK            *Westland, 28 April 1995*
### Stacy Mitchell

Having left the cars, I think it would have been a walk of approximately half an hour to the platform. When we got to the platform I walked straight on with everybody else. I found myself in front and towards the right-hand of the platform. There was only one person to my right and that was Paul Chisholm.

We were standing there and looking over the edge and could see a few trees and a few rocks but couldn't actually see the cave where the creek re-emerged. I remember looking over the edge to see how high it was. I estimated it to be about 25 metres and continued to talk to Paul Chisholm and to Jody Davis. He was standing to my right.

We would have been on the platform for about a minute before the incident. Suddenly I became aware of the fact that the platform was swaying a bit. There was a movement of some sort, I am not sure exactly what. The platform then suddenly began to tip forward. I can't say that it was a violent movement, but it was reasonably sudden. I don't think the platform fell straight away. It tipped first. It tipped right forward and would have certainly 45 degrees. I had my hand on the front rail and simply crouched down behind the rail. I recall thinking that if it was going to fall further, it would just rest on the ground directly in front and below.

Suddenly the platform just broke away and fell forward. It all happened very quickly. I can't state with certainty that I saw people fall over the front, but that seems likely . . .

I remember the platform falling and branches flicking against the front railing. The railings seemed to stay attached to the platform until I lost consciousness. I can't remember hitting the bottom. I first remember waking up lying on my right side, wedged between what I felt like two boulders. I was knocked out and I have no idea how long that was for. The only injuries that I suffered were a contusion on my lung, bruising round my kidney area and quite a lot of bruising generally down my right side.

*Stacy Mitchell was one of four Polytech students who survived the collapse of the viewing platform. Twelve students and a Department of Conservation officer were killed in the fall. Two surviving students gave evidence at an enquiry but two others were still too damaged to report on their experiences. A commission established that 'the platform was not constructed in accordance with sound building practice'.*

## BAITING THE FRENCH AT MURUROA ATOLL

*July 1995*

## Alice Richard Leney

I was the outboard mechanic on the *Rainbow Warrior* on both Mururoa trips in July and September 1995. I guess I'll start with the evening in July when we arrived off Mururoa. We had resupplied the *Vega* and changed some crew, and even though during resupply it was getting dark at the time, the French warships were starting to collect around us. We

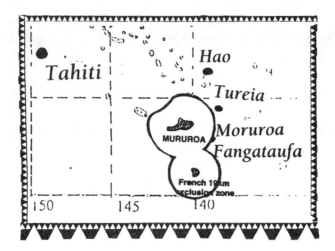

were 30 miles from Mururoa, but we hadn't reached the exclusion zone.

We'd done some testing of decoy devices that we'd made that were little home-made radar decoys, made up of old floats and bits of steel that looked like inflatables in the water on a radar screen. As it got dark, the famous fifth inflatable, with Hank Haazen, David McTaggart and Chris Robinson, slipped away. The French never even realised. About half an hour after they'd gone, we throw one of our decoy buoys over and then about another 20 minutes later we throw another one over and when the French see these on their radar they then have to go over and see what it is then it's hard for them to work out what it is in the water and this causes confusion among them. We had four of these things and we threw them periodically over the side until about 3.30 p.m., when we launched the other two inflatables. We had five inflatables altogether but one had slipped away with McTaggart earlier.

I was in one of those inflatables with Kate Leichi, who's a New Zealand woman, and the other inflatable had Todd Thompson, from the Bay of Islands, and Natisha, a French woman. We came away from the ship, the ship sailed on north. The French sent up a helicopter from one of these ships and tried to find us. They could see us on their radar but because we kept moving all the time, they couldn't actually pin us down. It looked like they were launching an inflatable. We could see boats hanging over the side but I don't think they actually launched them because it was dark and there was a swell. From what I've seen since, they're nothing like as used to going in little rubber boats as we are and we'd done an awful lot of training.

We followed the reef down until there was, like a bit of a nose, where the pass starts and we just shot around the nose. By this time the French warship, which was the one which had rammed the *Warrior*, was in the pass. We came round the corner, they saw us, they started to launch a boat. We were gone. We never saw them again. I didn't look back to see if the boat hit the water. We were into the lagoon, flat water, we were going. The whole purpose of our part of the role had been to draw the French warships off to allow the *Warrior* space to try and get in, which worked beautifully—they fell for it, hook, line and sinker.

So we were heading off across the lagoon. Right now the thing was to go for the drilling rig—we had lock boxes to chain ourselves on to it, in the boat, as part of the boat's equipment. There were two structures we could see quite clearly. It was hard to see if they were on land or in the water because they were both close to the land. We just took pot-chance and went for the left-hand one. Kate got the lock box out and swung it over my shoulder. I had it all set up with a rope through it— this is like a pike that you lock yourself into a bar in the middle.

We screamed up to this thing, and just as we came real close I realised you could drive a boat right in, right under the drilling rig itself. There was this walkway, a gantry sort of thing, walking across. So we just screamed in right under that. Kate jumped up, I sort of slow the boat up, she grabs the walkway, I jump up, climb up the framework and there was this workman's ladder that was tied up right at the end of the walkway. Where it ended I could just reach out and grab this other platform . . . this is about 20 feet off the ground . . . I swung myself over into there . . . At this point I see French legionnaires running up the deck, so I quickly pull down the lock box, slip it through the handrail and lock myself through the handrails on the drilling rig and sit down. Well, the French come screaming up . . . three or four of them came and then they started wrenching at my arms because they thought I was hanging on to my arm inside this pipe. Well, they pulled me round and I kept saying to them, 'I'm chained in it.' I've got a bit of French and I can tell them 'Whoa, Whoa,' and that I want someone who speaks English.

So they were wondering what to do and then they found another lock box very similar in another boat, so they then inspected this thing and it was like, 'Oh we see what's going on.' They cut the padding out of the end of the pipe and they pulled my arms as far as they could and then a guy got a long knife and cut through the velcro on my wrist and got my hand off, so it was end of story.

They carried me down, because we were non-violent protestors. They put us on a boat, they took us away to the gendarmerie on the atoll.

*Thirty-two boats, 11 from New Zealand, protested about French nuclear tests at Mururoa Atoll. The protestors may have had some effect for, 14 months later, the French Government signed the Comprehensive Test Ban Treaty.*

## THE GENERAL ELECTION                                    *1996*

### David Armstrong

Out of Levin I notice a well-built hitchhiker dressed in the classic White Trash uniform of white track shoes, black jeans and T-shirt, and wrap-around sunglasses—not to mention tatts on the biceps.

'G'day mate, name's Zak,' he says enthusiastically and gets in. He informs me he is on his way to Paraparaumu. 'It's a good place to pick up muff,' he says, 'especially young muff.'

It's going to be a long trip.

Zak informs me he's just finished his PD early. My hands stiffen around the steering wheel. I don't dare ask what he's doing the PD for, but when Zak is not chopping gorse he's a solo dad with two girls.

'Their mother drinks too much—she's an alcoholic. It'd break my heart, but we'd go to the pub together, she'd get drunk and start chatting up some pretty young boy, and I'd know she was going to go home and root him,' says Zak.

I'm fascinated, but don't know exactly how far I should delve into the personal life of Zak.

'If you were in a bad relationship it's probably best that you're bringing your kids up alone.' I stammer.

'Oath,' agrees Zak, 'that's what the bloke at Anger Management said.'

Oh fuck, I'm giving a lift to Woody Harrelson in *Natural Born Killers*.

'He said, if a woman causes you to feel bad and beat her up, you're better off without her.'

'I agree,' I squeak. 'Did you find anger management helped?' I ask, purely out of self-interest. I didn't want to fuck this guy off.

'Oath,' he says, 'it was bloody good. Now I just worry about myself, go to the gym every day and work on my body,' he explains, flexing his massive arms. 'Sure I take a few things to make my muscles develop better, but I'm doing well.'

'Good on you,' I say, trying not to let my voice shake too much. Fuck, steroids make one even more irrational than shock.

'Yep, I'm in bloody good shape now, not like after the stabbing.'

Oh shit.

I take a big deep breath and get the run-down on the stabbing—not to mention the wonderful help of the in-laws. Apparently even though Zak's wife was off with toyboys, her family have a lot of time for him.

'You know,' he tells me, 'her Dad turned up with fifty bucks the other day to buy presents for the girls, and I go and stay with them all the time. They say to me "You know Zak, our daughter was crazy to leave you".'

'That's really nice,' I reply and try to concentrate on the road.

'Same with her younger sister.'

Oh no, I feel another story coming on.

'It was amazing eh!' says Zak. 'I went to stay with her parents and I was in the sleepout and my wife's younger sister comes in while I'm watching *Shortland Street*. She asks if she can sit on the couch with me. "You know," she says, "I've always liked you, my sister was mad to give you up!" Well the next thing you know her and I start pashing on the couch. So I take her onto the bed, undress her and we go for it.'

'Sounds just like an episode of *Shortland Street*,' I quip.

Zak looks at me blankly. I wonder if he's about to knock my head off. He pauses, then lets out an enormous laugh, 'Yeah, I suppose it does,' he says, chuckling loudly. 'Afterwards I told her she was a much better root than her sister, and she was eh. Nice slim legs, my wife's let herself go to fat a bit eh.'

If I wasn't holding the steering wheel, both hands would be over my eyes. I can't believe this shit.

'Then she told me that when she came to visit us a few years ago with her boyfriend, he rooted my wife while I was out.'

We're nearing Waikanae. The White Trashfest will soon end, thank goodness. Zak will visit a nightclub and seek out some young muff and I'll be free to go home to my old muff.

Zak asks me to stop at a rest area where he can have a piss on the side of the road. I suggest we stop at a garage instead—'You know what the fucking pigs are like about dudes pissing in public,' I say, trying to sound tough by using his vernacular.

We chat about his daughters, who he obviously loves and does his best for. He's much happier with his domestic situation now.

'Yep, my wife and I are better off apart. There's no way I'm ever going back to her, the reconciliation was a waste of time,' declares Zak.

Reconciliation?

'We got back together for a short time last year, but it all broke up when I discovered I had contracted gonorrhoea from her,' reports Zak as I almost drive into a Shetland pony grazing a paddock at the Lindale Farm.

Just before we arrive at Paraparaumu, Zak asks me what I do. I tell him I'm writing a book about the election.

'Well,' he says, 'I've made my mind up. I'm voting for Helen Clark— the country needs a woman Prime Minister and I reckon Helen's great.'

So there you have it. If a wife-beating, muff-chasing, ex-bouncer on steroids is going to vote for Helen Clark, then surely she will be this country's next Prime Minister. And maybe Zak's right—perhaps we do need a bit of muff running the country?

We finally arrive at Paraparaumu and he graciously thanks me for the ride.

## AUCKLAND POWER CRISIS                    *February 1998*

## Maryanne Gardiner and Alan Mummery

*Maryanne*: To have a place down here opposite a commercial port overlooking the sea is so exciting. I'm at the stage in my life when I don't ever want to see another washing line or tricycle or dog in my garden again. In fact, I love having no garden.

We were at Piha having a nice little blot-out. When you live in an apartment you've got to have an escape. So we go out there and we don't watch television—we don't listen to radios—any kind of radios. So we hadn't read any newspapers on the weekend.

We came home on Sunday night, didn't watch the television news, so we didn't know what was going on. We found out from somebody ringing up and leaving a message on our answer phone—Would we like to stay with them?—What are you poor people doing? And we thought, what are they talking about?

And when we found out there really *was* a crisis—I mean we'd heard mention of it all week, Alan took it quite seriously but I just said, 'Oh come on we'll pretend we're camping. We love candles. We like reading to each other. We'll just stay here. We don't need power. We've got a view and the port of Auckland lights.' Alan said 'I think it's more serious than this.'

*Alan*: I explained that the water supply requires electric pumps to take the water to the head of the building and soon that water which feeds the building by gravity will run away and won't be replaced and the sewage system would stop.

*Maryanne*: But I just had another glass of wine and wouldn't listen to any of this. So we went to bed and about two o'clock in the morning I woke up and said to Alan 'This could be serious.' I then said, 'Let's do something now,' and got out of bed and cleaned the freezer. I'm not going to waste all this food! I also phoned some poor person in the orchestra. 'Could you tell me the code for the hall because I need to get in to put all my food in the freezer . . . '

At nearly 3.00 a.m. on Sunday we're driving up Symonds Street through to Mount Eden with a whole car full of frozen food.

*Alan*: Going there, was a police roadblock and they stopped and asked us where we'd come from and said, 'Thank you sir. That'll be fine. Where are you going?' There was someone wandering round with a very large microphone plus video camera. There was an awful smell and there was something on the road that looked like a squashed spleen. We were quite pleased to leave the area. We still don't know what it was . . .

*Maryanne*: So we deposited all our food and drove home again, thinking 'Shall we use the lift?' I'm saying, 'Life's too short to be stuck in a lift for four hours or all night—It would be too frightening and too hot. I want to go to my bed.'

Where will I put my car. If I can't get it out of the garage do I leave it in? Or, if I can't get it out, do I leave it in the street? Will it be done over by derelict downtown Auckland, which is pretty bad anyway. I mean the city's in a terrible state. There's a lineup of derelict buildings down here, we're in pre-Britomart territory.

*Alan*: Plus there is very little street cleaning going on down town. The lovely wind sculpture and pond underneath is empty and full of rubbish. Even such streets as High Street look as though they're never cleaned, so without power for a week it's a very bleak prospect of what the CBD of Auckland will be like.

*Maryanne*: You hear about people being stuck in lifts 34 floors up and Ooh six hours! There's a six hour delay to get out of lifts.

*Alan*: At one stage there were 48 lifts jammed with people in them, and by that time the delay for the rescue teams was mounting up to six hours for these poor people.

*Maryanne*: It's very hot. The height of summer. The humidity's revolting. I don't like the idea of being stuck in a lift at all.

*Alan*: The front doors of the building are normally closed and can only be opened with a swipe-card. With the doors permanently open the building no longer has security. Because no one'll know when the power goes off, and it could be at 3.30 a.m., for example, the building would be insecure. Street kids could come in or anybody who felt like having a look around.

*Maryanne*: And also because the buildings are so dark, anybody can wander round.

*Alan*: No one would know—so one of the options is to employ a security person to sit at the doors 24 hours a day just on the prospect that the power might go off. I feel that it's most unreasonable that we should have to pay for something like this. I believe the supplier of the commodity should pay.

*Maryanne*: I can't think what on earth I'm going to wear for a week!— I know this sounds really pathetic but we are in for a busy week. We have an opening night this week of our major concert with Julian Lloyd Webber and a wonderful Mexican conductor Enrique Diemecke. What happens if people can't go to the concert? Our orchestra has really got financial problems. Whose fault is that? We're still going to have to pay the conductor and the soloist. The fact that Kermadec restaurant throw out $8000 worth of frozen food is a pain in the butt—I really felt for them . . . perhaps employ six or eight staff. Do they tell them to go home? Who pays for the staff? Tough!

*Maryanne Gardiner, development manager with the Auckland Philharmonia Orchestra, and Alan Mummery, yacht designer and architect, left their inner city apartment to stay with friends in Remuera during the power crisis.*

# Sources

Armstrong, David. (The General Election, 1996) *True Colours*. David Bateman, Auckland, 1997.

Ashwin, Bernard Carl. (Cabinet Hears Britain Declare War on Germany, 1939.) From Ashwin's diary.

Awatere Huata, Donna. (Maori Land March, 1975.) Donna Awatere Huata, *My Journey*. Seaview Press, 1996.

Banks, John. (Flying to Wellington, 1981.) Paul Goldsmith, *John Banks. A Biography*. Penguin, Auckland, 1997.

Banks, Sir Joseph. ('Dr Solander and myself . . . landed without much difficulty.' 1769.) J.C. Beaglehole, ed., *Endeavour Journal*, Vol. II, Sydney, 1962.

Batten, Jean. (The *Gull* lands at Auckland Airport, 1936.) Jean Batten, *My Life*. Harrap, London, 1938.

Baxter, Archibald. (No. 1 Field Punishment, 1918.) Archibald Baxter, *We Will Not Cease*. Cape Catley Press, Picton, 1980.

Best, Ensign. (Auckland's First Horse Race. 1842.) M.N. Taylor, ed., *The Journal of Ensign Best*. Turnbull Library Monograph, Government Printer, Wellington, 1966.

Bird, Herbert. (The Mail Must Get Through, 1901.) Frank Fyfe, *The Pride of the Valley*. 1980.

Booth, Pat. (Mr Asia Rumbled, 1978–79.) *Deadline. My Story*. Penguin, Auckland, 1997.

Boultbee, John. (Utu at Stewart Island, 1827.) Starke, ed., *Journal of a Rambler*. Oxford University Press, Auckland, 1986.

Brockie, Walter. (Arriving in New Zealand, 1921.) Letter.

Brunner, Thomas. (Negotiating the Buller Gorge, 1847.) *Journal of an Expedition to Explore the Interior of the Middle Island, New Zealand, 1846–8*. Published in the *Nelson Examiner*, 30 September–21 October, 1848.

Carey, Brigadier-General George. (Waikato Battle, 1864.) John Featon, *The Waikato War 1863–1864*. John Henry Field, Auckland, 1880.

Carmen. (Wellington Mayoral Campaign Launched, 1977.) *Carmen: My Life* as told to Paul Martin. Benton Ross, Auckland, 1988.

Chorlton, Barbara. (Growing Up in Lyall Bay, 1920. School Holidays Up Country, 1928.) Diary. Alexander Turnbull Library, NLNZ, MS. No. xi.

*Christchurch Press* Reporters. (The Brunnerton Mine Disaster, 1896.) *Christchurch Press*, 27 March 1896.

Clark, Colin. (Waterfront Dispute, 1951.) Letter.

Colenso, William. (Signing of the

Treaty of Waitangi, 1840.) *The Authentic and Genuine History of the Signing of the Treaty of Waitangi.* Government Print, Wellington, 1890.

Colenso, William. (Frolicking Naked in the Snow, 1851.) *An Account of visits and crossings over, the Ruahine Mountain Range, Hawke's Bay, New Zealand, and the natural history of that region performed 1845–1847.* Read before the Hawke's Bay Philosophical Institute in 1878. Reprinted at the *Daily Telegraph* Office, Napier, 1884.

Cook, James. (First European to Set Foot on New Zealand. 1769.) J.C. Beaglehole, ed., *The Journals of Captain James Cook. Volume I. The Voyage of the Endeavour 1768–1771.* Cambridge, 1955.

Cook, James. (Modern Man Meets Ancient Man and His Daughters, 1773.) *A Voyage towards the South Pole and Round the World, performed in His Majesty's Ships, the* Resolution *and* Adventure. London, 1777.

Cooke, Harold Fuller. ('It is my intention to come out on Thursday', 1941.) H.A. Willis, *Man-hunt. The Story of Stanley Graham.* Whitcoulls, Christchurch, 1979.

Cox, James. (No Work in Hawke's Bay, 1893. 'Hope some work will come my way soon', 1915.) Diary. Alexander Turnbull Library, NZNL, MS 4296–5 & 26.

Cresswell, D'Arcy. (Tea with the Mayor of Wanganui, 1920.) Court testimony reported in the *Otago Daily Times*, May 28, 1920.

Crozet, Julien. (Frenchmen Fraternising with the Savages in the Bay of Islands, 1772.) Roth H. Ling, *Crozet's voyage to Tasmania, New Zealand, and the Ladrone Islands, and the Philippines in the years 1771–1772.* Truslove and Shirley, London, 1891.

Darwin, Charles. (Visiting Waimate, 1835.) *The Voyage of the* Beagle. Dent, 1845.

Davies, Sonja. (Protesting the Springbok Tour, 1981.) *Marching on . . .* Random House, Auckland, 1997.

Donegal, Ellen. (The Depression Hits Donegal Flat, early 1930s.) Christine Hunt, *I'm Ninety-Five . . . Any Objection? Folk History from the South Island.* Reed Methuen, Auckland, 1985.

Drew, S.H. (Pelican up the Wanganui River, 1889.) Ross B. O'Rourke ed., *The Drew/Hector Letters (1880–1899).* Museum of New Zealand/Te Papa, Wellington, 1996.

Du Chateau, Robyn. (Meeting the Right People in Heretaunga, early 1960s.) Jane Tollerton, *60s Chicks Hit the Nineties.* Penguin, Auckland, 1997.

Edmunds, Zita. (Turning Point, 1985.) Glenn Busch, ed., *You are My Darling Zita.* Godwit, Auckland, 1991.

Ell, George, Henry. (Vindicating Public Purity, 1898.) Evidence given at a governmental enquiry into the New Zealand Police Force. *Appendices to the Journals of the House of Representatives*, Vol. III, 1898.

*Evening Post* Reporters. (Off to the War, Wellington, 1899.) *Evening Post*, 22 October 1899.

Ellis, Cyril. (Tangiwai Disaster, 1953.) New Zealand Press Association, 25 December 1953.

Fenwick, Lt. Colonel P.C. (Burying the Dead at Gallipoli, 1915.) Diary Kippenberger Military Archive and Research Library, Army Museum, Waiouru.

Forster, J.G.A. (Cook's Men Clear Bush at Dusky Sound, 1773.) *A*

*Voyage Round the World in His Britannic Majesty's Ship Resolution*. Vol. 1, 1777.

France, Doctor. (Visiting the Karori Lunatic Asylum 1871.) The Appendices to the Journals of the Legislative Council 1870–75.

Fraser, George. (The Hulk Does Stillwater, 1951.) *Seeing Red: Undercover in 1950s New Zealand*. Dunmore Press, Palmerston North, 1995.

Freyberg, General Bernard. (The Fighting at Passchendaele, 1917.) Paul Freyberg, *Bernard Freyberg, VC: Soldier of Two Nations*. Hodder and Stoughton, Auckland, 1991.

Freyberg, General Bernard. (Battle for the Mareth Line, 1943.) *Documents Relating to New Zealand's Participation in the Second World War 1939–45*. Vol. II. War Histories Branch, Department of Internal Affairs, 1951.

Gardiner Maryanne and Alan Mummery (Auckland Power Crisis, 1998.) Radio New Zealand interview.

Gawith, Trooper Herbert H. (Giving the Boers Jip, 1900.) *Boer War Diary of Herbert H. Gawith No. 2245, 6th New Zealand Contingent*. Alexander Turnbull Library, MS Papers 2317.

Gibbs, Darren. (Dialling 111, Aramoana, 1990.) Bill O'Brien, *Aramoana: Twenty-two Hours of Terror*. Penguin, Auckland, 1991.

Gilshnan, Edward. (The Stratford Fire Storm, 1868.) *Evening Post*, 20 January 1886.

Glennie, John. (*The* Rose-Nöelle *Makes Land, 1990.*) John Glennie, Jane Phare, *The Spirit of* Rose-Nöelle. Viking, Auckland, 1990.

Godley, Charlotte. (Queen's Birthday Ball Aboard the *Meander*, 1850. A Drowning in Lyttelton Harbour, 1851.) *Letters from Early New Zealand*. Whitcombe & Tombs, Christchurch, 1951.

Gordon, Dr Doris. (War's End and Influenza Strikes, 1918.) *Back Blocks Baby-Doctor—an Autobiography*. Faber and Faber, London, 1950.

Grey, Zane. (Fighting the Black Marlin off the Bay of Islands, 1920s.) *Tales of the Angler's Eldorado, New Zealand*. 1926. Republished as *Angler's Eldorado: Zane Grey in New Zealand*. A.H. and A.W. Reed, Auckland, © Zane Grey Inc. 1982.

Harker, Jack S. (HMNZS *Achilles* in Action off the River Plate, 1939.) *HMNZS Achilles*. Collins, Auckland, 1980.

Harney, Vita. (Escaping the Murchison Earthquake, 1929.) Harney Collection. Alexander Turnbull Library, NLNZ, MS 1440.

Harper, H.W. (Parson Calls on Kaniere Gold Miners, 1866.) *Letters from New Zealand*. Hugh Rees, London, 1914.

Harsant, Florence. (Drunks Fighting Like Dogs at Tolaga Bay, 1914.) *They Called Me Te Maari*. Whitcoulls, Christchurch, 1979.

Haszard, Amelia. (Trapped Under Tarawera Ash, 1886.) *New Zealand Herald*, 1886, and the *Weekly Graphic and New Zealand Mail*, 1912.

Haydn, George. (Hungarian Refugee's First Job in New Zealand, 1940.) Anne Beaglehole, *A Small Price to Pay. Refugees from Hitler in New Zealand 1936–46*. Allen and Unwin and the Historical Branch, Department of Internal Affairs, Wellington, 1988.

Hayward, Margaret. (Norman Kirk's Days and Nights, 1974.) *Diary of the Kirk Years*. Reed Cape Catley, 1981.

Hepburn, Alex W. (Annual School Picnic, about 1906.) *Henderson School and District Jubilee Booklet*, 1933.

Hewitt, Brian. (Data Entry Error, 1978.) Justice Mahon, Report of the Royal Commission to Inquire into the Crash on Mt Erebus, Antarctica of a DC10 Aircraft Operated by Air New Zealand Ltd, 1981.

Hillary, Edmund. (Knocking Off Mount Everest, 1953.) Steven Barnett, & Jim Sullivan. *In Their Own Words: From the Sound Archives of Radio New Zealand.* GP Books, Wellington, 1988.

Hiroki. ('Cry for me', 1882.) Dick Scott, *Ask that Mountain: The Story of Parihaka*, Reed-Southern Cross, Auckland, 1975.

Holland, Sidney. (Undreamt-of Success, 1951.) Alexander Turnbull Library, NZNL, MS 1624–103.

Holyoake, Roger. (Kiwi Keith's High-flying Kites, about 1947.) Verbatim account.

Hope, Arthur. (Backcountry Snow in Canterbury, 1895.) William Vance, *High Endeavour: Story of the Mackenzie Country*, Reed, Auckland, 1995.

Huata (see Awatere)

Hull, Archie. (Life is Good if You've Got the Guts) Diary. Alexander Turnbull Library, MS X. 4254.

Jackson, Captain William. (Carbine and Revolver Attack South of Auckland. 1863.) John Featon, *The Waikato War 1863–1864*. John Henry Field, Auckland, 1880.

Jonas, Captain Alfred ('I respectfully beg to appeal', 1918.) Max Avery, *The Strange Case of Captain Jonas. Historical Review.* Whakatane, 44:1996.

Jones, Bob. (Sunday Night at the Peter Pan Cabaret, 1974.) *Memories of Muldoon.* Canterbury University Press, Christchurch, 1997.

Joyce, Bronwyn. (The Edgecumbe Earthquake, 1987.) *Historical Review.* Whakatane, 45: 1 May 1997.

King, F. Truby. (Advice to Mothers, 1909.) Address to the Society for the Promotion of Health of Women and Children, 1909.

King, Jill, (The Queen Visits Stratford, 1954.) Letter.

Kingsford-Smith, Squadron Leader. (First Trans-Tasman Flight, 1928.) Alexander Turnbull Library, MS Paper 3524.

Lange, David. (The Oxford Debate, 1985.) *Nuclear Free. The New Zealand Way.* Penguin, Auckland, 1990.

Lee, John A. (Escaping Burnham Industrial School, about 1905.) *Delinquent Days.* Collins, Auckland, 1967 and (Parliamentary Proceedings, 1937.) *The John A Lee's Diaries 1936–40.* Whitcoulls, Christchurch, 1981.

Leney, Alice Richard. (Baiting the French at Mururoa Atoll 1995.) Claudia Pond Eley ed., *Protest at Mururoa: First-hand accounts from the New Zealand-based flotilla.* Tandem Press, Auckland, 1990.

Luoni, Warrant Officer George (Shot Down in the Pacific, 1943.) Keith Mulligan, 'Kittyhawks and Coconuts'. *New Zealand WINGS*, 1995.

Makeriti. (Collecting Potatoes Near Whakarewarewa, 1870s.) *The Old-Time Maori.* Victor Gollancz, London, 1938.

Maning, Frederick Edward. (The Spirit Calls, 1830s.) *Old New Zealand.* Whitcomb & Tombs, Christchurch, 1863.

Mansfield, Katherine. (Jumping the Baby Up and Down at Waipunga 1907.) Vincent

O'Sullivan, Margaret Scott, eds., *The Collected Letters of Katherine Mansfield. Vol. I. 1903–1917.* Clarendon, London, 1984.

Markham, Edward. ('I do not know that I ever cried in parting from a Girl before', 1834.) E.H. McCormack, ed., *New Zealand, Or Recollections of It.* Alexander Turnbull Library Monograph. Government Printer, Wellington, 1963.

Marsden, Samuel. (First Christian Service at Bay of Islands, 1814.) Elder, John Rawson, eds., *The Letters and Journals of Samuel Marsden 1765–1838.* Coulls Somerville Wilkie and A.H. Reed for the Otago University Council, 1932.

Massey, Frank. (General Kippenberger Loses his Feet at Cassino, 1944.) Glynn Harper, *Kippenberger: An Inspired New Zealand Commander.* Harper Collins, Auckland, 1997.

Massey, William. (The Bombay Football Club, 1922.) Alexander Turnbull Library, MS 5266.

Maynard, Felix and Alexandre Dumas. (Harpooning Whales off Banks Peninsula, 1838. A Fair Exchange in Lyttelton Harbour, 1838.) *Les Beleiniers (The Whalers).* Translated by F.W. Reed. Hutchinson, London, 1937.

McDonald, Henry. (Lifeboat Adrift off South Africa 1874.) Sir Henry Brett, *White Wings.* Reprinted Capper Press, Christchurch, 1976.

McFadden, Suzanne. (The America's Cup Comes to New Zealand, 1995.) *New Zealand Herald,* 25 May 1995.

McIntosh, Alistair. (Hotel Service, 1947.) Ian McGibbon, ed., *Undiplomatic Dialogue: Letters between Carl Berendsen and Alistair McIntosh 1943–1952.* Auckland University Press, Ministry of Foreign Affairs and Trade, and the Historical Branch, Department of Internal Affairs, 1993.

McNeill, Augusta. ('I was treated in a cold, cruel and unkind manner', 1865.) Letters in the records of the Female Middle Class Emigration Society, London.

Meurant, Ross. (Confronting the Anti-apartheid Protestors, 1981.) *The Red Squad Story . . .* Harlen, Auckland, 1982.

Mitchell, Stacy. (Falling into Cave Creek, 1995.) Report of the Commission of Inquiry into the Collapse of a Viewing Platform at Cave Creek near Punakaiki on the West Coast. Department of Internal Affairs, GP Print, Wellington, 1996.

Monita, Eru (Welcoming the New Launch at Uawa (Tolaga Bay) 1901.) *Te Puke Ki Hikurangi* newspaper. Translated by Margaret Orbell. *History Now* Vol. 3, No. 1. May, 1997.

Muldoon, Robert. (Visiting Rio and Berlin, 1967.) *Number 38.* Reed Methuen, Auckland, 1986.

Murry, John. ('I don't like to be shot at like a bird', 1795.) *Journal of the Endeavour, 1795* (MS in Peabody Museum, Salem); quoted in Anne Salmond, *Between Worlds.* Viking, Auckland, 1997.

Nash, Nancy. (Ballantyne's Fire, 1947.) Testimony presented to the Royal Commission into the Fire at J. Ballantyne and Co. 1948. National Archives microfilm.

Newland, Olly. (Share Market Crash, Auckland, 1987.) *Lost Property. The Crash of '87 . . . and the Aftershock.* Harper Collins, Auckland, 1994.

*New Zealand Graphic and Ladies Home Journal* Reporter. ('At Home' – Government House, 1893.) *New Zealand Graphic and Ladies Home Journal*, 29 July 1893.

*New Zealand Herald* Reporter. (Richard Seddon Welcomes the All Blacks Home, 1906.) *New Zealand Herald*, 6 March 1906.

New Zealand Press Association Reporter. (Napier Mortuary After the Big Quake, 1931.)

Nicholas, J.L. (Escaped Convicts Recaptured, Bay of Islands, 1814. First Cattle and Horses Landed at Bay of Islands, 1814.) *Narrative of a Voyage to New Zealand. Vol. 1*, 1817.

Nicholls, Margueretta. (Ballantyne's Fire, 1947.) Testimony presented to the Royal Commission into the Fire at J. Ballantyne and Co. 1948. National Archives microfilm.

Oates, Jane. ('My children has had to go bare futed', 1865.) Bethlyn Watters, Oates family papers 1852–91. Alexander Turnbull Library, NLNZ, MS 3932–5.

O'Connell, Therese. (First Holy Communion, 1958.) Jane Tollerton, *Convent Girls*. Penguin, Auckland, 1994.

*Otago Daily Times* Reporter. (The Prince of Wales Welcomed to Dunedin, 1920.) *Otago Daily Times* 20 May, 1920.

Palmer, Robert. (The Lonely Shepherd, 1864.) *Robert Palmer farm diary 1864*. Fyffe Family Papers, Canterbury Museum Manuscripts Department.

Park, Ruth. (Ahuriri Lagoon Turns to Dry Land, 1931. Farewelling the Troops, 1940.) *A Fence Around the Cuckoo*. Penguin, Melbourne, 1992.

Parker, Pauline. (Moidering Mother, 1954.) Julia Glamizina and

Alison Laurie, *Parker and Hume. A Lesbian View*. New Woman's Press, Auckland, 1991.

Phillips, Redmond Bernard. (Juvenile Delinquency in Reefton, early 1920s) *The People on the Verandah*. Alexander Turnbull Library, NLNZ, Unpublished MS Papers 4333.

*Pioneer* Reporter. (Mackenzie's Dog in Court, 1855.) The *Pioneer*, Timaru, 1906–7.

*Port Nicholson Spectator* Reporter. (First Operation Under General Anaesthetic in Wellington, 1847.) *Port Nicholson Spectator*, 29 September 1847.

Pouhawaiki, Ihaia. (Massacre at Akaroa, 1830.) H.C. Jacobson, *Tales of Banks Peninsula*. Akaroa Mail Office, 1883.

Rangiamoa. (Lament for the Dispossessed, 1860s.) Margaret Orbell, *Waiata. Maori Songs in History*. Reed, Auckland, 1991.

Reid, H. Murray. (Bombardment at El Alamein, 1942.) *The Turning Point: With the New Zealand Engineers at El Alamein*. Collins, Auckland, 1944.

Rennie, J. (Aftermath of the S.S. *Tararua* Sinking, 1881.) Joan Macintosh, *The Wreck of the Tararua*. A.H. and A.W. Reed, Wellington, 1970.

Richmond, Anne. ('My time is very full', 1884.) Guy H. Schofield, ed., *The Richmond-Atkinson Papers*. Government Printer, Wellington, 1960.

Robertson, Second Lieutenant Keith. (Mutiny at POW Camp, 1943.) Proceedings of a Court of Enquiry on Mutiny at Prisoner of War Camp, Featherston, New Zealand. New Zealand Military Forces, Wellington, 1943.

Rosel, Carl Frederick. (Christmas Day in Paremoremo, 1970.) Peter Williams, *A Passion for*

*Justice.* Shoal Bay Press, Christchurch, 1997.

Rutherford, Ernest. (Winning the Nobel prize, 1908.) A.S. Eve, *Rutherford. Being the Life and Letters of the Rt. Hon. Lord Rutherford,* O.M. Cambridge, 1939.

Ryan, Kevin. (Milan Brych Unmasked, 1974.) *Justice Without Fear or Favour.* Hodder Moa Beckett, Auckland, 1997.

Savage, Michael Joseph. (Labour Victory, 1935.) Barry Gustafson, *Cradle to the Grave. A Biography of Michael Joseph Savage.* Reed Methuen, Auckland, 1986.

Scott, Tom. (New Year's Eve Party, 1980.) *New Zealand Listener,* 12 January, 1980.

Scrimgeour, C.G. (The Unemployed Riot in Queen Street, 1932.) C.G. Scrimgeour, John A. Lee, Tony Simpson, *The Scrim-Lee Papers.* A.H. and A.W. Reed, Wellington, 1976.

Shadbolt, Tim. (Anti-Vietnam Demos in Auckland, 1968.) *Bullshit & Jellybeans.* Alister Taylor, Wellington, 1971.

Sinclair, Keith. (Vietnam Teach-in, 1965.) *Half Way Round the Harbour. An Autobiography.* Penguin, Auckland, 1993.

Smith, Dr Peter Eccles. (Qui Nhon Hospital, 1969.) *Letters from a Viet Nam Hospital.* Reed, Wellington, 1969.

Snell, Peter. (The World Mile Record, 1962.) Peter Snell, Garth Gilmour, *No Bugles, No Drums.* Minerva, Auckland, 1965.

Soulas (Father Soulas, also known as Pa Hoani Papita.) (Sister Joseph Given her Instructions, 1885.) Jessie Munro, *The Story of Suzanne Aubert.* Auckland University Press and Bridget Williams Books, Auckland, 1996.

*Southland Times* Reporter (Minnie Dean Hanged at Invercargill, 1895.) *Southland Times,* August 12 1895.

Tasman, Abel. (New Zealand Espied, 1642. Violence at Murderers Bay, 1642.) J.E. Heere, *Abel Janszoon Tasman: His Life and Labours.* Amsterdam, 1898.

Te Rangi Hiroa. (Doctoring to the Troops at Gallipoli, 1915.) J.B. Condliffe, *Te Rangi Hiroa. The Life of Sir Peter Buck.* Whitcombe and Tombs, Christchurch, 1971.

Te Taniwha, Horeta, (Cook's Visit Recalled, 1852.) Anne Salmond, *Two Worlds.* Viking, Auckland, 1991.

Te Uatorikiriki. (Broken-hearted at Cloudy Bay, about 1840.) Te Ahukaramu Charles Royal, trans., *Kati au i konei (Let me here abide). A collection of songs from Ngati Toa, rangatira and Ngati Raukawa.* Huia, Wellington, 1994.

Thomas, Arthur Allan. (Statement to Police, 1970.) David A. Yallop, *Beyond Reasonable Doubt.* Hodder and Stoughton, Auckland, 1978.

Trevithick, Gay. ('Move or nod your head if you can hear us', 1944.) Lawrence Watt, *Mates and Mayhem. World War II: Frontline Kiwis Remember.* HarperCollins, Auckland, 1996.

Trollope, Anthony. (Coaching through Otago, 1872.) *Australia and New Zealand.* Chapman & Hall, London, 1874.

von Haast, Julius. (German Hospitality near Motueka, 1859.) *The Life and Times of Sir Julius von Haast.* P. von Haast, 1948.

Watson, Herbert. (The Sporting Life, 1919.) Alexander Turnbull Library, NZNL, MS papers 5714–017.

Watson, John. (Retreat from Greece and Crete, 1941.) Alison Parr,

*Silent Casualties: New Zealand's Unspoken Legacy of the Second World War.* Tandem Press, Auckland, 1995.

Westmacott, Lieutenant H.H. Spencer. (Landing at Gallipoli, 1915.) Alexander Turnbull Library, NZNL, MS No. 0847.

Woolf, Ada. (Saved from the Sinking Wahine, 1968.) Letter to her family, 1968. Alexander Turnbull Library, NLNZ, MS 87–138.

'Mr X'. (Work in the Bakehouse, 1890.) Report of the Royal Commission appointed to enquire into certain relationships between employers of a certain kind of labour and the persons employed therein. (The 'Sweating Commission'.) Appendices to the Journals of the House of Representatives. III. H–5, 1890.

## ACKNOWLEDGEMENTS

Thanks are due to the following for permission to reprint extracts from the publications listed:

A.H. & A. W. Reed for *The Wreck of the Tararua* by Joan Macintosh (1970), *The Scrim-Lee Papers* by C.G. Scrimgeour, John A. Lee and Tony Simpson (1976), *Tales of the Angler's Eldorado, New Zealand* (1926), republished as *Angler's Eldorado: Zane Grey in New Zealand*, © Zane Grey Inc (1982); Alister Taylor for *Bullshit and Jellybeans* by Tim Shadbolt (1971); Allen and Unwin for *A Small Price to Pay. Refugees from Hitler in New Zealand 1936–46* by Anne Beaglehole (1988); Auckland University Press and Ministry of Foreign Affairs and Industry for *Undiplomatic Dialogue: Letters between Carl Berendsen and Alistair McIntosh 1943–1952* edited by Ian McGibbon (1993); Auckland University Press, Bridget Williams Press and Home of Compassion Archives for *The Story of Sister Aubert* by Jessie Munro (1996); Benton Ross for *Carmen—My Life* as told to Paul Martin (1988); Canterbury Museum for *Robert Palmer farm diary 1864* from the Fyffe Family Papers; Canterbury University History Department for 'An oil launch for Uawa,' translated by Margaret Orbell, from *History Now*, Vol 3. No. 1, (1997); Canterbury University Press for *Memories of Muldoon* by Bob Jones (1997); Cape Catley Press for *We Will Not Cease* by Archibald Baxter (1980); Clarendon for *The Collected Letters of Katherine Mansfield. Vol. I 1903–1917* edited by Vincent O'Sullivan and Margaret Scott (1984); Collins for *HMNZS Achilles* by Jack S. Harker (1980), *The Turning Point: With the New Zealand Engineers at El Alamein* by H. Murray Reid (1944); David Bateman for *True Colours* by David Armstrong (1997); Dunmore Press for *Seeing Red: Undercover in 1950s New Zealand* by George Fraser (1995); Faber and Faber for *Back Blocks Baby-Doctor—an Autobiography* by Dr Doris Gordon (1950); Fyfe, Mary, John, Adam, and Anne for *The Pride of the Valley,* edited by Frank Fyfe (1980); Godwit Press for *You are*

*My Darling Zita* edited by Glenn Busch (1991); Government Printer *New Zealand, Or Recollections of It* edited by E. H. McCormack (1963), *The Journal of Ensign Best* edited by M. N. Taylor, A Turnbull Library Monograph (1966); Govt Print for *The Richmond-Atkinson Papers* edited by Guy Schofield (1960); GP Books for *In Their Own Words from the Sound Archives of Radio New Zealand* by Stephen Barnett and Jim Sullivan (1988); Harlen Publishing for *The Red Squad Story* by Ross Meurant (1982); Harper Collins for *Lost Property, The Crash of '87 and the Aftershock* by Olly Newland (1994), *Mates and Mayhem, World War II: Frontline Kiwis Remember* by Lawrence Watt (1996), *Kippenberger: An Inspired New Zealand Commander* by Glynn Harper (1997); Hodder Moa Beckett for *Justice Without Fear or Favour* by Kevin Ryan (1997); Hodder and Stoughton for *Beyond Reasonable Doubt* by David A. Yallop (1978), *Bernard Freyberg, VC: Soldier of Two Nations* by Paul Freyberg (1991); Seaview Press for *My Journey* by Donna Awatere Huata (1996); Huia Publishers for *Kati au i konei (Let me here abide). A collection of songs from Ngati Toa, rangatira and Ngati Raukawa,* translated by Te Ahukaramu Charles Royal (1994); Minerva for *No bugles, no drums* by Peter Snell and Garth Gilmour (1965); *New Zealand Herald* for 'The America's Cup comes to New Zealand', by Suzanne McFadden, May 25 1995; *New Zealand Listener* for 'Rhubarb, rhubarb', by Tom Scott, January 12 1980; New Zealand Press Association for 'Tangiwai Disaster' by Cyril Ellis, 25 December 1953; *New Zealand WINGS* for 'Kittyhawks and Coconuts' by Keith Mulligan (1995); Oxford University Press for *Journal of a Rambler* edited by June Starke (1986); Peabody Museum, Salem, USA for *Journal of the Endeavour* by John Murry (1795); Penguin Books New Zealand for *Nuclear Free. The New Zealand Way* by David Lange (1990), *The Spirit of Rose-Noëlle* by John Glennie and Jane Phare (1990), *Aramoana: Twenty-two Hours of Terror* by Bill O'Brien (1991), *Two Worlds* by Anne Salmond (1991), *Half Way Round the Harbour: An Autobiography* by Keith Sinclair (1993), *Convent Girls* by Jane Tollerton (1994), *Between Worlds* by Anne Salmond (1997), *Deadline, My Story* by Pat Booth (1997), *John Banks. A Biography* by Paul Goldsmith (1997), *60s Chicks Hit the Nineties* by Jane Tollerton (1997); Penguin Books Australia for *A Fence around the Cuckoo* by Ruth Park (1992); Random House for *Marching on . . .* by Sonja Davies (1997); Radio New Zealand for interview with Maryanne Gardiner and Alan Mummery Gardiner (1998); Reed for *Letters from a Viet Nam Hospital* by Dr Peter Eccles Smith (1969), *Waiata. Maori Songs in History* by Margaret Orbell (1991), *High Endeavour: Story of the Mackenzie Country* by William Vance (1995); Reed

Cape Catley for *Diary of the Kirk Years* by Margaret Hayward (1981); Reed Methuen for *I'm Ninety-Five . . . Any Objection? Folk History from the South Island* compiled by Christine Hunt (1985), *Cradle to the Grave, A Biography of Michael Joseph Savage* by Barry Gustafson (1986), *Number 38* by Robert Muldoon (1986); Reed-Southern Cross for *Ask That Mountain: The Story of Parihaka* by Dick Scott (1975); Shoal Bay Press for *A Passion for Justice* by Peter Williams QC (1997); Tandem Press for *Protest at Mururoa: First-hand accounts from the New Zealand-based flotilla* edited by Claudia Pond Ely (1990), *Silent Casualties: New Zealand's Unspoken Legacy of the Second World War* by Allison Parr (1995); Whakatane and District Historical Society for 'The Edgecumbe Earthquake' by Bronwyn Joyce, *Bay of Plenty Journal of History*, 45:1. May (1997), 'The Strange Case of Captain Jonas' by Max Avery, *Bay of Plenty Journal of History*, 44 (1996); Whitcomb and Tombs for *Letters from Early New Zealand* by Charlotte Godley (1951), *Old New Zealand* by Frederick Maning (1956), *Te Rangi Hiroa. The Life of Sir Peter Buck* edited by J.B. Condliffe (1971); Whitcoulls for *Manhunt. The Story of Stanley Graham* by H.A. Willis (1979), *They Called Me Te Maari* by Florence Harsant (1979), *The John A Lee's Diaries 1936–40* by John A. Lee (1981).

# INDEX